COMPLETE ADVANCED LEVEL MATHEMATICS

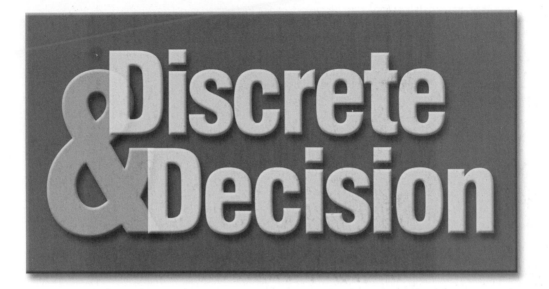

Discrete &Decision

Ian Bloomfield • John Stevens

Published in 2002 by:
Nelson Thornes Ltd
Delta Place
27 Bath Road
CHELTENHAM
GL53 7TH
United Kingdom

01 02 03 04 05 06/ 10 9 8 7 6 5 4 3 2 1

A catalogue record for this book is available from the British Library

ISBN 0 7487 6456 9

Illustrations by Peters and Zabransky
Page make-up by Mathematical Composition Setters Ltd

Printed and bound in Great Britain by Scotprint

Acknowledgements
The publishers thank the following for permission to reproduce copyright material:
Photodisc 31 (NT): 228

The authors and publishers are grateful to Edexcel, OCR and AQA for permission to
reproduce questions from their past examination papers. AQA(AEB)/AQA
examination questions are reproduced by permission of the Assessment and
Qualifications Alliance. Any answers and mark schemes included have not been
provided by the examining boards, they are the sole responsibility of the authors
and may not necessarily constitute the only possible solutions

Contents

Acknowledgements   ii

About the Authors   vi

Introduction   vii

1   Algorithms   **1**
   1.1   Definition and Notation   1
   1.2   Properties   4

2   Sorting, Searching and Packing   **7**
   2.1   Searching – Linear and Indexed   7
   2.2   Searching – Binary and Tree Searches   8
   2.3   Sorting –Linear Algorithms   11
   2.4   Shell Sort   17
   2.5   Quicksort   18
   2.6   Bin-packing   20

3   Graph Theory   **26**
   3.1   Language and Notation   26
   3.2   Modelling Networks with Graphs   30
   3.3   Eulerian, Bipartite and Complete Graphs   31
   3.4   Planarity   35

4   Spanning Trees   **46**
   4.1   Kruskal's Algorithm   47
   4.2   Prim's Algorithm   51
   4.3   Prim with a Matrix

5   Shortest Paths   **64**
   5.1   Dijkstra's Algorithm   64
   5.2   Dijkstra for all Paths   69
   5.3   Floyd's Algorithm

6   Route Inspection   **80**
   6.1   The Route Inspection Problem   80

7   Travelling Salesperson Problems   **89**
   7.1   The Classical Problem   89
   7.2   Nearest Neighbour Algorithm   93
   7.3   Upper Bounds and Improvements   97
   7.4   Lower Bounds   99
   7.5   Scheduling   101

8   Critical Path Analysis   **111**
   8.1   Formulation and Notation   111
   8.2   Solving   117
   8.3   Float   121
   8.4   Cascade (Gantt) charts   124
   8.5   Scheduling and Resources   125
   8.6   Crashing a Network   128

Contents

9 Linear Programming **139**
9.1 Variables, Constraints and Graphs 142
9.2 Optimisation 143
9.3 Integer Solutions 145
9.4 Multiple Solutions 147
9.5 Slack Variables and Interpretation 148
9.6 Minimisation Problems 150

10 The Simplex Method **157**
10.1 The Simplex Algorithm 157
10.2 Two Stage Algorithm – Artificial Variables 163
10.3 The big M method 167

11 Matchings **174**
11.1 Modelling with Bipartite Graphs 174
11.2 Maximum Matching Algorithm 177

12 Allocation and Transportation **188**
12.1 Minimum Cost Allocations 188
12.2 The Hungarian Algorithm 191
12.3 Transportation Problems 196
12.4 Testing for Optimality 201
12.5 Improving a Solution 204

13 Network Flow **212**
13.1 Formulation and Notation 212
13.2 Solutions 215
13.3 Cuts and Optimality 217
13.4 The Labelling Algorithm 219

14 Dynamic Programming **230**
14.1 Principles and Notation 230
14.2 Common Applications 234

15 Game Theory **244**
15.1 Zero-sum Games 244
15.2 Stategy Dominance 247
15.3 Mixed Strategies 249
15.4 Linear Programming Solutions 252

16 Decision Trees **260**
16.1 Formulation 260
16.2 Solution 262

17 Simulation **272**
17.1 Single Event Models 272
17.2 Queuing 276
17.3 Reliability 278

18 Recurrence Relations **289**
18.1 Exploring Sequences 289
18.2 Linear First Order 290
18.3 Second Order Homogeneous 292
18.4 Second Order Non-homogeneous 294

19 Logic and Boolean Algebra   **300**
    19.1 Propositional Logic   300
    19.2 Switching Circuits   302
    19.3 Truth Tables   304
    19.4 Combinational Circuits   308
    19.5 Boolean Algegbra   311

20 Coding   **318**
    20.1 Check digits   319
    20.2 Binary Codes   322
    20.3 Hamming Distance   324
    20.4 Linear Codes and Parity Check Matrices   326

Answers   **335**

Index   **370**

About the Authors

Ian Bloomfield teaches mathematics and ICT in a Norfolk College where he was Head of Department for a number of years. He has been involved for several years in the development of Discrete & Decision Mathematics at A-level, is a coursework moderator and leads teacher training days nationally.

John Stevens teaches mathematics in a Cambridge College. He has been involved for several years in the development of Discrete & Decision Mathematics at A-level.

Introduction

This book covers all the requirements for **Discrete & Decision Mathematics** from all the latest Advanced Level specifications and course requirements for AS and A-level Mathematics. It will provide you with:

- Comprehensive coverage and clear explanations of all Discrete & Decision Mathematics topics and skills.

- Numerous exercises and worked examples with questions and clear diagrams.

- Precise and comprehensive teaching text with clear progression.

- Margin notes that provide supporting commentary on key topics, formulas and other aspects of the work.

- A full index to the topics covered.

  Chapters in the book contain a number of **key features**:

- **What you need to know** sections covering prerequisite knowledge for a chapter.

- **Review** sections with practice questions on what you need to know.

- **Worked Examples** and supporting commentary with clear diagrams built up in stages to show the application of the methods being studied.

- **Technique** and **Contextual Exercises** to give thorough practice in all concepts and skills.

- **Consolidation A** and **B Exercises**, much of which is actual examination questions, to build on the work in a chapter and provide practice in a variety of question types.

- **Applications and Extensions** as a support to coursework, and to develop computer-based means of solving the problems in the chapter.

- A **summary** of all the key concepts covered.

1 Algorithms

Throughout this book of Discrete and Decision Mathematics, you will study methodical approaches to problem solving. In many cases the examples will be relatively simple and you will undoubtedly find some that you could solve by inspection or by trial and error. However, by taking a methodical approach you are acquiring skills which can later be applied to much larger problems. You should therefore take time to work through this chapter, and to seek to understand the algorithms that are used throughout the rest of the book.

1.1 Definition and Notation

Any process with a sequence of steps or instructions contains an algorithm, from simple arithmetic to complex computer programmes, from buttering bread to cooking a gourmet meal. By following the instructions a fixed outcome is guaranteed, unless there is some random or chance element within the process, or the inputs are changed.

Some algorithms have multiple solutions – all equally good – caused by an arbitrary choice during the process.

There are a variety of ways of describing or writing out an algorithm. In the following examples, we are going to look at three approaches. In each case we will consider the algorithm for the mathematical function Factorial.

Factorial is defined for positive integers as all the numbers from the chosen one down to one multiplied together. For example, 4! (pronounced 'four factorial') is $4 \times 3 \times 2 \times 1 = 24$.

Example 1 – Flow Chart

Using the following boxes, describe the algorithm to calculate a factorial with a flow chart.

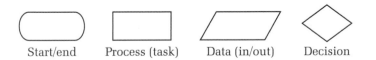

Start/end   Process (task)   Data (in/out)   Decision

Solution

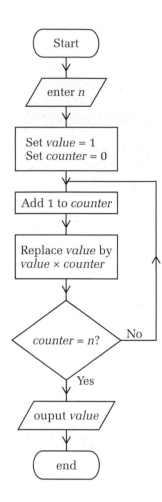

Example 2 – Structured Code

Use structured code to describe the algorithm to calculate a factorial.

Solution

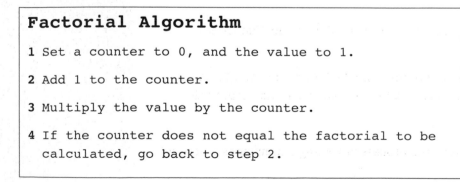

> **Factorial Algorithm**
>
> **1** Set a counter to 0, and the value to 1.
>
> **2** Add 1 to the counter.
>
> **3** Multiply the value by the counter.
>
> **4** If the counter does not equal the factorial to be calculated, go back to step 2.

This is the notation generally used throughout the book.

Example 3 – Spreadsheet

Use a spreadsheet to calculate a factorial.

Solution

The formulae (in *MS Excel*) would be:

	A	B
1	Enter Factorial:	5
2	Counter	Value
3	1	=1
4	=A3+1	=IF(A4<=$B$1,B3*A4,"")
5	=A4+1	=IF(A5<=$B$1,B4*A5,"")
6	=A5+1	=IF(A6<=$B$1,B5*A6,"")
7	=A6+1	=IF(A7<=$B$1,B6*A7,"")
8	=A7+1	=IF(A8<=$B$1,B7*A8,"")
9	=A8+1	=IF(A9<=$B$1,B8*A9,"")
10	=A9+1	=IF(A10<=$B$1,B9*A10,"")
11	=A10+1	=IF(A11<=$B$1,B10*A11,"")
12	=A11+1	=IF(A12<=$B$1,B11*A12,"")

giving the results

	A	B
1	Enter Factorial:	5
2	Counter	Value
3	1	1
4	2	2
5	3	6
6	4	24
7	5	120
8	6	
9	7	
10	8	
11	9	
12	10	

1.1 Definition and Notation

Exercise

Contextual

1 Algorithms do not have to be mathematical. Write down an algorithm for carrying out a three-point turn when driving.

2 You should do this question twice, once using structured code and once using a flow chart.

An examiner has to find the mean mark for 200 scripts that he has marked.

a Write an algorithm that will input the 200 marks and add them up.
b Extend the algorithm to calculate the mean mark and output this mean mark.

3 Create a flow chart to show the process of writing a number as a product of its prime factors.

1.2 Properties

Simple linear algorithms, which have a sequence of steps to be done in a fixed sequence, will stop when the last instruction is reached. However, many algorithms have a branch or decision involved, and it is then important that we ensure that the algorithm will eventually finish and not go on for ever around a loop.

For any algorithm which has the potential to take a significant amount of time/number of operations, we may want to consider its complexity, or order. The order of an algorithm is a measure of the amount of work to be done in proportion to the size of the problem given. So an algorithm which will require work in proportion to the square of the problem size is said to have **order n-squared**, written $O(n^2)$.

Some algorithms have logarithmic complexity. This is explained where it occurs in the text.

Example 1 – Stopping Conditions

Explain the stopping condition used in the factorial algorithm of section 1.1, and give examples of when it will not work.

Solution

In our factorial algorithm, we introduced a test to check whether our counter had reached the number whose factorial we were calculating. This will eventually be satisfied and cause the algorithm to stop, provided that the factorial to be found is a positive integer. If, however, we try to calculate a negative factorial, say $(-3)!$, or a fractional one, say $4\frac{1}{2}!$, the counter will continue to increase indefinitely.

Example 2 – Complexity

Nina is hosting a dinner party at which there will be n guests (not including herself). She is concerned about three tasks which she has to do.

a Sending out the invitations
b Organising the seating pattern for dinner
c Introducing everyone to each other

Analyse the complexity of each of these tasks.

Solution

a Nina has to send out n invitations. Each one is a single task so this is therefore $O(n)$.
b Assuming that Nina sits at the head of the table, there are n people to choose from to sit to her left. That leaves $n-1$ to choose the next

person from, and so on. The total number of choices is
$n \times (n-1) \times (n-2) \times (n-3) \times (n-4) \times \cdots \times 3 \times 2 \times 1 = n!$ so the task is $O(n!)$

c The first guest to arrive must be introduced to the other $n-1$ as they arrive; the second will meet $n-2$, etc. The total number of introductions is therefore $(n - 1) + (n - 2) + (n - 3) + (n - 4) + \cdots + 2 + 1 = \frac{1}{2}n(n-1)$. For large n, the '-1' has very little effect and the sum is quite close to $\frac{1}{2}n^2$. This is proportional to n^2 so we say that this task is $O(n^2)$

This formula is often quoted and is proved in Pure Mathematics.

1.2 Properties

Exercise

Contextual

1 In Exercise 1.1 question 3 you wrote an algorithm for expressing a number as a product of its prime factors. Explain the stopping condition in your algorithm, and state any conditions under which it would fail.

2 A task is $O(n)$ and takes 10 minutes to carry out on a set of 12 items.

   a How long will it take to carry out the task on a set of 48 items?
   b How long will it take to carry out the task on a set of 6 items?

3 A task is $O(n^2)$ and takes 10 minutes to carry out on a set of 12 items.

   a How long will it take to carry out the task on a set of 48 items?
   b How long will it take to carry out the task on a set of 6 items?

4 A task is $O(n!)$ and takes 10 minutes to carry out on a set of 12 items. (Give your answer to these questions in standard form.)

   a How long will it take to carry out the task on a set of 48 items?
   b How long will it take to carry out the task on a set of 6 items?

5 Below is an algorithm for sorting numbers.

```
1 Cut pieces of spaghetti (uncooked) to length to
  represent each of your numbers.

2 Place all the pieces of spaghetti on to a flat
  surface, and line them up against a common base
  line.

3 Pick out the longest piece of spaghetti.

4 Repeat step 3 until you reach the last piece.
```

a What is the order of complexity of this algorithm?

b Why does this work with people but not for computers?

c Under what circumstances might this algorithm fail?

Applications and Extensions

Recursion

A recursive algorithm is one which is defined in terms of itself. Give a recursive definition for factorial, and explain the stopping condition.

Summary

- An **algorithm** is a set of instructions for a task.

- Algorithms can be written in a variety of formats including **flow chart**, **structured code**, and **computer language**.

- The **Complexity**, or **Order**, of an algorithm is a measure of the amount of work needed to complete the task expressed in terms of the size of the problem.

- An algorithm which includes repetition needs a means of stopping when the task is completed.

2 Sorting, Searching and Packing

What you need to know

● The definition of the order (complexity) of an algorithm

Review

1 State whether each of the following is $O(n)$, $O(n^2)$ or $O(n^3)$.

  a Using bricks to make a solid platform, n by $2n$ by 0.5 metres.
  b Finding a book on a shelf where n is the length of the shelf.
  c Blowing up an inflatable ball, radius n cm.

2 **a** A task is $O(n)$. If it takes 15 minutes to carry out the task on a set of 20 items, how long will it take to carry out the task on a set of 60 items?
  b A task is $O(n^2)$. If it takes 15 minutes to carry out the task on a set of 20 items, how long will it take to carry out the task on a set of 60 items?

2.1 Searching – Linear and Indexed

The very simplest way of searching for something is to start at the beginning, and keep looking until you find it! This is a **linear** search.

On average, you will have to check half the items.

An indexed search, as its name suggests, uses an index to speed up the search. Whilst it is possible for a search to be **fully indexed** (that is, every item is individually referenced in the index), it is more common to use one or more levels of index, followed by a linear search.

On average, you will have to search halfway through each index.

Example 1

Hazel is going to see her new friend Joanne, who lives at 'The Beeches', Autumn Drive. How does she find the house, using a linear search?

Solution

She walks along Autumn Drive from the beginning, checking each house name in turn until she finds 'The Beeches'. Then she stops.

Example 2

Darren cannot remember how to spell isomorphic. His dictionary has a tab down the page edges for each letter of the alphabet, and the first word on each page is printed in bold at the top of the page. How does he find the word?

Solution

He looks down the tabs until he finds the letter I. He opens the dictionary at this page, then turns pages one at a time until he finds words starting with IS. He then searches linearly through that page until he finds 'isomorphic'.

This indexed search uses two levels of indices, followed by a linear search.

2.1 Searching – Linear and Indexed

Exercise

Contextual

1 Jody is looking in the library for a book about the English Civil War. What would be a sensible strategy?

2 Karen wants to buy a bicycle. She knows there is a bicycle shop on the High Street, and can catch a bus that will drop her at the end of the High Street. How does she find the shop, using a linear search?

2.2 Searching – Binary and Tree Searches

If the items we are searching through are in random order, we do not have much choice other than to make a linear search. However, if they are ordered, we can considerably reduce the number of items we must check. One of the most common methods is the **Binary Search**. This works by continually halving the possibilities. However, if the items are stored in a tree, then a **Tree Search** will be needed.

Example 1 – Binary Search

Henry is thinking of a number between 1 and 100. Paul has to guess what it is. How should he guess?

Solution

Guess number	Paul's guess	Henry's response
1	50	Too big
2	25	Too small
3	37	Too small
4	44	Too big
5	40	Too small
6	42	Too big
7	41	Correct

Example 2 – Tree Search

A river is formed from a large number of tributaries, each of which starts from a natural spring. Alan is researching the water flow of the river, and wishes to check the flow at each spring, and at each place where flows merge. He labels each measuring point on his map, and then plans what order to go round them. What are his best choices?

You may be familiar with a tree diagram in statistics. A binary tree is one in which each branch splits in to two new ones.

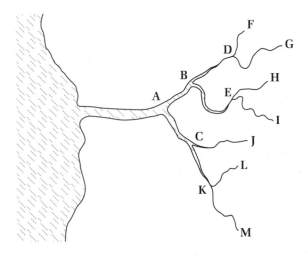

A more detailed definition of a tree can be found in Chapter 3.

Solution

The river system is a tree-like structure: we shall assume that Alan starts at the root of the tree – the full river flow. In a tree, we can define branches as being to the left (before) or the right (after) the node (junction). There are three methods of searching a tree – pre-order, in-order and post-order, which refer to whether the node is checked before any branches, between the left and right branches, or after the branches.

He decides to use a pre-order search, which means starting at the river mouth. When he reaches a junction he will measure the flow there, then he will do the entire left branch (with all its sub-branches), followed by the right.

He therefore starts at **A**, then heads for **B**. After **B** he goes to **D**, then on to **F**. As this is a leaf (end), he retraces to the previous node and, as the node is already checked, goes down the right branch to **G**. He must now retrace back until he finds a node that he has not done the right branch of (which will be **B**) and take this branch, taking flow measurements at **E**, then **H**, then **I**.

He now retraces his steps back to **A** (where he has already taken the measurement) and follows the right branch to **C**, **J**, **K**, **L**, **M** in that order, before returning to his starting point.

Alan's search aims to cover all possible points. Many searches would stop on finding a required item.

Activity

List the order in which the measurements will be taken if Alan uses

a an in-order (left, node, right) search or
b a post-order (left, right, node) search.

2.2 Searching – Binary and Tree Searches

Exercise

Contextual

1 You are playing a version of hangman, in which you guess each letter of the word in turn. Each time you guess, if you are wrong you are told whether the correct letter is earlier or later in the alphabet than your guess. What would be a sensible strategy?

2 You and a friend are playing a guessing game at a party. You each have a card marked with the shapes below. Your friend has chosen one of the shapes, and you have to find out which one. You are only allowed to use yes/no questions. Which three questions would let you find the right shape if:

a **i** your friend chose the square?
   ii your friend chose the circle?

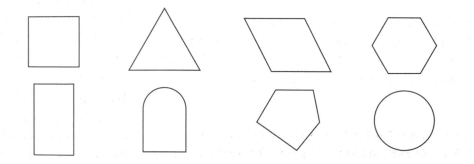

b Can you find a set of yes/no questions which will always let you get the right answer in 3 questions? (You may need to have a set of more than 3 questions).

3 Below is an extract from the family tree of Edward III.

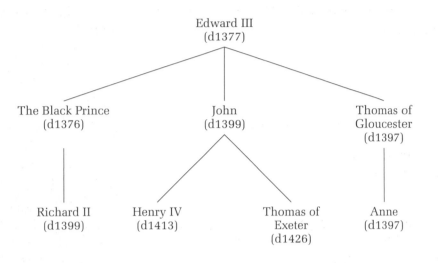

Mara and Ian are trying to find out when Thomas of Exeter died.

a Mara starts with the first node. She works her way down each branch in turn, keeping to the left and checking any node she passes through. When she reaches the end of a branch, she goes back up, and down any branches to the right.

List the order in which she checks each name until she reaches her target.

b Ian starts with the first node. He then checks all the nodes at the next level down, working from left to right. He continues like this until he finds his target.

List the order in which Ian checks each name.

c In general, is there a difference between the efficiency of these methods?

2.3 Sorting – Linear Algorithms

Linear sorting algorithms are those which, usually repeatedly, work through the data in the order in which it occurs, making adjustments to the order where appropriate at each step. They all require a checking of each value against a proportion of the others and are therefore $O(n^2)$ in complexity.

The most common one is **Bubble Sort**, which is considered in this section, together with **Shuttle Sort** and **Insertion Sort**. There are other

Sorting algorithms can be applied to any set of objects which have an implied order or sequence. However, for simplicity, it is common to consider a set of integers.

We start with distinct values – see page 14 for comments on sets with duplicate values.

linear sorting algorithms, and two more can be found in questions 1 and 2 of Exercise 2.3 Contextual.

The principle of Bubble Sort is to work through the list in sequence, comparing adjacent values and swapping them if they are in the wrong order. This is repeated until the ordering is complete.

Example 1 – Bubble

Avril is tidying the shelves in the library and finds that the encyclopaedia in six volumes has not been put back in order. They are very heavy so she can only manage to lift one out at a time, sliding the next one along the shelf and placing the one in her hand back on the shelf. How does she sort the books? How many 'moves' will she have to make?

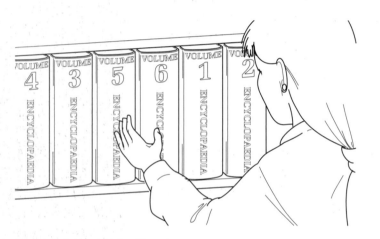

Complete A-Level Maths-Discrete

Solution

First pass:	4 3 5 6 1 2	compare (4, 3) and swap
	3 4 5 6 1 2	compare (4, 5)
	3 4 5 6 1 2	compare (5, 6)
	3 4 5 6 1 2	compare (6,1) and swap
	3 4 5 1 6 2	compare (6,2) and swap
Second Pass	3 4 5 1 2 6	compare (3, 4), (4, 5), (5, 1) and swap this
	3 4 1 5 2 6	compare and swap (5,2)
	3 4 1 2 5 6	compare (5,6)
Third Pass	3 4 1 2 5 6	compare (3, 4), (4, 1) and swap this
	3 1 4 2 5 6	compare and swap (4, 2)
	3 1 2 4 5 6	compare (4, 5), (5, 6)

In future, we will only start a new line of working after a swap has taken place.

Fourth Pass	3 1 2 4 5 6	compare and swap (3, 1)
	1 3 2 4 5 6	compare and swap (3, 2)
	1 2 3 4 5 6	compare (3, 4), (4, 5), (5, 6)

Fifth Pass

No values needed to be swapped so we have finished.

Total number of moves 3 + 2 + 2 + 2 = 9

Analysis

Notice that at each pass, at least one value is added to its correct position from the right-hand end. It is therefore possible to amend the algorithm to stop one sooner each time.

Bubble Sort takes its name from the large items 'bubbling' through to the end of the list on each pass.

The **Shuttle Sort** algorithm has the opposite effect in that small items work to the beginning of the list. The method says that whenever a smaller item is found and swapped, it is then compared with its other predecessors until its natural position is found. Thus at any given time, the items already considered form a sorted sub-list.

Example 2 – Shuttle

Avril decides that having taken a book off the shelf, she can hold it whilst sliding several books, one at a time, along the shelf until the rightful place for the one she is holding is found. How does she sort the books? How many sliding moves will she have to make?

Solution

4 3 5 6 1 2	compare (4, 3), remove 3, slide 4 and replace 3 [1 sliding move]
3 4 5 6 1 2	compare 4 and 5
3 4 5 6 1 2	compare 5 and 6
3 4 5 6 1 2	compare (6, 1), remove 1, slide 6; compare and slide 5, compare and slide 4, compare and slide 3, and then replace 1 [4 sliding moves]
1 3 4 5 6 2	compare (6, 2), remove 2, slide 6, compare and slide 5, compare and slide 4, compare and slide 3, compare but do not slide 1 and re-insert 2 [4 sliding moves]

Shuttle Sort takes its name from the forward and backward motion through the list. The name is occasionally also applied to the shaker sort, in which the bubble sort algorithm is applied alternately left-to-right, then right-to-left.

Total number of moves 1 + 4 + 4 = 9

Insertion Sort is based on a series of linear searches, and constructs a new list in order. It is particularly effective where moving the items is difficult since it guarantees moving each item once, and once only, most of the work being in making comparisons.

Insertion Sort Algorithm

1 Search the current list for the smallest value.

2 Move this value to the first available place in a new list.

3 Repeat steps 1 and 2 until all items have been added to the new list.

Example 3 – Insertion

A carnival procession is to include a parade of 8 classic cars which are currently parked in alphabetical order in a nearby car park. Each car has a card on the windscreen giving its age. Show how the steward can sort them into order by age in the procession.

Solution

The cars are: Austin A40 (1959), Ford Anglia (1949), Hillman Imp (1963), Jaguar E-Type (1964), Lotus Elite (1962), Morris Oxford (1961), Triumph Herald (1960), VW Beetle (1953).

The steward walks along the line of cars checking the windscreen cards: he looks at the first car and remembers 1959. He then looks at the second and decides that 1949 is earlier so remembers this instead. He continues to look at each of the others in turn, but does not find anything before 1949. Having reached the end of the row, he knows that the 1949 Ford Anglia is the oldest, and sends it down to the exit.

He now walks along the row a second time, checking the remaining seven cars in the same way, and will choose the VW Beetle.

On the third, fourth, fifth and sixth walks he will select the Austin A40, the Triumph Herald, the Morris Oxford and the Lotus Elite respectively.

On the seventh walk he checks the remaining two and sends the Hillman Imp forward. This only leaves the Jaguar, which must therefore be the most recent, and can be sent to join the back of the procession.

Lists containing duplicate values

Duplicate values are not a problem provided that the algorithm has been clearly defined. For example, in the linear sorting algorithms, the comparison should be of the form 'if the right-most value of the pair is the greater then swap their positions'; this will leave equal values unchanged thus avoiding an unnecessary exchange. In Quicksort (see section 2.5) a decision must be made as to whether they are placed in the left or the right sub-list when a duplicate to the pivot is found.

2.3 Sorting – Linear Algorithms

Exercise

Technique

1 Use Bubble Sort to sort the following list of numbers into ascending order: 3, 6, 2, 7, 4, 1, 5

a How many swaps are made?

b How many comparisons are made if you always check to the end of the list?

c How many comparisons could you save if you remember that the last value is correct, and reduce the number of comparisons by one each time you go through?

2 Use Shuttle Sort to sort the following list of numbers into ascending order: 3, 6, 2, 7, 4, 1, 5

a How many swaps are made?

b How many comparisons are made?

3 Use Insertion Sort to sort the following list of numbers into ascending order:

3, 6, 2, 7, 4, 1, 5

a How many comparisons are made when you are looking for the smallest value in the list?

b How many 'swaps' are made (where a swap is moving a number from the unsorted list to the sorted list)?

Contextual

1 The **Selection with Interchange algorithm** is:

```
1 Starting from the left, take each value in turn as
  the key value.

2 Compare the key value with each value to its right
  in turn, remembering the position of the smallest.
```

```
3 When you have checked them all, swap the key value
  with the smallest value found.

4 Continue with the next key value, until the last
  one is reached.
```

Use this to sort the following list of numbers:

3, 6, 2, 7, 4, 1, 5

2 The **Exchange Sort algorithm** is:

```
1 Starting from the left, take each position in turn
  as the key position.

2 Compare the item in the key position with each
  subsequent item to its right in turn, swapping if
  necessary after each comparison, retaining the key
  position even though the value in it will have
  changed.

3 Continue with each subsequent key position until
  the last one is reached.
```

Use this to sort the following list of numbers:

3, 6, 2, 7, 4, 1, 5

3 A child is putting a Russian doll back together. The dolls are currently in the order below. Before putting the doll together, the child wants to get the dolls lined up in the correct order, starting with the largest.

a How many comparisons are made when putting the dolls in order?
b How many 'swaps' are made (where a swap is moving a number from the unsorted list to the sorted list)?

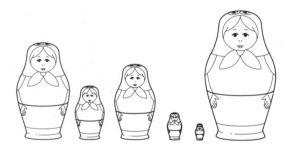

2.4 Shell Sort

Shell Sort applies a Linear Sorting Algorithm (usually Bubble Sort) a number of times, making comparisons across intervals which eventually decrease down to 1. For example, if the intervals were 3 and 1, we would first compare $1^{st}/4^{th}/7^{th}/10^{th}$ etc, $2^{nd}/5^{th}/8^{th}/11^{th}$ etc, $3^{rd}/6^{th}/9^{th}/12^{th}$ etc until each of these sub-lists was sorted, then sort on an interval of size 1 as before.

The analysis is difficult, but it has been shown to be considerably more efficient than the sample linear algorithms described in the previous section.

The Shell Sort algorithm was first published in 1959 by D L Shell of the General Electric Company, Cincinnati, Ohio.

Example 1

Sort the following list of numbers, using the Shell Sort algorithm with steps of size 3, then size 1:

3, 2, 5, 7, 6, 4, 8, 1

Solution

First phase: step size 3

First Pass   3 2 **5** 7 6 **4** 8 1

Compare 1st with 4th (3, 7), 2nd with 5th (2, 6), 3rd with 6th (5, 4) and swap

3 2 4 **7** 6 **5** **8** **1**

Compare 4th with 7th (7, 8), 5th with 8th (6, 1) and swap giving

3 2 4 7 1 5 8

Second Pass   3 **2** 4 7 **1** 5 8 6

Compare 1st with 4th (3, 7), 2nd with 5th (2, 1) and swap

3 1 **4** 7 **2** 5 **8** **6**

Compare 3rd with 6th (4, 5), 4th with 7th (7, 8), 5th with 8th (2, 6)

There are no more swaps to be made on this step size

Second phase: size 1

First Pass   3 1 4 7 2 5 8 6
                  1 3 4 7 2 5 8 6
                  1 3 4 2 7 5 8 6
                  1 3 4 2 5 7 8 6

Second Pass   1 3 4 2 5 7 6 8

Third Pass   1 3 2 4 5 6 7 8

Analysis

Notice that the number of exchanges compared to an ordinary Bubble Sort has been reduced because some of the earlier ones moved objects further in one exchange.

For large sets of data, step sizes of $\frac{1}{2}(3^k - 1)$ are believed by many to be the most efficient; this gives the sequence 1, 4, 13, 40, ... which are, of course, used in reverse order.

k is an integer counter, allowing us to calculate a sequence of values for the step sizes, starting with $k = 1$.

2.4 Shell Sort

Exercise

Technique

Use Shell Sort to sort the following lists, using step sizes of 3 and 1.

1 7, 8, 3, 6, 5, 1, 2, 9, 4

2 12, 14, 8, 10, 16, 4, 18, 2, 6

3 49, 56, 7, 21, 63, 35, 14, 28, 42

2.5 Quicksort

Quicksort is a 'divide and conquer' algorithm. The principle is to split each list to be sorted into 3: – a pivot value, and two sub-lists, one containing only values less than the pivot, the other containing only values greater than the pivot. Within each sub-list, the original order is maintained.

At each step the number of sub-lists is doubling, and their length is, on average, halving. Therefore after m iterations there will be 2^m sub-lists. When $2^m = n$ (the number of values to be sorted), m is proportional to the logarithm of n. At each iteration there are n values to be subdivided, so on average the algorithm is O($n \log n$). However, in the worst scenario, it can still be O(n^2).

A logarithm is the inverse of an exponential function. There is a different logarithm function for each exponential ($\log_2$ for 2^m, $\log_{10}$ or log for 10^m etc). However, as all logarithms are proportional to each other, it does not matter which we use for our analysis.

Sometimes the pivot value is taken as the middle (left middle if the list contains an even number of values) and we shall use this in our example. However, as the list is unordered, the first value is just as likely to be suitable and is easier to find.

Example 1

Miss Johnson has a pile of exam papers which have to be ranked in order of merit. She has enough desk space to split them in to a number of piles so she decides to use Quicksort. Show how she does this.

Solution

Miss Johnson notes that there are 10 papers so the 'middle' is the 5th paper which has a mark of 71% on it. She sorts the remaining papers so that they are the correct side of this one.

She now has two sets of papers to deal with: the left set has six papers, and the middle (left of) is the 57% so she splits according to that, whilst the right has three papers, of which the middle is the 93% which happens to be the highest.

She now has a number of small piles – one with three in and two with two. She deals with these in the same way.

All her piles have now gone, the papers are all single, so she can gather them up in order.

2.5 Quicksort

Exercise

Technique

Use Quicksort to sort the following lists. In each case, use the first number in the list as the pivot.

1 7, 8, 3, 6, 5, 1, 2, 9, 4

2 12, 14, 8, 10, 16, 4, 18, 2, 6

3 49, 56, 7, 21, 63, 35, 14, 28, 42

2.6 Bin-packing

The principle of Bin-packing is that a number of objects of differing sizes have to be fitted into bins of a uniform fixed size. The simplest algorithm for Bin-packing is the first-fit algorithm. This states that each item is placed in the first available bin.

"Bin" is used to describe objects such as boxes, shelves, planks which can be filled by items or cut into varying sizes

Example 1 – First fit

A builder is replacing the guttering on a series of roof-gables. He needs the following lengths of guttering:

0.7 m, 2.1 m, 0.8 m, 0.6 m, 1.9 m, 1.3 m, 0.3 m, 0.8 m, 0.4 m

Guttering is sold in lengths of 3 metres. How many lengths should he buy and how should he cut it?

Solution

The following diagram shows the end result, with the numbers in brackets showing the order in which the pieces were cut (this would not normally be included in a solution).

0.7 (1)	2.1 (2)		0.2
0.8 (3)	0.6 (4)	1.3 (6)	0.3 (7)
1.9 (5)		0.8 (8)	0.3
0.4 (9)	2.6		

0.7 m is cut from the first length leaving 2.3 metres.

2.1 m is cut from the 2.3 metres, leaving 0.2 metres.

0.8 m is cut from a second length (since the 0.2 m left over is not big enough), leaving 2.2 m.

0.6 m is cut from the 2.2 m, leaving 1.6 m.

Since neither remnant is big enough, a third piece is now used to cut the 1.9 m length, leaving 1.1 m.

1.3 m is cut from the 1.6 m remnant, leaving 0.3 m, which is used next.

0.8 m is cut from the 1.1 m remnant, leaving 0.3 m.

Since none of the remaining remnants are long enough, a fourth length is needed to cut the final piece of 0.4 m.

The builder therefore needs to purchase 4 lengths if he is to cut the lengths in this manner.

This would appear not to be optimal and an alternative algorithm is required. A significant improvement can often be obtained by sorting the items into decreasing order of size first.

Example 2 – First fit decreasing

Find a solution to the previous problem by using the first-fit decreasing algorithm. Show by calculation the minimum number of lengths that will be required.

Solution

First the required lengths are sorted in to decreasing order of size.

2.1, 1.9, 1.3, 0.8, 0.8, 0.7, 0.6, 0.4, 0.3

Now applying the first-fit algorithm as before, we get the following cutting pattern:

2.1 (1)		0.8 (4)	0.1
1.9 (2)		0.8 (5)	0.3 (9)
1.3 (3)	0.7 (6)	0.6 (7)	0.4 (8)

The total of all the required lengths is 8.9 metres. Dividing this by 3 metres (the purchased lengths) gives 2.967 lengths required. Therefore

Bin-packing is an heuristic algorithm and this improvement is not guaranteed to give the optimum solution.

Unless this calculation gives an integer result, it is always necessary to round it up.

the requirements cannot be cut from 2 lengths so at least 3 will be required. In this case we have found a solution which can be achieved with 3 lengths.

2.6 Bin-packing

Exercise

Contextual

1 An electrician needs a number of pieces of cable of the following lengths: 4 m, 3 m, 5 m, 1 m, 6 m, 6 m, 2 m, 7 m, 4 m, 2 m. Show how all these pieces can be cut from two 20 m lengths of cable.

2 A Media Studies student has asked a friend to record a number of programmes for them while they are away on holiday. The lengths of the programmes, in minutes, are given below.

30 25 75 90 30 30 25 20 90 100 25

  a What is the minimum number of 3 hour video tapes which will be needed?
  b What solution is given using the first fit decreasing algorithm?
  c Find a solution using the minimum number of tapes

Consolidation

Exercise A

1 **a** Use a Bubble Sort algorithm to rearrange the following numbers into ascending order, showing the new arrangement after each pass.
    4, 7, 13, 26, 8, 15, 6, 56
  b Find the maximum number of comparisons needed to rearrange a list of eight numbers into ascending order.

(AQA)

2 Use the Quicksort algorithm to rearrange the following numbers into ascending order, showing the new arrangement at each stage. Take the first number in any list as the pivot.

9, 5, 7, 11, 2, 8, 6, 17

(AQA)

3 Use the Binary Search algorithm to locate the name GREGORY in the following list.

1   ARCHER
2   BOWEN
3   COUTTS
4   DENYER
5   EATWELL
6   FULLER
7   GRANT
8   GREGORY
9   LEECH
10 PENNY
11 THOMPSON

4 Andy wants to record the following twelve TV programmes onto video tape. Each video tape has space for up to three hours of programmes.

Programme	A	B	C	D	E	F	G	H	I	J	K	L
Length (hours)	$\frac{1}{2}$	$\frac{1}{2}$	$\frac{3}{4}$	1	1	1	1	$1\frac{1}{2}$	$1\frac{1}{2}$	$1\frac{3}{4}$	2	2

a   Suppose that Andy records the programmes in the order A to L using the first fit algorithm. Find the number of tapes needed, and show which programmes are recorded onto which tape.

b   Suppose instead that Andy is transferring the programmes from previously recorded tapes, so that they can be copied in any order, and that Andy uses the first fit decreasing algorithm. Find the number of tapes needed, and show which programmes are recorded onto which tape.

(OCR)

Exercise B

1 Use the Bubble Sort algorithm to rearrange the following numbers into ascending order, showing the new arrangement after each pass.

5, 3, 12, 19, 11, 14, 2, 10

(AQA Modified)

2 Use the Quicksort algorithm to rearrange the following numbers into ascending order, showing the new arrangement at each stage. Take the first number in any list as the pivot.

5, 3, 12, 19, 11, 14, 2, 10

(AQA Modified)

3 Use the Binary Search algorithm to locate the name DENYER in the following list.

1   ARCHER
2   BOWEN
3   COUTTS
4   DENYER
5   EATWELL
6   FULLER
7   GRANT
8   GREGORY
9   LEECH
10 PENNY
11 THOMPSON

4 Andy wants to record the following twelve TV programmes onto video tape. Each video tape has space for up to three hours of programmes.

Programme	A	B	C	D	E	F	G	H	I	J	K	L
Length (hours)	$\frac{1}{2}$	$\frac{1}{4}$	$\frac{1}{2}$	$\frac{3}{4}$	$1\frac{1}{4}$	1	$\frac{1}{4}$	$\frac{1}{4}$	1	$1\frac{1}{4}$	$1\frac{1}{2}$	$\frac{1}{2}$

a Suppose that Andy records the programmes in the order A to L using the first fit algorithm. Find the number of tapes needed, and show which programmes are recorded onto which tape.

b Suppose instead that Andy is transferring the programmes from previously recorded tapes, so that they can be copied in any order, and that Andy uses the first fit decreasing algorithm. Find the number of tapes needed, and show which programmes are recorded onto which tape.

(OCR)

Applications and Extensions

Battleships

In the game of battleships, your opponent has hidden boats of varying length on a grid of squares. You guess one square at a time and are told 'hit' or 'miss'. Investigate different strategies for searching the grid, depending on how many squares long the boats still to find are.

Shell Sort step sizes

Try using different combinations of step sizes to test the hypothesis that step sizes of $\frac{1}{2}(3^k - 1)$ are the most efficient.

Packing in more than one dimension

How would you apply the packing algorithms from section 2.6 when dealing with 2-dimensional shapes?

Summary

- In a **linear** search, you may have to check every item to find the one required.

- In an **indexed** search, one or more levels of indices enable the scope of the search to be reduced.

- In a **binary** search, the items must be already ordered, the middle item is repeatedly checked and half the list rejected.

- In a **tree** search, we eventually need to check each node, and everything below it. An **in-order** search will consider the left branch, then the current node, then the right branch, whilst a **pre-order** search studies the current node before any branches, and a **post-order** search will leave the current node until after all its branches.

- There are a number of $O(n^2)$ **sorting** algorithms, including Bubble Sort and Insertion Sort. They all work by making a series of comparisons and exchanges.

- **Quicksort** is a divide and conquer algorithm which is in best case $O(n \log n)$.

- **Shell Sort** is a variation on the $O(n^2)$ sorts which initially uses larger step sizes to move items larger distances with less work.

- **Bin packing** describes problems where varying sized items need grouping together efficiently subject to a maximum group size.

- The **first-fit** algorithm places items in to bins in the order in which they occur, whilst the first-fit decreasing algorithm sorts them into descending order of size first.

3 Graph Theory

3.1 Language and Notation

In this section, we look at the language and notation of graphs and how it can be used to model problems and help us to solve them.

Example 1

The following is a simplified map of the Hong Kong MRT in 2002, with some stations omitted. Describe this map using mathematical language.

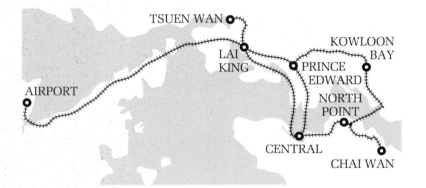

Solution

The map consists of a number of **vertices** (nodes), connected together by **edges** (arcs). We can analyse the vertices by counting the number of edges incident at each one, which we call the **order** (valency) of the vertex.

For example there is a vertex of order 4 at Lai King, and a vertex of order 1 at Chai Wan.

Since it is possible to find a route from any vertex to any other, we say that the graph is **connected**. Since there are no duplicate edges (i.e. two edges between the same pair of vertices) and no **loops** (an edge with both ends at the same vertex) we say that the graph is **simple**.

There are two **cycles**, one of which is North Point–Kowloon Bay–Prince Edward–Central–North Point.

There are a number of different words used in graph theory – we will generally use vertex, edge and order but the other words are equivalent.

Example 2

Represent the Hong Kong map from example 1 in a table and discuss alternative graphical representations.

Solution

The following **adjacency matrix** represents the graph. In this case a 1 indicates the existence of a direct route between the locations.

	Airport	Tsuen Wan	Lai King	Central	Prince Edward	Kowloon Bay	North Point	Chai Wan
Airport	—	0	1	0	0	0	0	0
Tsuen Wan	0	—	1	0	0	0	0	0
Lai King	1	1	—	1	1	0	0	0
Central	0	0	1	—	1	0	1	0
Prince Edward	0	0	1	1	—	1	0	0
Kowloon Bay	0	0	0	0	1	—	1	0
North Point	0	0	0	1	0	1	—	1
Chai Wan	0	0	0	0	0	0	1	—

A dash is used where the vertex is repeated (and no connection is therefore needed).

The following graphs correspond to the same information, but are clearly different from each other, and the original map.

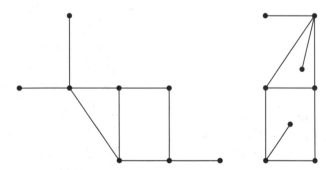

Since the connectivity has not changed and the underlying data is therefore the same, these graphs are said to be **isomorphic** to each other. With an appropriate choice of vertex labelling, they could be represented by the same adjacency matrix.

For two graphs to be isomorphic, it is necessary that they have the same number of vertices of each order. However, these vertices must also be connected together in the same manner.

Isomorphic is derived from the Greek words isos meaning equal and morphe meaning form.

Example 3

Here is a map of the roads in the town centre in Barsett. Represent this as an adjacency matrix.

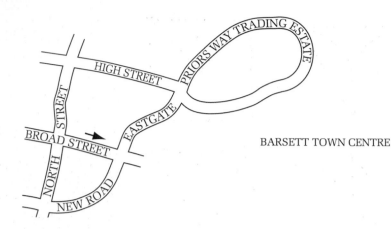

BARSETT TOWN CENTRE

Solution

We first label the five junctions clockwise from the junction of New Road and North Street, A to E.

		To				
		A	**B**	**C**	**D**	**E**
From	**A**	—	1	0	0	1
	B	1	—	1	0	1
	C	0	1	—	1	0
	D	0	0	1	2	1
	E	1	0	0	1	—

The adjacency matrix shows the number of connections between each pair of vertices. We therefore need to use a 2 for D to D because there is a loop which can be used in either direction, whilst E to B is 0 because B to E is a one-way street.

It is standard practice to use 'From' and 'To' as here, and this will be assumed in future examples and exercises.

3.1 Language and Notation

Exercise

Technique

1 From the eight graphs below, pick out the four pairs which are isomorphic to each other.

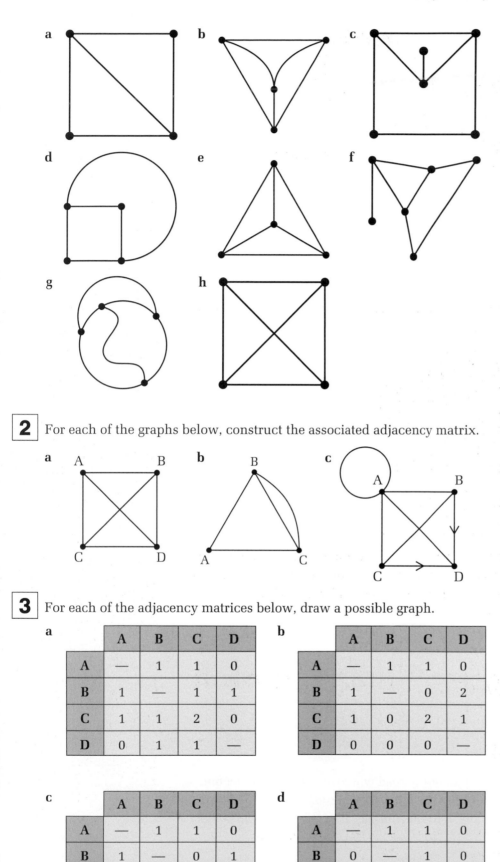

2 For each of the graphs below, construct the associated adjacency matrix.

3 For each of the adjacency matrices below, draw a possible graph.

a

	A	B	C	D
A	—	1	1	0
B	1	—	1	1
C	1	1	2	0
D	0	1	1	—

b

	A	B	C	D
A	—	1	1	0
B	1	—	0	2
C	1	0	2	1
D	0	0	0	—

c

	A	B	C	D
A	—	1	1	0
B	1	—	0	1
C	1	1	—	1
D	0	1	1	—

d

	A	B	C	D
A	—	1	1	0
B	0	—	1	0
C	0	0	—	1
D	1	1	0	—

3.2 Modelling Networks with Graphs

Graphs can be used to represent different aspects of the problem which is being modelled. We define **a network** as being a graph carrying information such as lengths, costs or times as **weights** on the edges.

Example

Construct a **distance matrix** for Barsett town centre (the approximate road lengths have been added to the map).

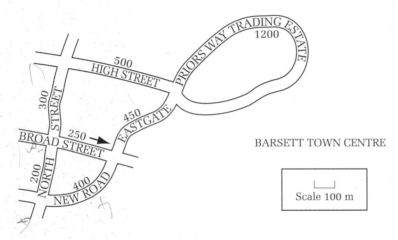

BARSETT TOWN CENTRE

Scale 100 m

Solution

Using the same labelling for the road junctions, we can complete the table.

	A	B	C	D	E
A	—	200			400
B	200	—	300		250
C		300	—	450	
D			450	1200	400
E	400			400	—

The matrix shows the length of the road wherever a direct connection exists. D to D therefore shows the length of the road around the Priors Way Trading Estate, whilst E to B is null because it is a one-way street the other way.

Chapter 5 develops algorithms for finding shortest distances which would enable this matrix to be filled in for other journeys.

3.2 Modelling Networks with Graphs

Exercise

Contextual

For each of the networks below, construct the associated distance matrix.

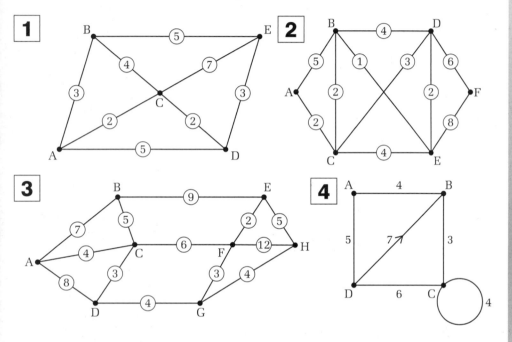

3.3 Eulerian, Bipartite and Complete Graphs

Activity – Handshaking

Four people meet at a party and decide to shake hands, but each one wants to shake a different number of hands to all the others. Since the first person can only shake three others, that leaves at most two for the second, one for the third and therefore none for the fourth. This cannot happen because the first person must shake the fourth person's hand.

Investigate for different sized groups of people. What do you notice about the total of all the numbers of hands shaken (valency of the vertices)? How does it relate to the number of handshakes (edges) that took place?

Example 1 – Eulerian

Many of you will have seen the following diagram:

 The problem here is to draw the diagram without taking the pencil off the paper, and without drawing any line twice.

Solution

It can be achieved by starting at one of the lower vertices, and there are a number of possible solutions, including

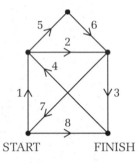

START   FINISH

The graph is traversable because all the vertices except the two at the bottom are of even order. If a vertex is of even order, then every time that the vertex is reached along a previously unused edge, there will be another edge available on which the route can continue. If it is possible to traverse a graph and finish at the start vertex, it is called **Eulerian**. The above example where the start and finish are different is known as **semi-Eulerian**. Therefore an Eulerian graph will have all vertices of even order, whilst a semi-Eulerian will have two odd-order vertices, with the remainder even-ordered. This concept will be used in Chapter 7.

Leonhard Euler was an 18th century Swiss mathematician whose many contributions include some graph theory.

Example 2 – Bipartite

There are four wholesale warehouses which can supply goods to each of six stores according to the following table:

Wholesaler	Store
A	P, Q, T
B	R, S, T
C	P, R, T, V
D	Q, S, V

Represent this information as a graph.

Solution

By arranging the vertices in two groups, it is possible to draw the graph so that every edge has one end in each group.

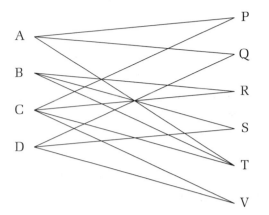

This is called a **Bipartite** (two part) graph. Such graphs can be used to represent matching, allocation and transportation problems (see Chapters 11 and 12)

Example 3 – Complete Graphs

Draw a simple connected graph with four vertices of order three, and a bipartite graph with a set of three and a set of two vertices, of order two and three respectively.

Solution

      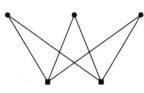

These graphs are called **complete** graphs.

The first, because there is a single edge between each and every pair of vertices. The first is often denoted K_4, the complete graph for four vertices.

The second because there is a single edge connecting each of the possible pairings between the two sets of vertices, and no connections between vertices in the same set. This is denoted $K_{3,2}$, the complete bipartite graph for sets of three and two vertices.

In this example, we have used circles and squares to distinguish between the two sets of vertices in our bipartite graph.

3.3 Eulerian, Bipartite and Complete Graphs

Exercise

Technique

1 State whether the following graphs are Eulerian, semi-Eulerian or neither.

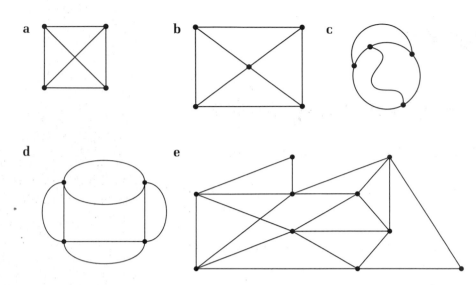

2 Represent the information in each of the following tables using a bipartite graph.

a

Player	Role
Klusener	Batsman, Bowler
Hick	Batsman, Slip Fielder, Bowler
Russell	Wicket-keeper, Batsman
Stewart	Wicket-keeper, Batsman
Atherton	Batsman, Slip Fielder

b

Country	Sea coast on
UK	North Sea, Atlantic Ocean
Norway	Atlantic, North Sea, Baltic
Russia	Baltic, Arctic Ocean, Pacific Ocean, Black Sea
Spain	Atlantic Ocean, Mediterranean
Turkey	Mediterranean, Black Sea

3 Draw the following graphs:

    a K_6 **b** $K_{4,2}$

3.4 Planarity

Activity - Crossing edges

Try to draw the graphs K_4, K_5 and $K_{3,3}$ without any edges crossing.

A graph in which there are no crossing edges is called a **planar graph**. It is planar if it *can* be drawn without crossing edges, even though there may currently be some. You should have found that K_4 is planar (though the common drawing is a square with two diagonals which cross over), but that K_5 and $K_{3,3}$ are not. **Kuratowski's theorem** uses this to show that a graph is planar only if it does not contain K_5 or $K_{3,3}$ within it. Putting this the other way round, if a **sub-graph** (some of the vertices and their associated edges) can be found which is either K_5 or $K_{3,3}$, it is not possible to avoid crossing edges, and the graph is not planar.

Planarity is important in applications such as the design of electronic circuits.

Example 1

Show that this graph is not planar.

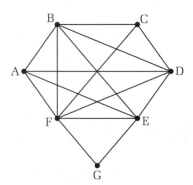

Solution

Deleting the vertices C and G, and all the edges associated with them leaves the following graph:

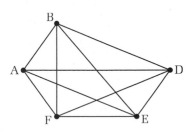

This is K_5 which is not planar, therefore the original graph is not planar.

Example 2

Show that this graph is not planar.

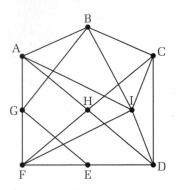

Solution

Delete edges BG, BI and GE (shown here as dotted lines)

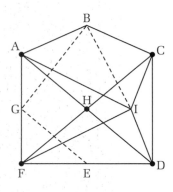

Note that vertices B, G and E are now of order 2. Their labels have been retained, but they are no longer marked as vertices. This means that there is now a direct connection between each of A and C, A and F, and F and D.

Similarly, I is no longer treated as a vertex. The edges AI and ID are treated as a single edge AD. We do the same with edges CI and IF.

There are now direct connections between each and every pair of vertices from the set A, C, D, F and H, forming K_5.

Since the graph contains K_5 as a **sub graph**, it is not planar.

Example 3

At this point we need to define a Hamiltonian cycle. This is a cycle which visits every vertex in a graph, without repetition.

Use the following algorithm to check whether or not the accompanying graph is planar.

Planarity Algorithm

1 Find a Hamiltonian cycle (every vertex joined to form a continuous chain) and redraw the graph so that this forms a polygon with all other edges inside it.

2 Select an edge to remain inside the polygon, and move outside the polygon any edges which cross it, without them crossing each other. If this cannot be done — stop, graph is not planar.

3 For any crossings remaining inside the polygon, try to move one of the edges involved to the outside of the polygon, without it creating any new crossings.

4 Repeat step 3 until all possible edge moves and all crossings have been considered. If there is still at least one crossing it is not planar, otherwise you have succeeded.

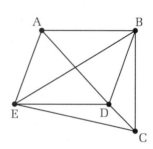

Solution

There is a Hamiltonian cycle A-B-C-D-E-A so this sequence of edges is drawn to form the perimeter of the polygon, and all the other edges are placed inside.

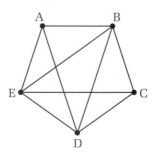

We choose (arbitrarily) to keep the edge BE inside the polygon, and therefore move AD to the outside.

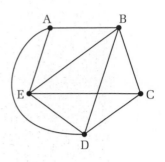

As BD and CE still cross we must consider each of these. Choosing to keep BD inside is not useful as we cannot then put CE outside without it crossing AD. However, if we keep CE inside and move BD a planar graph can be achieved.

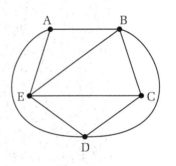

3.4 Planarity

Exercise

Technique

1 Redraw the following graphs in planar form.

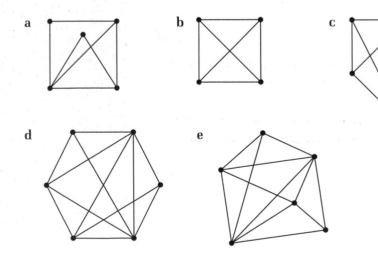

2 By showing that they contain either K_5 or $K_{3,3}$, as a subgraph show that the following graphs are non-planar.

a

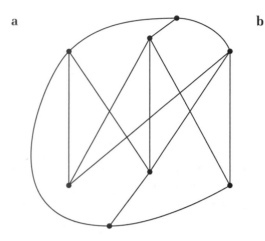

b

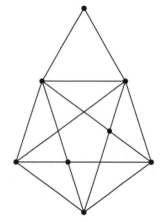

Consolidation

Exercise A

1 The caller at a barn dance asks 4 males and 4 females to arrange themselves so that the females are each holding hands with two other people, whilst the males are each holding hands with just one other person.

Draw graphs using [○] to represent a female and [×] to represent a male, to show all possible different arrangements in which this can be achieved.

You are not required to consider the number of ways in which arrangements may be formed. In other words you should regard the males as being indistinguishable from each other, and likewise for the females.

(AEB)

2 **a** A simple connected graph has 7 vertices, all having the same degree d. Give the possible values of d, and for each value of d give the number of edges of the graph.
b Another simple connected graph has 8 vertices, all having the same degree d. Draw such a graph with $d = 3$, and give the other possible values of d.

(AEB)

3 G is the graph illustrated with 6 vertices and 5 edges.

a What is the smallest number of edges which must be added to **G** in order to make a connected graph. Illustrate one such graph.
b What is the smallest number of edges which must be added to **G** to make a Hamiltonian graph? Illustrate one such graph, clearly pointing out a Hamiltonian cycle.
c What is the smallest number of edges which must be added to **G** in order to make an Eulerian graph. Illustrate one such graph.
d Show how the addition of 4 edges to **G** can create a graph which is not planar. Explain briefly how you know this graph is not planar.

(AQA)

4 Draw a bipartite graph to represent information in the following table.

Student	Subjects studied
A	W, X
B	Y
C	Z
D	X, Y

5 For the graph below

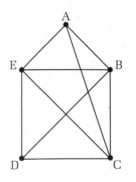

a state whether it is Eulerian, semi-Eulerian or neither
b show that the graph can be redrawn in planar form.

Exercise B

1 **a** Prove that the graph **G** is non-planar.

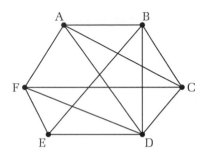

b **i** Show that the following graph, **G**, contains a subdivision of $K_{3,3}$, as a sub-graph:

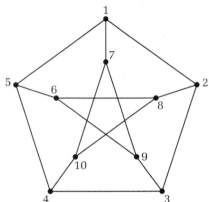

ii What does the fact that **G** has a sub-graph which is a subdivision of $K_{3,3}$ tell you about **G**?

(AQA)

2 **a** **b**

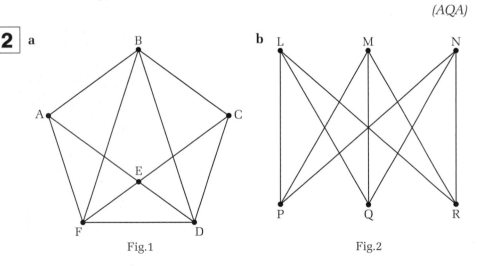

Fig.1   Fig.2

Use the planarity algorithm for graphs to determine which, if either, of the graphs shown in Fig 1 and Fig 2 is planar.

(EDEXCEL)

3 **a** A, B, C and D are the vertices of the complete graph K_4. List all the paths from A to B (i.e. routes passing through particular vertices only once).

b How many paths are there from A to B in the complete graph on the vertices {A, B, C, D, E}?

c Which of the graphs in parts **a** and **b** are Eulerian, and why?

(AQA)

4

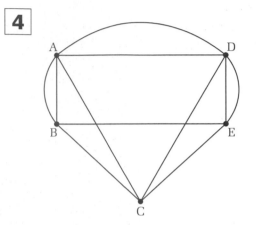

a Write down the orders of the nodes in the above graph, and deduce that the graph is semi-Eulerian.

b A semi-Eulerian trail is a path that traverses every arc once and only once. Explain why, for any semi-Eulerian trail on the graph in part (a), two of the arcs AC, BC, DC and EC must be traversed moving towards C and two traversed moving away from C.

c Redraw the graph in part (a) to show that it is planar.

d Show that it is impossible to add a vertex, F, joined to each of A, B, C, D and E, in such a way that the resulting graph is still planar.

(OCR)

5 **a** State whether the graph below is Eulerian, semi-Eulerian or neither.

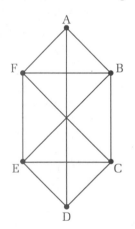

b By finding a subdivision of $K_{3,3}$, show that the graph is non-planar.

Applications and Extensions

The colouring problem

If you look at a map of the world, you will notice that it has been coloured so that no country is the same colour as any of the countries it borders (although it may be the same as a country which it only touches at a corner). This makes it much easier to tell the countries apart.

It is possible to use a graph to help colour in a map in this way. The vertices represent the countries. Edges indicate that countries share a common border.

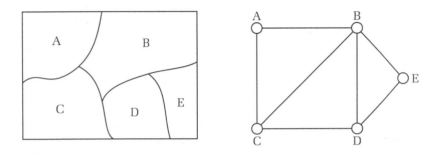

In the example below, vertex A was coloured "grey" first. This meant that B and C could not be "grey". D can be "grey", meaning that E cannot. The next stage was to colour B black. C and E cannot be black, so a third colour is needed. C was coloured white; E can also be white, and the map is finished.

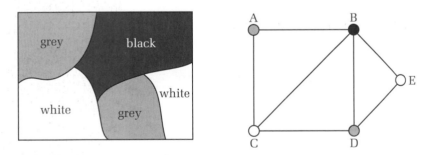

Investigate the minimum number of colours needed to colour any map.

Measuring jugs

In the film Die Hard III, Bruce Willis and Samuel L. Jackson are challenged to measure out exactly 4 litres of water into a large container, using only a 5 litre and a 3 litre jug. It is possible to use graph theory to keep track of the possible choices.

In the graph below, the vertices represent the contents of each jug and the container; edges show how to move from one possible vertex to another.

0, 0, 0 = all containers empty

5, 0, 0 = 5 l jug full: 3 l and large container empty

2, 0, 3 = 2 l in 5 l jug: 0 in 3 l jug: 3 l in large container

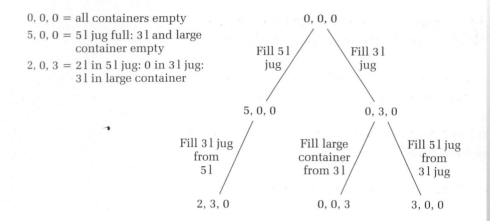

By continuing the graph, find a possible solution.

This technique can also be applied to the river crossing problems you may find in other books.

Summary

- A **graph** consists of **vertices** (**nodes**, points) and **edges** (**arcs**, lines).

- The **order** or **valency** of a vertex is the number of ends of edges at that vertex.

- The total order of all the vertices in a graph will always be an even number, equal to twice the number of edges.

- A **loop** is an edge with both ends connected to the same vertex.

- In a **simple** graph there is no more than one edge between any pair of vertices, and there are no loops.

- In a **connected** graph it is possible to find a route between every pair of vertices.

- A sequence of edges, starting and finishing at the same vertex and never repeating an edge is a **cycle**.

- A **Hamiltonian cycle** is one which visits every vertex exactly once.

- A graph can be represented by an **adjacency matrix** which shows how many edges exist between each pair of vertices.

- A **network** is a graph with weighted edges (representing distance, cost etc.). These can also be shown in a matrix, often called a **distance matrix**.

- Two graphs are said to be **isomorphic** if they could be represented (possibly by re-labelling vertices) by the same adjacency matrix.

- An **Eulerian** graph will have at most two odd vertices. It is possible to traverse every edge exactly once in a continuous sequence.

- In a **Bipartite** graph, it is possible to split the vertices into two groups so that every edge is a link between the two groups.

- A **complete** graph is a **simple** graph with every possible connection included.

- A **planar** graph can be drawn on a flat surface without any edges crossing.

4 Spanning Trees

What you need to know

● The language and notation of graphs

● The definition of a tree

Review

State which of the following are trees:

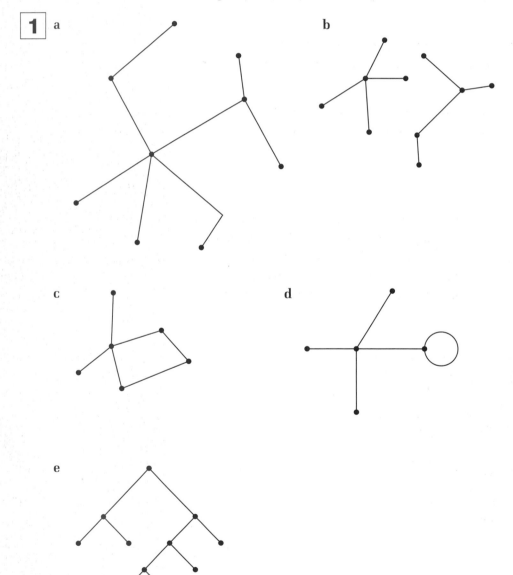

1 **a**   **b**

c   **d**

e

4.1 Kruskal's Algorithm

The most common reason for constructing a Spanning Tree is to find a minimum connector. That is, to ensure that all vertices are connected together (possibly via others) in the cheapest way.

Kruskal's algorithm is the most intuitive way of solving this problem, in that it seeks always to use the edge of least weight. This 'miserly' approach means that it is sometimes referred to as a **greedy algorithm.**

So named because it was first published by JB Kruskal in the proceedings of the American Mathematical Society in 1956.

```
Kruskal's Algorithm

1 Select the smallest edge in the graph (if more than
  one equally small, choose arbitrarily): this is the
  first edge in your solution.

2 Select the smallest unused edge in the original
  graph and, as long as it will not form a cycle, add
  it to your solution.

3 Repeat step 2 until all vertices are connected
  (this will require n - 1 edges for n vertices).
```

Example

Cable-2-U is setting up a new cable television network. Their system has a base station in the local business park (P) and 6 hubs (A-F) which then serve the local areas. They want to connect the hubs as cheaply as possible. The following graph shows the cost of each connection (in units of £10 000). Which cables should they lay and how much will it cost them?

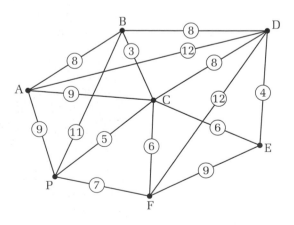

Solution

The edge with the lowest weight is BC so this edge is selected first.

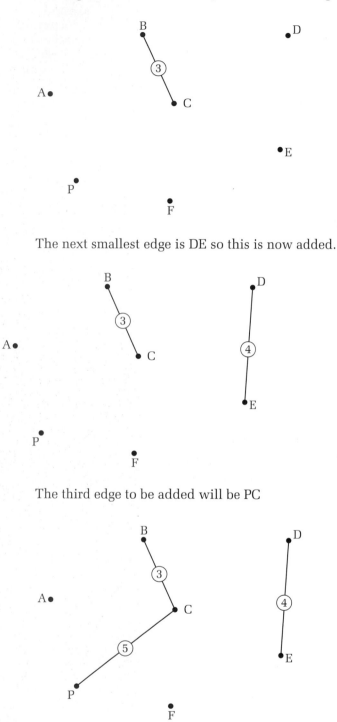

The next smallest edge is DE so this is now added.

The third edge to be added will be PC

For the fourth edge we have a choice of two edges of length 6. We will arbitrarily choose CE.

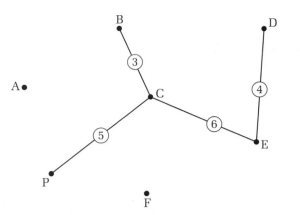

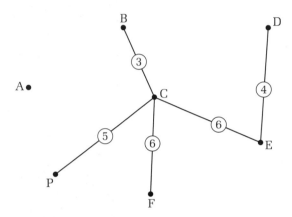

For the fifth edge we will now choose CF.

The next smallest edge is PF, but this would form a cycle (P is already connected to F via C). Instead we consider the edges of length 8; both BD and CD would form cycles, but AB does not so we add this to our tree.

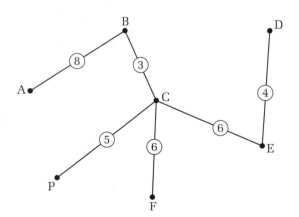

We have now used 6 edges, so our 7 vertices must be connected.

The sum of the selected edges is 32 so the total cost for Cable-2-U will be £320 000.

Note about uniqueness

Although we made an arbitrary choice during this example, the final solution was unique because both choices were subsequently used. However, it is possible to achieve different Minimum Spanning Trees for the same graph as the following diagram demonstrates (note that although the trees are not isomorphic, they do have the same total edge weight).

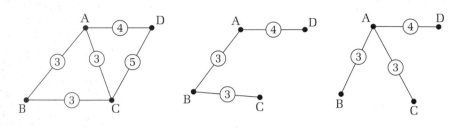

4.1 Kruskal's Algorithm

Exercise

Technique

Use Kruskal's Algorithm to find the Minimum Spanning Tree for each of the diagrams below.

1

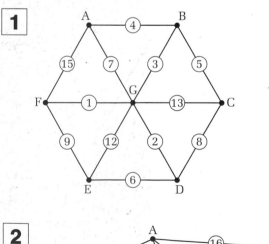

2

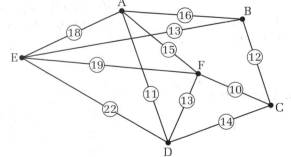

3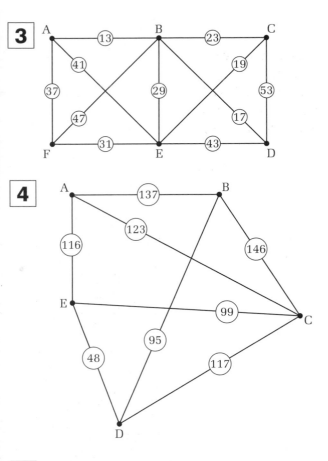

4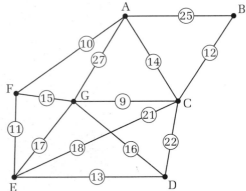

5

4.2 Prim's Algorithm

The difficulty with Kruskal's algorithm is that, for a large graph, it is difficult to check whether or not choosing a particular edge will form a loop.

Prim's Algorithm takes a more systematic approach, which we will develop in the following example.

R C Prim is credited with first publishing this algorithm in 1957.

Example

Apply Prim's algorithm, to the Cable-2-U.example from section 4.1.

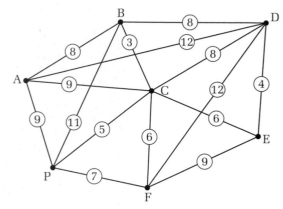

Start from the Business Park (P).

Solution

We need to fix a starting point, in this case P. Since P must be connected to at least one other vertex, we will choose the nearest, which is C.

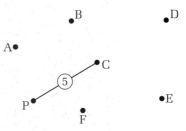

Now consider these two vertices. They must be connected by at least one edge to one or more of the remaining vertices so we consider all possibilities from both and choose the cheapest, which is CB.

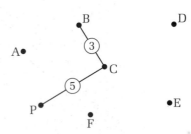

We repeat this, adding CE (arbitrary choice, could have chosen CF), then ED, then CF and finally AB.

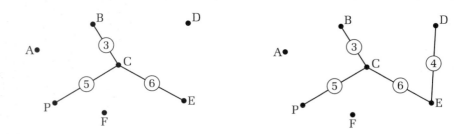

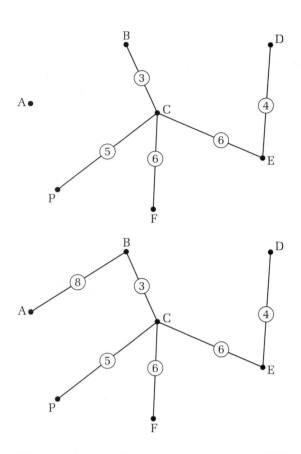

When we have added $n - 1$ vertices, we will have connected all the vertices into our tree, and therefore will have constructed the MST.

Since the solution is identical to that achieved through Kruskal's Algorithm, it is important to show the order in which the vertices have been added to show that the algorithm has been applied correctly.

This can be achieved either by listing the edges in the order added, or by numbering them on the tree.

Prim's Algorithm

1 Select (arbitrarily) a start vertex and make this part of your solution.

2 Consider all the edges which connect any vertex already in your solution to one not in the solution, and choose the smallest, adding it to the solution.

3 Repeat step 2 until all vertices have been added (this will require $n - 1$ edges for n vertices).

4.2 Prim's Algorithm

Exercise

Technique

Use Prim's algorithm to find the Minimum Spanning Tree for the networks in Exercise 4.1. In each case, start at the specified vertex.

1 Start at A.

2 Start at B.

3 Start at C.

4 Start at D.

5 Start at E.

4.3 Prim with a Matrix

Many problems come in a matrix format rather than as a graph. If the number of vertices is large, it is often not practical to draw the graph and a method of finding the Minimum Spanning Tree directly from the matrix is needed.

Prim's algorithm is suitable for this as the following example shows. The principle is to delete rows and add columns, to indicate which vertices have been connected and which still need connecting. The algorithm is given in full at the end of the example.

Data such as mileage charts often come in triangular form: for Prim's algorithm to work it is necessary to complete the table.

Example

Cable-2-U were provided with their costs in the following table:

	P	A	B	C	D	E	F
P		9	11	5			7
A	9		8	9	12		
B	11	8		3	8		
C	5	9	3		8	6	6
D		12	8	8		4	12
E				6	4		9
F				6	12	9	

Use Prim's algorithm without drawing the network to find the Minimum Connector.

Solution

We will again choose to start at the Business Park (P) so we highlight this column and delete the corresponding row.

	P	A	B	C	D	E	F
P		9	11	5			7
A	9		8	9	12		
B	11	8		3	8		
C	5	9	3		8	6	6
D		12	8	8		4	12
E				6	4		9
F				6	12	9	

We select the smallest value in the highlighted row, which is 5, corresponding to vertex C. We highlight the column and delete the row corresponding to C.

	P	A	B	C	D	E	F
P		9	11	5			7
A	9		8	9	12		
B	11	8		3	8		
C	⑤	9	3		8	6	6
D		12	8	8		4	12
E				6	4		9
F				6	12	9	

This is the equivalent to the first diagram in solution on page 51, with edge PC added.

We continue to look for vertices not yet connected (not deleted) that can be reached from those already selected (highlighted) so we next select the 3 in column C as the smallest available, highlighting column B and deleting the corresponding row.

	P	A	B	C	D	E	F
P		9	11	5			7
A	9		8	9	12		
B	11	8		③	8		
C	⑤	9	3		8	6	6
D		12	8	8		4	12
E				6	4		9
F				6	12	9	

Continuing in the same way we pick one of the 6s next: say CF.

	P	A	B	C	D	E	F
P		9	11	5			7
A	9		8	9	12		
B	11	8		③	8		
C	⑤	9	3		8	6	6
D		12	8	8		4	12
E				6	4		9
F				⑥	12	9	

Then the 6 from C to E.

	P	A	B	C	D	E	F
P		9	11	5			7
A	9		8	9	12		
B	11	8		③	8		
C	⑤	9	3		8	6	6
D		12	8	8		4	12
E				⑥	4		9
F				⑥	12	9	

Then the 4 from E to D.

	P	A	B	C	D	E	F
P		9	11	5			7
A	9		8	9	12		
B	11	8		③	8		
C	⑤	9	3		8	6	6
D		12	8	8		④	12
E				⑥	4		9
F				⑥	12	9	

And finally the 8 from B to A.

	P	A	B	C	D	E	F
P		9	11	5			7
A	9		⑧	9	12		
B	11	8		③	8		
C	⑤	9	3		8	6	6
D		12	8	8		④	12
E				⑥	4		9
F				⑥	12	9	

The total length of the Minimum Spanning Tree can be found by adding all the circled values.

$5+8+3+6+6+4=32$

```
Prim's Algorithm for a matrix

1 Select (arbitrarily) a start vertex. Highlight its
  column and delete its row.

2 Consider highlighted, non-deleted values and pick
  the smallest. Add the corresponding edge to the
  solution, delete the row that it was in, and
  highlight the corresponding column.

3 Repeat step 2 until all columns have been
  highlighted.
```

4.3 Prim with a Matrix

Exercise

Technique

The tables below give the distances between vertices in a network. Use Prim's Algorithm, starting at the specified vertex, to find the Minimum Spanning Tree.

1 **a** Start at A.

	A	B	C	D	E	F
A	–	3	5	8	11	3
B	3	–	9	12	7	8
C	5	9	–	4	13	6
D	8	12	4	–	5	1
E	11	7	13	5	–	12
F	3	8	6	1	12	–

b Start at C.

	A	B	C	D	E	F
A	–	4	1	3	13	8
B	4	–	9	11	2	14
C	1	9	–	10	12	6
D	3	11	10	–	5	15
E	13	2	12	5	–	7
F	8	14	6	15	7	–

c Start at D.

	A	B	C	D	E	F
A	–	6	7	14	13	
B	6	–	10	13	12	4
C	7	10	–		8	2
D	14	13		–	11	5
E	13	12	8	11	–	9
F		4	2	5	9	–

d Start at E.

	A	B	C	D	E	F
A	–	34	57	33	90	29
B	34	–	87	45	73	37
C	57	87	–	67	48	12
D	33	45	67	–	92	18
E	90	73	48	92	–	32
F	29	37	12	18	32	–

e Start at B

	A	B	C	D	E	F
A	–	7	5	11	14	8
B	7	–	12	2	15	9
C	5	12	–	7	11	12
D	11	2	7	–	4	8
E	14	15	11	4	–	9
F	8	9	12	8	9	–

Consolidation

Exercise A

1 For each of the graphs below, find the Minimum Spanning Tree using

i Kruskal's Algorithm

ii Prim's Algorithm, starting at vertex A.

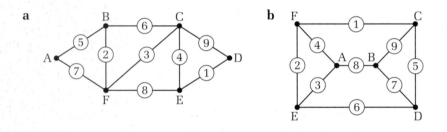

2 A world-wide family consists of people A, B, C, D, E, F and G. The minimum cost of a phone-call, in pence, between any pair of them is shown in the following table.

	A	B	C	D	E	F	G
A	–	80	20	95	10	20	10
B	80	–	70	45	60	70	80
C	20	70	–	80	60	25	25
D	95	45	80	–	70	80	90
E	10	60	60	70	–	25	15
F	20	70	25	80	25	–	30
G	10	80	25	90	15	30	–

Person A wishes to pass on a piece of news to all the other family members, either directly or by the message being passed on by other phone calls.

a By applying Prim's algorithm to the matrix (or otherwise) find the minimum cost of notifying the whole family of the news.

b Person A joins a telephone discount scheme which halves the cost of all phone calls to and from him. Without repeating the algorithm, state how this would affect your answer to part (a) and calculate the new minimum cost of notifying the whole family. *(AQA)*

3 A mathematician is writing a chapter of a book. In this chapter she wishes to start from result A, which was proved in an earlier chapter, to prove results B, C, D and E. There are many ways in which she can do this, since she can prove some results from others. She would like to do it as efficiently as possible, so that the total number of lines of proof is as small as possible.

The numbers of lines of proof required to establish one result directly from another are given in the following table.

		Result to be proved			
		B	**C**	**D**	**E**
Proved result	**A**	10	9	–	15
	B	–	15	20	7
	C	15	–	11	12
	D	20	11	–	5
	E	7	12	5	–

For example, she can prove B from A in 10 lines.

a Of the two graphs shown below, one represents a possible solution, the other does not. State, with a reason, which does not represent a solution, and give the number of lines of proof required for the other.

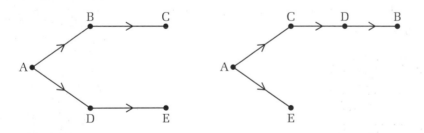

b Use the following algorithm to find an efficient way for the mathematician to prove all the results B, C, D and E from A. Draw a graph representing your solution and give the total number of lines of proof.

step 1 Start with A proved.
step 2 Prove the result that can be proved in the minimum number of lines from a proved result.
step 3 Repeat step 2 until all results are proved.

c Suppose that the mathematician subsequently discovers that she can prove C from D in only 8 instead of 11 lines. (It still takes 11 lines to prove D from C, and all other figures are similarly unaffected).

What difference does this make to the solution?

In this case, does the algorithm succeed in finding the best solution in the corresponding digraph? Justify your answer. *(AQA)*

4 A company has offices in six towns, A, B, C, D, E and F. The costs, in £, of travelling between these towns are shown in the table.

Town	A	B	C	D	E	F
A	–	15	26	13	14	25
B	15	–	16	16	25	13
C	26	16	–	38	16	15
D	13	16	38	–	15	19
E	14	25	16	15	–	14
F	25	13	15	19	14	–

Use Prim's algorithm starting by deleting row A, to find the cheapest way of connecting the six towns. You should show all your working and indicate the order in which the towns were included. *(OCR)*

Exercise B

1 For each of the graphs below, find the Minimum Spanning Tree using

i Kruskal's Algorithm
ii Prim's Algorithm, starting at vertex A

a

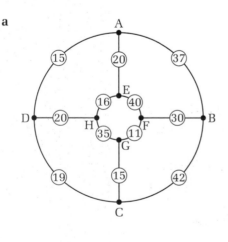

b

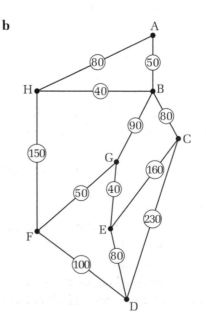

2 The table below shows the shortest distance, in metres, between various buildings in a university. The university wishes to install an internal telephone network, linking these buildings. Find the minimum length of cable needed.

	Maths	Humanities	Medicine	Sciences	Administration	Music
Maths	–	700	800	200	600	700
Humanities	700	–	250	600	200	100
Medicine	800	250	–	700	300	350
Sciences	200	600	700	–	600	650
Administration	600	200	300	600	–	100
Music	700	100	350	650	100	–

3 A school wishes to link six computers. One is in the school office and one in each of rooms A, B, C, D and E. Cables need to be laid to connect the computers. The school wishes to use a minimum total length of cable.

The table shows the shortest distances, in metres, between the various sites.

	Office	A	B	C	D	E
Office	–	8	16	12	10	14
A	8	–	14	13	11	9
B	16	14	–	12	15	11
C	12	13	12	–	11	8
D	10	11	15	11	–	10
E	14	9	11	8	10	–

a Starting at the school office, use Prim's algorithm to find a Minimum Spanning Tree. Indicate the order in which you select edges and draw your final tree.

b Using your answer to part (a), calculate the minimum total length of cable required. *(EDEXCEL)*

4 The following matrix shows the costs of connecting together each possible pair from six computer terminals.

The computers are to be connected together so that, for any pair of computers, there should either be a direct link between them or a link

	A	B	C	D	E	F
A		120	200	140	135	250
B	120		230	75	130	80
C	200	230		160	160	120
D	140	75	160		200	85
E	135	130	160	200		150
F	250	80	120	85	150	

via one or more other computers. Use an appropriate algorithm to find the cheapest way of connecting these computers. Show your result on a network and give the total cost. *(AEB)*

Applications and Extensions

Edge deletion
Kruskal's algorithm works by adding short edges to an incomplete tree. An alternative approach is to delete long edges from the original network until you are left with a tree of minimum length.

Try using this method on some of the networks in this chapter. Try writing an algorithm to do this.

Redundancy
Minimum Spanning Trees represent the cheapest way of connecting a set of vertices. In reality, there are other factors to consider. For example, when designing a computer network, the designers will want to avoid a situation where a fault on one edge causes the whole network to crash. They will also be aware that some vertices are more important than others. In particular, they will probably want there to be several connections to the main server.

Investigate ways of modifying MSTs so that a fault on one edge causes minimum disruption.

Summary

- A **Minimum Spanning Tree** is a tree which connects every vertex in the graph, with the minimum total edge weight.

- For a graph with n vertices, a spanning tree will always have $n - 1$ edges.

- **Kruskal's algorithm** is a greedy algorithm, selecting smallest weight edges.

- **Prim's algorithm** works outward from a starting vertex until all vertices have been included.

- Prim's algorithm can be applied to a table (matrix) without drawing the graph.

5 Shortest Paths

What you need to know

● The language and notation of graphs

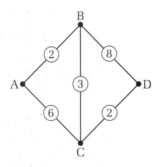

1 How many different paths are there from A to D in this network?

2 If the numbers on the edges represent distance, which of the above is the shortest path from A to D?

A **shortest path** is a route from one vertex to another using the smallest overall sum of edge weights. It will never use an edge more than once, nor visit a vertex more than once.

5.1 Dijkstra's Algorithm

The shortest path across a network is not always the most obvious, in that it may not use the shortest edges as the following example will show.

Dijkstra's algorithm takes a 'local' view, in that it only ever considers going one vertex on from what it is already sure of.

```
Dijkstra's Algorithm

This algorithm makes uses of boxes at the vertices
to keep track of the workings.
```

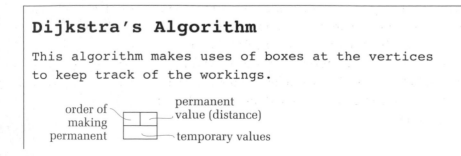

Apart from the order box, all other variables are distances from the start vertex.

1 Begin by giving the start vertex order label 1 and permanent (distance) label 0. Then put in temporary values at each vertex you can reach directly from the start. These temporary values are their distance from the start.

2 Pick the vertex with the smallest temporary value, and make that value permanent. Put in the correct order label. This is now the current vertex.
   If there is more than one equally small temporary value, make an arbitrary choice.

   Consider each of the vertices (which are not yet permanently labelled) which you can reach directly from the current vertex. Calculate a temporary value by adding its distance from the current vertex to the permanent value of the current vertex. If this is less than the existing temporary value, change it, otherwise ignore it.

   Repeat this step until you have a permanent value at your target vertex. Note that you must consider all temporary values, not just the ones you have just updated, when looking for the smallest.

3 Trace back to find the route used, commencing with your target and using at each step the edge which generated the permanent label. Write it down forwards, giving the total distance covered.
   If you have a choice of edges, this indicates that there is more than one route of optimum length.

Example 1

Patrick wants to build a small water-feature in his garden which requires an electricity supply. He wants to lay the cable under his existing paved paths so that there is no risk of damaging it when digging his garden. Since he does not want to have to lift and re-lay more paving than is absolutely necessary, he wants to find the shortest route from his fuse box near the garage door (G) to the pond (P). The following plan shows the layout of his garden. What route should he use and how many 50 cm slabs will he have to lift and relay?

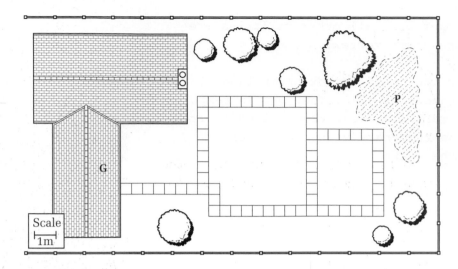

Solution

The plan is translated in to the following graph, with boxes added at the
vertices to allow us to record our values as we apply Dijkstra's algorithm.
The edge weights are the number of slabs to be lifted on that section of
the path.

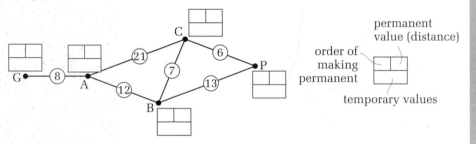

We start by labelling vertex G with a 1 for its order, and a 0 for the
permanent value. We then place the temporary value of 8 at A.

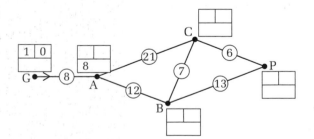

The algorithm then says to pick the vertex with the smallest temporary
value which, since there is only one, must be A. This vertex is labelled
with order 2, and distance 8. It is also helpful to add an arrow along the
edge we have just used (GA).

We must then update temporary values of vertices which can be reached
from A, taking the value 8 from A and adding to it the length of the
respective edge. So B has a temporary value of $8 + 12 = 20$, and C is
$8 + 21 = 29$.

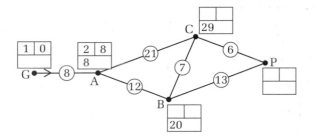

The smallest temporary value is the 20 at B, so B is permanently labelled, an arrow is added to AB, and the temporary values at C and P are updated.

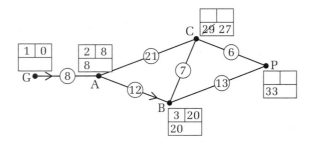

The smallest temporary value is now at C, so we label up as before. The temporary value at P is unchanged because the route from C is no better than we already have.

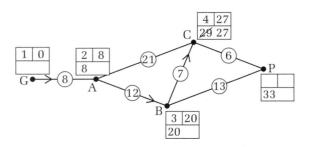

P is now the only unlabelled vertex, and receives the order label 5 and permanent distance of 33. Since this can be achieved from both B and C, we place an arrow on both edges

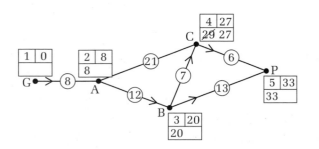

We now track back from the pond to the garage door and can use (in reverse) the edges we placed the arrows on.

From P we could have come from C, which came from B, which came from A, which came from G, so our route is G-A-B-C-P, length 33 slabs.

In this example, BP was the same length as BCP so we could also have found the solution G-A-B-P with the same length.

Analysis

The algorithm will always find the optimum solution for an undirected graph with positive edge weights. In doing so, all vertices with a permanent label will have their shortest distance from the start vertex given (for example, the shortest route to C from G is G-A-B-C with 27 slabs). If there are any vertices which have not yet been labelled, they can be included by continuing the algorithm.

In the worst case scenario (a complete graph), the algorithm will take n steps, considering an average of $\frac{n}{2}$ vertices each time. Therefore, it has complexity $n \times \frac{n}{2} = O(n^2)$.

For a definition of complexity, see Chapter 1.

5.1 Dijkstra'a Algorithm

Exercise

Technique

1 Use Dijkstra's algorithm to find the shortest path from A to E on the network below.

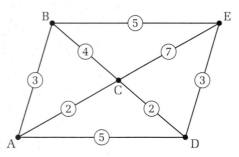

2 Use Dijkstra's algorithm to find the shortest path from A to F on the network below.

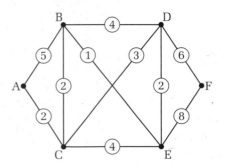

3 Use Dijkstra's algorithm to find the shortest path from A to H on the network below.

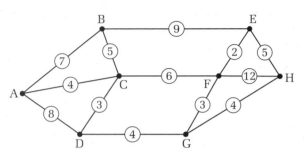

4 Use Dijkstra's algorithm to find the shortest path from A to G on the network below.

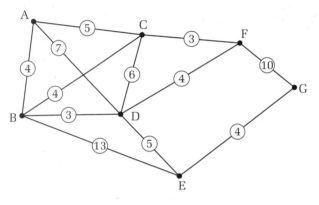

5 Use Dijkstra's algorithm to find the shortest path from A to G on the network below.

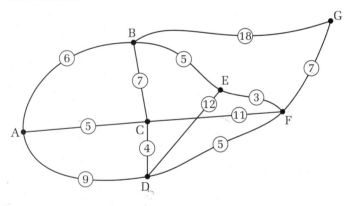

5.2 Dijkstra for all Paths

By applying Dijkstra's algorithm repeatedly, using each vertex in turn as the start vertex, a table of shortest paths between all possible pairs of vertices can be constructed. Because it is the algorithm discussed in Section 5.1 as being $O(n^2)$, applied n times, its complexity is $O(n^3)$.

Example 1

By applying Dijkstra's algorithm from each vertex in turn, complete the table of distances for this graph.

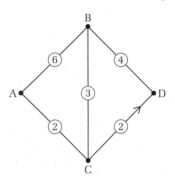

CD is a directional edge and can only be used one-way from C to D

Solution

Starting from A: Starting from B:

Starting from C: Starting from D:

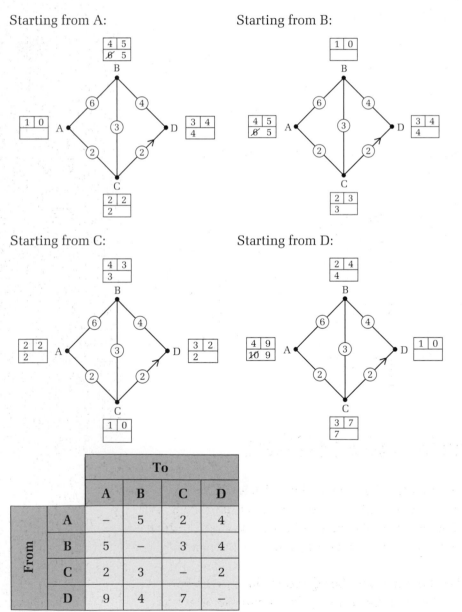

		To		
	A	**B**	**C**	**D**
A	–	5	2	4
B	5	–	3	4
C	2	3	–	2
D	9	4	7	–

Although a direct edge AB exists, the route ACB is shorter.

5.2 Dijkstra for all Paths

Exercise

Technique

1 By applying Dijkstra's algorithm from each vertex in turn, complete the table of shortest distances.

		To		
	A	**B**	**C**	**D**
A	–			
B		–		
C			–	
D				–

(From label on left side)

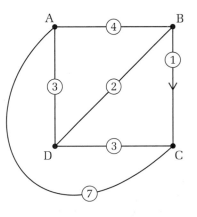

2 By applying Dijkstra's algorithm from each vertex in turn, complete the table of shortest distances.

			To		
	A	**B**	**C**	**D**	**E**
A	–				
B		–			
C			–		
D				–	
E					–

(From label on left side)

5.3 Floyd's Algorithm

Floyd's Algorithm is another $O(n^3)$ algorithm, but is based on the manipulation of matrices. Two matrices are required; one containing the distances, or weights, of the edges, the other being a route matrix giving information about the vertices on the shortest path.

Each vertex is considered in turn, and the algorithm checks whether a route exists which is better than the current (often non-existent) route.

71

Floyd's Algorithm

1 Set a matrix the same size as the distance matrix, with the first column all set to A, the second to B etc.

2 Select a vertex and highlight its row and column in the distance matrix, and the corresponding column (only) in the route matrix.

3 For each non-highlighted element in the matrix, add together the highlighted values in its row and column and, if the sum is less than the current value, replace it.

4 If a replacement has been made, replace the corresponding value in the route matrix with the highlighted value in the same row.

5 Repeat steps 2—4 until all the vertices have been done.

Example

Apply Floyd's algorithm to find all shortest paths in this network, and explain the use of the route matrix.

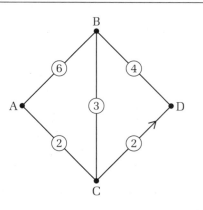

Solution

The initial distance matrix is, with corresponding route matrix.

	A	B	C	D
A	–	6	2	
B	6	–	3	4
C	2	3	–	2
D		4		–

	A	B	C	D
A	A	B	C	D
B	A	B	C	D
C	A	B	C	D
D	A	B	C	D

Some notations use the infinity sign ∞ for *no connection* such as AD.

The vertex names are generally omitted and we will do so from here onwards.

Selecting the first vertex, and highlighting the column in both matrices, and the row in the first, gives the following matrices.

–	6	2	
6	–	3	4
2	3	–	2
	4		–

A	B	C	D
A	B	C	D
A	B	C	D
A	B	C	D

The first value to consider is B to C, but 6 + 2 = 8 so we retain the existing 3 because it is shorter. The same is true for all the other values and, for D to C, there is no connection from D to A to use so this remains blank.

We continue to the next vertex, again highlighting the row and columns. This time we can make improvements to AD, DA and DC, replacing the blank spaces with a connection via B and updating the route matrix.

–	6	2	**10**
6	–	3	4
2	3	–	2
10	4	**7**	–

A	B	C	**B**
A	B	C	D
A	B	C	D
B	B	**B**	D

We have emboldened those elements which have been changed.

We continue by considering vertex C. This gives improved routes for AB, AD, BA and DA.

–	5	2	4
5	–	3	4
2	3	–	2
9	4	7	–

A	**C**	C	**C**
C	B	C	D
A	B	C	D
C	B	**B**	D

Finally we must consider vertex D, for which there is no further improvement in our example.

Comparing the distance matrix with the example in section 5.2 we see that they are the same.

In the route matrix we can see, for example, that the shortest path from A to C is to go direct to C. However, for the route AD, we should go from A to C and then seek the best route from C, which is direct to D.

		To			
		A	B	C	D
From	A	A	C	C	C
	B	C	B	C	D
	C	A	B	C	D
	D	C	B	B	D

5.3 Floyd's Algorithm

Exercise

Technique

Apply Floyd's algorithm to the networks represented by the following matrices.

 1 a

	A	B	C	D
A	–	2		3
B	2	–	4	1
C		4	–	3
D	3	1	3	–

b

	A	B	C	D
A	–	4	3	2
B	4	–	2	
C	3	2	–	
D	2			–

c

	A	B	C	D
A	–	3		
B	3	–	5	2
C		5	–	
D		2		–

Consolidation

Exercise A

1 The network shows the distances in kilometres of various routes between points S, T, U, V, W, X, Y, Z.

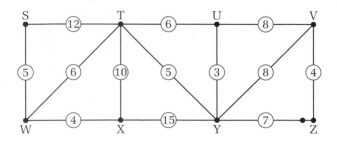

Use Dijkstra's algorithm to find the shortest path from S to Z. Show your working on the diagram.

(AQA)

2 The following network shows the time, in minutes, to travel between ten towns.

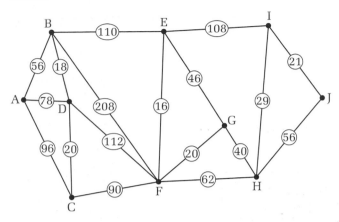

a Use Dijkstra's algorithm to find the minimum time to travel from A to J, and state the route.

b A new road is to be constructed connecting D to E. Find the time needed for travelling this section of road if the overall minimum journey time to travel from A to J is reduced by 10 minutes. State the new route.

(AQA)

3 Use Dijkstra's algorithm to find the shortest distance, and the corresponding shortest path, from B to F in the network below.

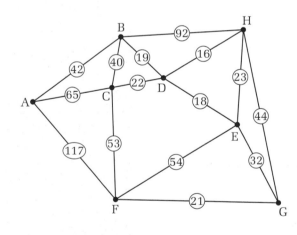

(AQA)

4

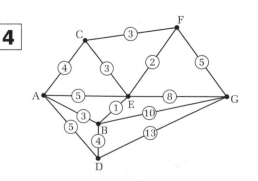

a Show fully the use of Dijkstra's algorithm to find the shortest path through the graph from A to G. Display the path clearly and state its length.

b It can be shown that a trial and improvement solution to the shortest path problem could take more than $(n-2)!$ computations for a network with n vertices. Using Dijkstra's algorithm requires a maximum of $\frac{1}{2}(5n^2 - 3n) + 1$ computations. Evaluate these expressions when $n = 7$ and $n = 70$, and comment on these values.

(AQA)

5 Apply Floyd's algorithm to the networks represented by the following matrices.

a

	A	B	C	D
A	–	4	3	
B	4	–	2	
C	3	2	–	1
D			1	–

b

	A	B	C	D
A	–		2	2
B		–		1
C	2		–	
D	2	1		–

Exercise B

1

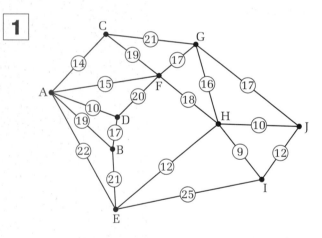

The network models the roads linking 10 towns. The number on each edge is the journey time, in minutes, along that road.

Alice lives in town A and works in town J.

a Use Dijkstra's algorithm to find the quickest route for Alice to travel to work each morning.

On her return journey from work one day Alice wishes to call in at the supermarket located in town C.

b Find her new quickest route home.

(EDEXCEL)

2 A network is represented by the matrix in the table below, in which the values are the distances, in miles, between the vertices P, Q, R, S and T.

There is no direct route between P and T.

	P	Q	R	S	T
P	–	2	3	6	
Q	2	–	2	2	7
R	3	2	–	2	5
S	6	2	2	–	3
T		7	5	3	–

    a   Draw and label the network represented by this matrix.

    b   Use Dijkstra's algorithm to find the shortest route from P to T.

(OCR modified)

3 A couple are eloping to Gretna Green when they notice that the cars ahead of them have come to a complete standstill because of an accident. They turn off the main road and consult the map.

The network below represents the roads that the couple can use to get from the accident (A) to Gretna Green (G). The length of each section of road is shown in miles.

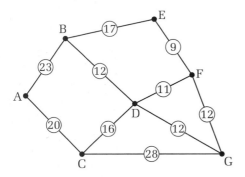

    a   Use Dijkstra's algorithm to find the shortest route from A to G. Show all your workings clearly.

       Before reaching B, the couple decide to stop at F for the night.

    b   Write down the shortest route from A to F.

(Oxford)

4 The diagram shows a number of satellite towns A, B, C, D, E and F surrounding a city, K. The number on each edge gives the length of the road in km.

Use Dijkstra's algorithm to find the shortest route from A to E in the network.

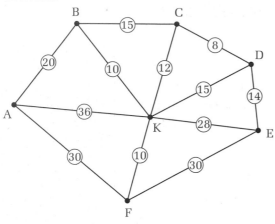

(EDEXCEL)

5 Apply Floyd's algorithm to the network represented by the following matrix.

	A	B	C	D	E
A	–	2			3
B	2	–	2		4
C		2	–	3	6
D			3	–	4
E	3	4	6	4	–

Applications and Extensions

Refinements

Dijkstra's algorithm provides a way of solving straightforward Shortest Path problems. In reality, there are often additional factors that have to be considered. Some of these are listed below. Think about how you would deal with these factors.

a Time not distance

The shortest distance is not always the quickest. Routes using motorways may be longer than routes using A roads, but they may be quicker.

b Varying values

The weights on a network may not be constant. Average speeds may vary according to the time of day; there may be occasional hold-ups, the probability of which can be estimated.

c One way roads

d Bridges

The weights on a network can represent the maximum load allowed over a bridge on that route. In this case, the problem is compounded by needing to avoid edges below a minimum weight.

<u>Formulating as a Linear Programme</u>

By defining each edge as a variable taking the value 0 or 1 (these are called **indicator variables**), and considering the conditions required at each vertex, we can express our shortest path problem from Section 5.1 as a series of equations.

For example, $AB + AC = 1$ (there must be one edge leading from A in our path), and $AB = BC + BP$ (the number of paths being used leading in to B must equal the number being used leading out from B).

The expression $8GA + 12AB + 21AC + 7BC + 13BP + 6CP$ will give the length of our path, since it will give 1 times the value of the lengths for the edges we are using, and 0 times the lengths for those we are not. Our aim is then to minimise this.

This set of equations is known as a **linear programme**, the solution of which is dealt with in chapters 9 and 10. Alternatively, a computer package can be used.

Try writing the example used in Section 5.2 as a linear programme for each of the start vertices.

Summary

- A **shortest path** is a route from one vertex to another using the smallest overall sum of edge weights.

- **Dijkstra's algorithm** works from a start vertex, updating distances and produces the shortest path to each vertex from the chosen start.

- Dijkstra's algorithm can be applied repeatedly from each vertex to find all shortest paths in the network.

- **Floyd's algorithm** uses two matrices, one of distances, the other of routes, to find all shortest paths in a network.

- There are a number of variations on the theme of Shortest Paths which involve finding routes criteria other than minimum total length (see Application and Extension – Refinements).

6 Route Inspection

What you need to know

- The order of a vertex

- The definition of an Eulerian graph

- Algorithms for finding shortest paths between pairs of vertices

Review

1 Find the shortest route from S to T on each of the following graphs.

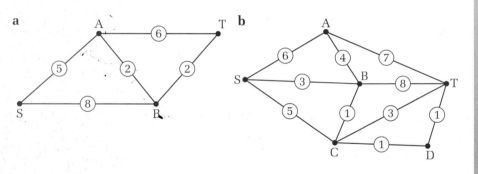

2 For each of the following graphs, state whether it is Eulerian, semi-Eulerian or neither.

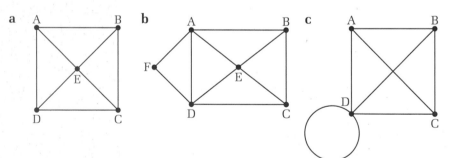

6.1 The Route Inspection Problem

Many problems which can be represented as a graph traversal problem are not Eulerian. In the following example we consider the method of solving one such problem.

Example

Barsett council have decided to instigate a weekly inspection of street lamps. This involves an inspection vehicle driving along each of the main routes in the central area to ensure that all lamps are working. What route should they take and how far is it?

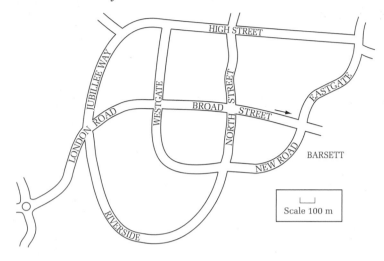

Solution

We first need to create a mathematical model of this problem by replacing the map with a simple network. We do not want street names, but instead give each vertex (junction) a letter name. We do not need to consider the roads leading off the edge of the map beyond each junction. The distances in metres have been added.

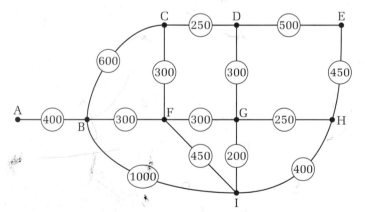

We need to make the graph traversable. The first step is to duplicate the edge AB. This has to be repeated because there is nowhere to go when we get to the roundabout at A other than back into the town. This has the effect of making B odd-ordered.

This now leaves us with four odd-ordered vertices, B, C, D and H. We consider the shortest routes between each possible pairing:

BC and DH is 600 + 550 = 1150
BD and CH is 850 + 800 = 1650
BH and CD is 850 + 250 = 1100

B because it becomes order 5 when we duplicate AB

The best pairing is therefore BH and CD so we duplicate these connections.

The total length of all edges in the original network was 5700 m. We have subsequently added a duplication of the edge AB = 400 m and the routes BH = 850 m and CD = 250 m, giving a total length of 7200 m or 7.2 km

There are lots of routes of this length which the inspection vehicle could take. One such would be EDCBFGHIGDCFIBABFGHE and clearly the reverse would also be valid (provided that we overlook any one-way streets).

For n vertices, there are $(n-1) \times (n-3) \times \cdots \times 1$ pairings
e.g. 6 vertices
$= 5 \times 3 \times 1 = 15$ ways,
8 vertices
$= 7 \times 5 \times 3 \times 1 = 105$ ways.

It soon becomes a lot of work!

6.1 The Route Inspection Problem

Exercise

Contextual

1 Each of the following diagrams represents a network of cables which needs to be inspected. For each network find the minimum distance which has to be repeated

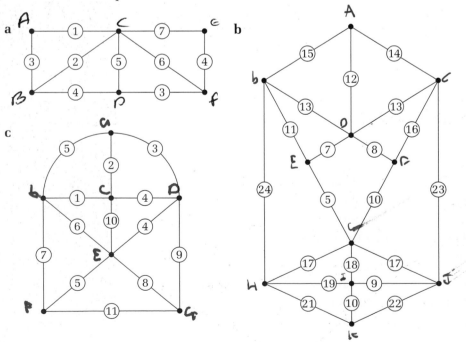

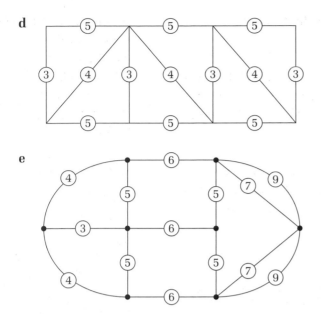

d

e

2 Each of the following matrices represents a network of cables which needs to be inspected. For each network:

i find the minimum distance which has to be repeated

ii find a possible route of minimum length which traverses all the edges.

a

	A	B	C	D	E
A	–	3	4		2
B	3	–			
C	4		–	6	
D			6	–	2
E	2			2	–

b

	A	B	C	D	E
A	2	3	1		5
B	3	–	4		
C	1	4	–	5	7
D			5	–	
E	5		7		–

Consolidation

Exercise A

1 The following diagram represents a network of cables which needs to be inspected.

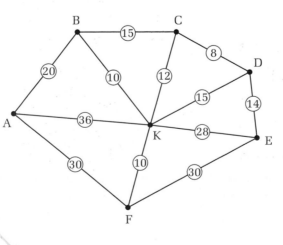

a Find the minimum distance which has to be repeated, given that the edge DE is part of the solution.

b Find a possible route of minimum length which traverses all the edges.

(EDEXCEL modified)

2 A local council is responsible for gritting roads.

The following diagram shows the lengths of roads, in miles, that have to be gritted.

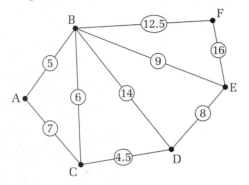

The gritter is based at A and must travel along all the roads, at least once, before returning to A.

a Explain why it is **not** possible to start from A and, by travelling along each road only once, return to A.

b Find an optimal 'Chinese postman' route around the network, starting and finishing at A. State the length of your route.

(AQA)

3 The edges of the network below represent roads in a small housing estate. There is only one road into and out of the estate, represented by edge AB. The lengths of the roads are shown in metres.

The total length of roads is 2300m.

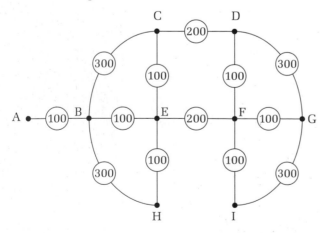

a A papergirl delivers to about 20% of the houses and therefore finds it worthwhile to cross from side to side of the road whilst making deliveries. Thus, she would **prefer** to walk along each road only once.

Use an appropriate algorithm to find the minimum total length of road along which she must walk if she starts and finishes her round at A. Indicate how you applied the algorithm.

b A postman delivers to about 80% of houses. He finds it best to deliver to one side of a road at a time. He therefore needs to walk along each road at least twice. If he starts and finishes at A, find the minimum distance that he must walk, justifying your answer.

c Suppose that the postman acquires a bicycle. This means that he would still like to travel along each road twice, but in opposite directions, so that he is always riding on the correct side of the road. Will this mean that he must travel further? Justify your answer.

(AQA)

4 The diagram shows the roads linking villages in an area covered by a district council. The numbers on the edges give the distances, in km, between the villages. After a storm a highways inspector wishes to travel along each road at least once.

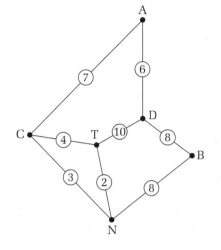

a Use an appropriate algorithm to find the minimum distance she must travel, starting and finishing at A.

b Write down a possible route which is of minimum length.

(EDEXCEL)

5 The following diagram represents a network of cables which needs to be inspected.

a Find the minimum distance which has to be repeated.

b Find a possible route of minimum length which traverses all the edges.

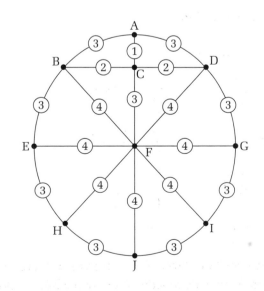

Exercise B

1 The following table represents a network of cables which needs to be inspected.

	A	B	C	D	E
A	–	5	–	3	7
B	5	–	5	–	4
C	–	5	–	6	3
D	3	–	6	–	2
E	7	4	3	2	–

a Find the minimum distance which has to be repeated

b Find a possible route of minimum length which traverses all the edges.

2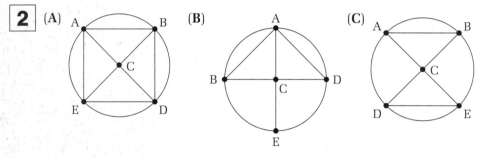

a By considering the order of each node, classify each of the graphs **A**, **B** and **C** as Eulerian, semi-Eulerian, or neither.

b Explain briefly how your classification in graph **A** relates to the problem of finding a route through the graph that includes each arc exactly once. Are there any restrictions on where such a route can start and finish?

(OCR)

3 The network is a representation of a system of roads. The lengths of the roads are shown in metres.

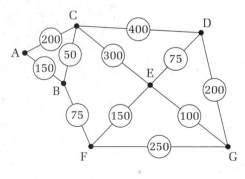

a List the odd vertices in the network.

b Explain why the graph is not Eulerian.

c By considering ways of pairing the odd vertices, find the shortest route, starting and finishing at A, which traverses each road at least once.

(AEB modified)

4 a Explain why the network below is not Eulerian.
  b By considering ways of pairing odd vertices, find a shortest route, starting and finishing at A, which traverses each road at least once. State the length of your route.

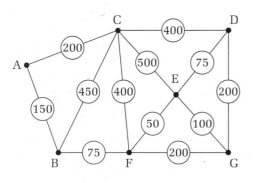

(AEB modified)

5 The following diagram represents a network of cables which needs to be inspected.

Find the minimum distance which has to be repeated.

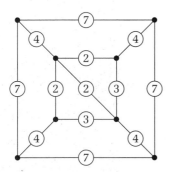

Applications and Extensions

Complexity

The length of time taken to solve a Route Inspection problem is dependent on the number of odd vertices. This is because an optimal solution can only be guaranteed by considering all possible pairs of odd vertices.

How many possible pairings are there of 2 odd vertices? Of 4? Of $2n$? What does this tell you about the complexity of the Route Inspection problem?

Formulating as a Linear Programme

Try formulating a Route Inspection problem as a Linear Programme. You will need to use indicator variables (see the Linear Programming Extension in Chapter 5). If you have access to an appropriate computer package, you could use this method to check your solutions.

Linear Programming is covered in Chapter 9.

Directed Edges

There are many situations in which the network would include directed edges. In this case you will need to amend your approach to incorporate these. There are quite simple cases in which there is not a solution, as the following diagram shows:

However, there are other cases where the algorithm can be adapted to incorporate a small number of directed edges. Investigate.

Sparse Graphs

Although the Route Inspection problem is theoretically complex, the amount of work is significantly reduced if the ratio of edges to vertices is very small. Such graphs are called sparse. How could the methods given in this chapter be adapted for these?

Summary

- **Route Inspection** problems involve travelling along each edge of the graph once, finishing at the starting vertex. This requires an **Eulerian** graph.

- Many practical problems will not be Eulerian. We therefore add edges to vertices of odd order until it becomes Eulerian. These are usually chosen to minimise the additional distance by considering all possible pairings of vertices with odd order.

7 Travelling Salesperson Problems

What you need to know

- The difference between a connected graph and a complete graph
- Algorithms for finding a Minimum Spanning Tree and shortest path

Review

1 Draw a complete graph with four vertices, and state the difference between this and a connected graph which is not complete.

2 Find a Minimum Spanning Tree for the following graph.

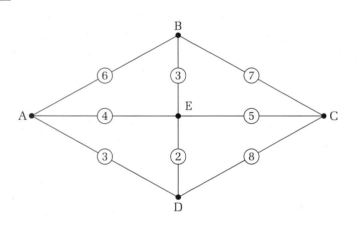

3 Find the shortest path from A to C on the graph in question 2.

7.1 The Classical Problem

The definition of a Travelling Salesperson Problem (TSP) is as follows: Traverse a network by visiting every vertex, returning to the starting point, at minimum cost. Cost can mean distance, time etc. – whatever the weights of the arcs represent.

In the Classical Problem this leads to a Hamiltonian Cycle.

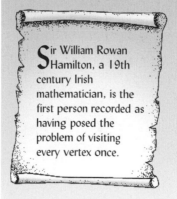

Sir William Rowan Hamilton, a 19th century Irish mathematician, is the first person recorded as having posed the problem of visiting every vertex once.

Example 1

Five signalling stations are located across a desert plain. Each has a transmitter/receiver built such that it has an uninterrupted line of sight to each of the others. The power required to transmit a 5-second signal between each pair is shown on the graph below. The operations manager, based at station A, wishes to ensure that all the stations are working by passing a signal round each station in turn, returning to him at A to verify completion. What sequence should he use to minimise the power consumption?

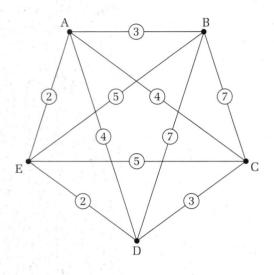

Solution

By trial and error, and a little intuition, we can deduce that the optimum route is A–B–C–D–E–A, of length 17. Notice that since this is a cycle, we could actually start/finish at any point and use the same route, or its reverse.

There is an alternative solution A–B–E–D–C–A of equal length.

Example 2

The following network represents the cost of using connections between 5 locations. By constructing a complete graph, find the minimum cost of visiting each location and returning to the starting point.

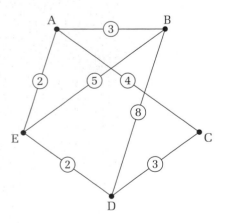

Solution

There are some difficulties in using the above graph as it stands. There is no direct connection shown between A and D for example, but we could of course make the connection via E of total cost 4, provided that we are permitting travel via intermediate vertices. There are two other missing edges, B to C and C to E. Furthermore, although there is a direct connection between B and D of cost 8, the route via E has total cost of 7 and is therefore cheaper.

To be sure that we have all the minimum costs, we must find the shortest path between all possible pairings, and then form a complete graph, thus converting our network to a Classical Problem. Floyd's algorithm is useful for this because it allows us to find the route used when a path consists of more than one edge.

Floyd's algorithm is explained in Section 5.3.

Our initial tables are:

	A	B	C	D	E
A	–	3	4		2
B	3	–		8	5
C	4		–	3	
D		8	3	–	2
E	2	5		2	–

	A	B	C	D	E
A	A	B	C	D	E
B	A	B	C	D	E
C	A	B	C	D	E
D	A	B	C	D	E
E	A	B	C	D	E

and the final tables after applying Floyd's Algorithm are:

	A	B	C	D	E
A	–	3	4	4	2
B	3	–	7	7	5
C	4	7	–	3	5
D	4	7	3	–	2
E	2	5	5	2	–

	A	B	C	D	E
A	A	B	C	E	E
B	A	B	A	E	E
C	A	A	C	D	D
D	E	E	C	D	E
E	A	B	D	D	E

We are therefore able to construct the following graph:

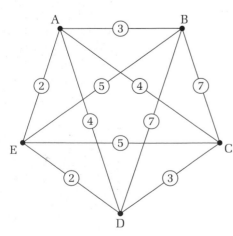

We have now changed this problem to a Classical Problem, in fact the same as Example 1 and so we know the solution, which was A–B–C–D–E–A. However, this solution includes the route B–C for which there was not a direct edge in the original graph for our practical problem, so we must replace it with B–A–C, giving a final solution to this problem of A–B–A–C–D–E–A.

When a problem has been modified, such as, transforming it to the Classical Problem with a complete graph, it is essential that the solution is interpreted in the context of the original problem.

7.1 The Classical Problem

Exercise

Technique

1 Find, by inspection, a minimum weight tour of the following graphs:

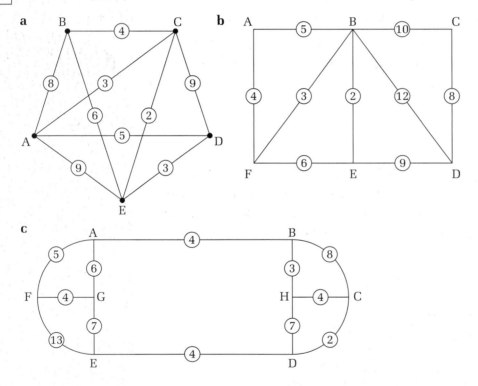

You should answer the following questions by inspection, rather than using Floyd's algorithm. You may find it easier to give your answers in matrix form.

2 Convert the network from question **1a** to its classical equivalent.

3 Convert the network from question **1b** to its classical equivalent.

4 Convert the network from question **1c** to its classical equivalent.

7.2 Nearest Neighbour Algorithm

So far, we have found solutions by inspection: this is clearly not going to be adequate for larger problems. We therefore need to develop an algorithmic approach to solving our problem. Unfortunately, Travelling Salesperson Problems cannot be solved in polynomial time: that is, we cannot write their complexity as $O(n^r)$ where n is the size of the problem and r is an integer. We therefore use an **heuristic** approach, a common and relatively simple example of which is the Nearest Neighbour Algorithm.

Nearest Neighbour Algorithm

1 Make the start vertex the current vertex.

2 Move from the current vertex to the nearest unvisited vertex, adding that edge to the tour.

3 Repeat step 2 until all vertices have been visited, then return from the final vertex to the start vertex by the shortest direct route.

The algorithm assumes a complete graph – The Classical Problem. Note the similarity, but also the difference between this algorithm and Prim's Algorithm for a Minimum Spanning Tree.

Example

Sanjay is going to cycle around his local area, delivering invitations to his birthday party to his friends' houses. The network below shows the distance between each house, each unit representing 0.1 km. What route does the Nearest Neighbour Algorithm advise him to take?

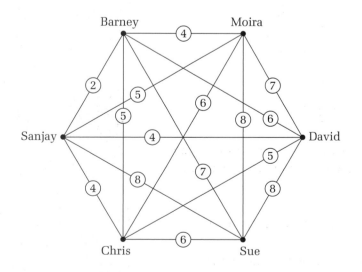

Solution

Sanjay clearly starts at his own house. The nearest house is Barney's so he will go there first.

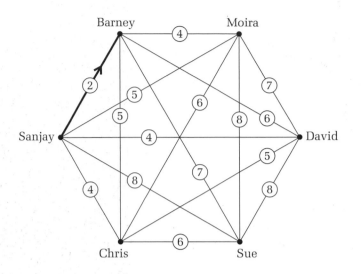

The nearest to Barney is Moira, so that is his next call.

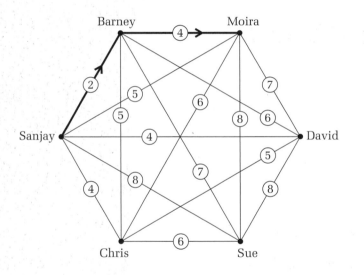

The shortest route would take him home – but he has not finished – so he goes to the next nearest which is Chris.

David is nearer than Sue so he goes there next.

Then he finally visits Sue, before returning home, giving the following network:

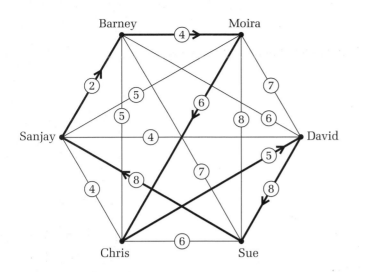

Therefore Sanjay will take the route Barney, Moira, Chris, David, Sue, home and will cycle a total distance of 33 units, or 3.3 km. In the next section, we will consider whether or not this is an efficient or optimal solution.

7.2 Nearest Neighbour Algorithm

Exercise

Technique

1 Apply the Nearest Neighbour Algorithm to this network, starting at vertex C.

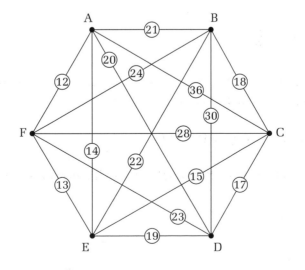

2 Apply the Nearest Neighbour Algorithm to this network starting at vertex D.

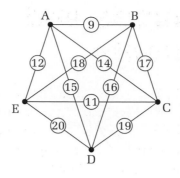

3 Apply the Nearest Neighbour Algorithm to this network, starting at vertex D.

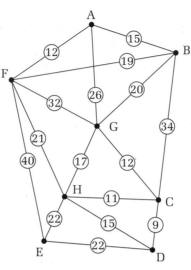

4 Apply the Nearest Neighbour Algorithm to this network, starting at each vertex in turn.

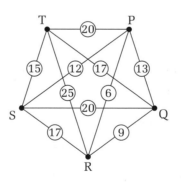

5 Apply the Nearest Neighbour Algorithm to this network, starting at each vertex in turn.

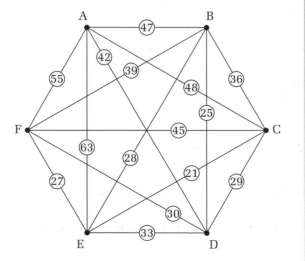

7.3 Upper Bounds and Improvements

In using the Nearest Neighbour Algorithm to construct a tour, we have constructed a solution which may not be optimal, but is feasible. We call this an upper bound of the optimum solution. Since it is not generally practical to check every possible route to be certain of optimality, it is common practice to seek to minimise the upper bound.

A standard approach is to choose each vertex in turn to be the starting node and apply the Nearest Neighbour Algorithm. This gives a series of values which can be compared and the smallest chosen (see Exercise 7.2 above, questions 4 and 5).

There are a number of other techniques which can be employed. Two of these, the interchange of vertices and making shortcuts from a crudely constructed tour based on doubling the Minimum Spanning Tree, are demonstrated in the following examples.

Example 1

Shorten Sanjay's journey from the previous section by interchanging the order of two of the vertices.

Solution

If we reverse the order of Chris and David, we get the route **Sanjay**, **Barney**, **Moira**, **David**, **Chris**, **Sue**, **Sanjay**.

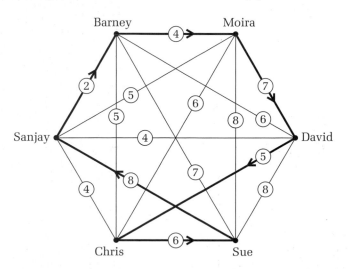

This is a slight improvement as it is only of length 32, or 3.2 km.

Changing the order of Chris and Sue, giving a route of length 31, or 3.1 km, would improve it further.

Example 2

Find an upper bound for Sanjay's journey by using a Minimum Spanning Tree and shortcuts.

Solution

The Minimum Spanning Tree, or MST, connects every vertex. Therefore, by traversing every edge of the MST twice, all vertices will be covered and will form a cycle.

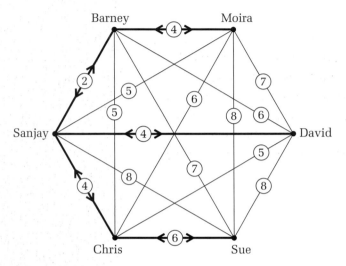

The length of the MST is 20, so we double this to get an upper bound of 40. This is, in itself, not a good upper bound as we are traversing every edge twice, albeit the shortest ones. We therefore look to make some shortcuts. For example, we could travel direct from Moira's to David's. This adds an edge of length 7, but saves doubling back to Barney's and home (lengths 4 and 2) followed by the direct route from home to David's (length 4) at this stage. We have therefore saved 3 overall and now have an upper bound of length of 37, or 3.7 km, as marked in the following diagram:

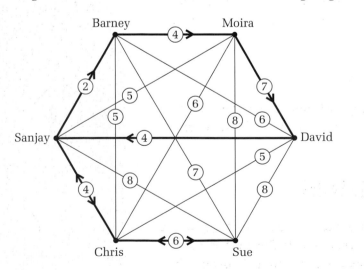

This process can be continued, but you must be very careful to ensure that a vertex does not become disconnected from the remainder of the network.

A further shortcut from David to Sue will result in the solution proposed but not shown at the end of Example 1.

7.3 Upper Bounds and Improvements

Exercise

Contextual

1 The Star Islands consist of the main island, Algor, and five small islands scattered around the coast. The inter-island ferry service runs regular shuttle services from Algor to each of the other five islands, at a cost of £1–£4 per single journey. The alternative is to hire a private ferry, at a cost of £6 per single journey between any two islands. The government inspector wishes to check the quayside safety arrangements at each harbour, having been flown in to the airport on the main island of Algor.

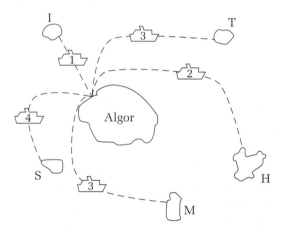

a By constructing a Minimum Spanning Tree, find an upper bound.

b Find a shortcut which improves this upper bound and implement it.

2 – 6

For each of the networks in Exercise 7.2

a find an upper bound by constructing a Minimum Spanning Tree.

b find a shortcut which improves this upper bound and implement it.

7.4 Lower Bounds

We have looked at the construction of upper bounds, and of improving them. However, these methods do not guarantee to find an optimal solution, and it would be helpful to have an indication of how much potential for improvement still exists. We therefore find a lower bound which is as large as possible and thus 'brackets' the optimal solution.

The method is to remove a vertex from the network, construct the Minimum Spanning Tree for the remaining vertices, and then add back in the two shortest edges from the vertex previously removed.

The following diagrams demonstrate a number of possible scenarios and show that this method will either find the optimal tour, or that any tour constructed from it will have to be greater.

In the first and third, a tour has not been achieved. Any different choice of edges used to create a tour will have a greater length, so this is a lower bound.

In the second, a tour has been achieved so this lower bound is also a solution.

Example

By removing each vertex in turn, find a series of lower bounds for Sanjay's journey. Hence state the range of values in which the optimum solution must lie, making this range as small as possible.

Solution

We remove the vertex representing Sanjay's house, and construct a Minimum Spanning Tree for the other five vertices, then add the two shortest edges from Sanjay (Barney, length 2, and one of the ones of length 4).

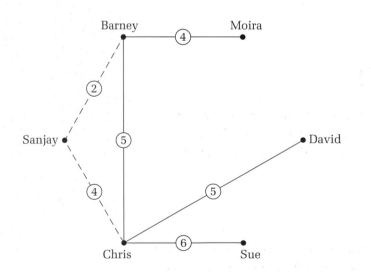

This can be repeated for the other vertices, and gives the following table of results.

Vertex removed	Sanjay	Barney	Moira	David	Sue	Chris
Length	26	26	26	25	27	27

We choose the largest of these, and say that our lower bound is 27, representing 2.7 km. Since we already have an upper bound of 3.1 km from Example 1 in the previous section, we can now say that Sanjay's optimum journey will be between 2.7 and 3.1 km.

7.4 Lower Bounds

Exercise

Technique

1 For the network in Exercise 7.2 question 1 find a lower bound using a Minimum Spanning Tree, initially deleting vertex A.

2 For the network in Exercise 7.2 question 2 find a lower bound using a Minimum Spanning Tree, initially deleting vertex B.

3 For the network in Exercise 7.2 question 3 find a lower bound using a Minimum Spanning Tree, initially deleting vertex H.

4 For the network in Exercise 7.2 question 4 find a lower bound using a Minimum Spanning Tree, initially deleting vertex Q.

5 For the network in Exercise 7.2 question 5 find a lower bound using a Minimum Spanning Tree, initially deleting vertex D.

7.5 Scheduling

There are a variety of situations which, although they do not involve travelling, can be represented by a complete graph and for which the solution is a Hamiltonian cycle, making the methods of this chapter appropriate.

Example

In a variety show at a theatre, there are six acts each requiring a different stage set, together with a prologue and a finale which require the same stage set. A compere does some stand-up comedy while the sets are changed. The following table gives the time taken to change the stage set between each act. Find lower and upper bounds for the amount of time the compere will be on stage, and suggest an order for the acts.

	P	A	B	C	D	E	F
Prologue/Finale (P)	–	2	3	1	5	4	2
Act A	2	–	2	3	5	3	4
Act B	3	2	–	6	4	1	3
Act C	1	3	6	–	2	5	4
Act D	5	5	4	2	–	4	5
Act E	4	3	1	5	4	–	6
Act F	2	4	3	4	5	6	–

Solution

Lower Bound: Removing P and finding the Minimum Spanning Tree for the remaining 6 vertices gives a tree of length 11.

Prim's Algorithm for a table would be appropriate here (Section 4.3).

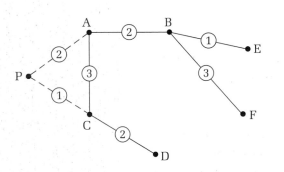

Adding the two shortest edges from P gives a lower bound of 14.

Upper Bound by Nearest Neighbour: Starting at P would go to C (1), D (2), B (4) [could equally have chosen E], E (1), A (3), F (4), P (2). Total length 17.

By interchanging B and E, we get P–C–D–E–B–A–F–P which is of length $1 + 2 + 4 + 1 + 2 + 4 + 2 = 16$. This is an improved upper bound which is very close to the lower bound and therefore probably optimal. Therefore this (or its reverse) is the order in which the acts should be performed, and the compere must prepare 16 minutes of fill-in.

7.5 Scheduling

Exercise

Contextual

1 A small engineering firm has a production line which is used to make batches of six different aero-engine components, A, B, C, D, E and F. The changeover times in minutes from the line being set up for one component to its being set up for another are given in the table below.

	A	B	C	D	E	F
A	–	60	100	40	50	70
B	60	–	90	50	40	40
C	100	90	–	80	60	80
D	40	50	80	–	70	50
E	50	40	60	70	–	70
F	70	40	80	50	70	–

a Each month, the production line is used to manufacture components A, B, C, D, E and F in succession. It is then set up ready to produce component A at the start of the following month.
  i How much time is taken up by the changeovers?
  ii Explain why your answer can be considered to be an *upper bound* to a particular Travelling Salesperson Problem.
  iii By using an appropriate algorithm, or otherwise, show how the engineering firm can reduce the amount of time spent on changeovers. Show sufficient working to make your method clear. You should aim to produce a time of at most 6 hours.
b By *initially ignoring component E*, find a lower bound for the time taken up by the changeovers in one month's complete production cycle.

(AQA)

Consolidation

Exercise A

1 A company, based in Rochdale, produces a free newspaper for distribution locally. The following table shows the six surrounding towns that receive the free paper. The figures represent the time, in minutes, to travel between the towns. The company delivery van has to travel from Rochdale to each one of the other towns, before returning to Rochdale.

	Rochdale	Castleton	Middleton	Shaw	Milnrow	Littleborough	Whitworth
Rochdale	–	3	7	8	6	5	4
Castleton	3	–	9	6	8	7.5	6.5
Middleton	7	9	–	14	12	11.5	12
Shaw	8	6	14	–	13	12	11
Milnrow	6	8	12	13	–	10	9
Littleborough	5	7.5	11.5	12	10	–	8
Whitworth	4	6.5	12	11	9	8	–

a Find a minimum connector for the seven towns, stating its length.

b Use the Nearest Neighbour Algorithm, starting from Rochdale, to find an upper bound for a tour of the seven towns.

c By deleting Rochdale from the minimum connector found in part (a), obtain a lower bound for a tour of the seven towns. *(AQA)*

2 An express pizza delivery company promises to deliver pizzas within 30 minutes of an order being telephoned in. Four customers telephone in orders at the same time. While the pizzas are cooking, which takes 10 minutes, a delivery route must be planned for the person who will deliver all four pizzas. The diagram below shows the pizza company P and the four customers A, B, C and D, and the accompanying table shows the travel times for each possible leg of a journey between them.

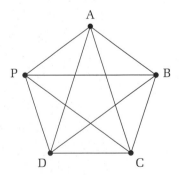

	P	A	B	C	D
P	–	5	3	4	2
A	5	–	1	4	4
B	3	1	–	3	5
C	4	4	3	–	7
D	2	4	5	7	–

The travel times shown exclude the time taken to stop at a customer's house and deliver the pizza; this stopping and delivery time is $2\frac{1}{2}$ minutes.

a Explain why a Travelling Salesperson solution taking less than 13 minutes guarantees that all four customers will get their pizzas (including stopping and delivery times) within 30 minutes of their telephone call.

b The pizzas are delivered using the Nearest Neighbour Algorithm, as follows.

> The first delivery is to the customer who is nearest to P (in the sense of having the shortest travel time).
>
> The second delivery is to the customer who is nearest the first one.
>
> The third delivery is to the customer nearest to the second who is still waiting for a pizza.
>
> The fourth delivery is to the remaining customer.

Write down the order in which the pizzas are delivered using this algorithm, and calculate how long the fourth customer has to wait for their pizza (including the stopping and delivery time).   *(OCR)*

3 This diagram shows a network connecting five vertices. The weights on the arcs represent distances in km. The direct route between any two vertices is always shorter than any indirect route.

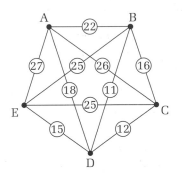

a Use the Nearest Neighbour Algorithm to find a route that starts at A and visits every other vertex once and once only before returning to A. Calculate the length of this route.

b By deleting vertex A and all arcs leading from A, find a lower bound for the length of the shortest cycle that visits every vertex.

c The lower bound obtained by deleting vertex B is 72 km. Explain whether or not this is a better lower bound than that obtained in part (b).

d The shortest cycle that visits every vertex in this network includes the longest arc and does not include the shortest arc. Find this cycle and give its length, justifying your answer.   *(OCR)*

4

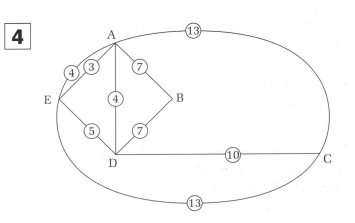

The network in the diagram shows a number of hostels in a national park and the possible paths joining them. The numbers on the edges give the lengths, in km, of the paths.

a Draw a complete network showing the shortest distances between the hostels. (You may do this by inspection. The application of an algorithm is not required.)

b Use the Nearest Neighbour Algorithm on the complete network to obtain an upper bound to the length of a tour in this network which starts at A and visits each hostel exactly once.

c Interpret your result in part (b) in terms of the original network.

(EDEXCEL)

5

	A	B	C	D	E	F	G
A	–	103	89	42	54	143	153
B	103	–	60	98	56	99	59
C	89	60	–	65	38	58	77
D	42	98	65	–	45	111	139
E	54	56	38	45	–	95	100
F	143	99	58	111	95	–	75
G	153	59	77	139	100	75	–

A computer supplier has outlets in seven cities A, B, C, D, E, F and G. The table shows the distances, in km, between the seven cities. Joan lives in city A and has to visit each city once to advise on displays. She wishes to plan a route, starting and finishing at A, visiting each city once and covering a minimum distance.

a Obtain a Minimum Spanning Tree for the network and draw this tree. Start with A and state the order in which the vertices are added.

Given that the network representing this problem is complete:

b Determine an initial upper bound for the length of the route travelled by Joan.

c Starting from your initial upper bound for the length of the route and using an appropriate method, find an upper bound which is less than 430 km.

d By deleting city A, determine a lower bound for the length of Joan's route.

(EDEXCEL)

Exercise B

1 The following matrix represents the distances between vertices in an undirected network. A missing entry indicates that there is no direct connection.

	A	B	C	D	E
A		2	1	6	3
B	2		5		10
C	1	5		2	
D	6		2		6
E	3	10		6	

a Draw the network.

b Use an appropriate algorithm to find the graph which is a minimum connector for the vertices of the network. Start from A and list the order in which you include edges. Give the length of your connector.

c A Hamiltonian cycle is a path visiting each vertex once and only once, and returning to the initial vertex. List all Hamiltonian cycles, taking vertex A as the initial and final vertex, and find a Hamiltonian cycle with the shortest length.

d It is often said that twice the length of the minimum connector is an upper bound for the solution to the travelling salesperson problem. Explain why, in this network, the minimum Hamiltonian cycle is greater than twice the length of the minimum connector.   *(AQA)*

2

	A	B	C	D	E	F
A	–	113	53	54	87	68
B	113	–	87	123	38	100
C	53	87	–	106	58	103
D	54	123	106	–	140	48
E	87	38	58	140	–	105
F	68	100	103	48	105	–

The table shows the distances, in km, between six towns.

a Starting from A, use Prim's algorithm to find a minimum connector and draw the Minimum Spanning Tree. You must make your method clear by stating the order in which the arcs are selected.

b i Hence form an initial upper bound for the solution to the Travelling Salesman Problem.

   ii Use a shortcut to reduce the upper bound to a value below 360.

c By deleting A, find a lower bound for the solution to the Travelling Salesman Problem.

d Use your answers to parts (b) and (c) to make a comment on the value of the optimal solution.

e Draw a diagram to show your best route.   *(EDEXCEL)*

3 The diagram below shows the location of some restaurants. The numbers represent the times taken by a delivery lorry from a catering supplies company. The lorry driver wishes to deliver to all the restaurants, starting and finishing at the company depot at A.

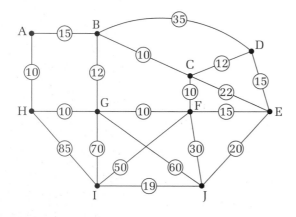

He applies the Nearest Neighbour algorithm.

a Give the route followed by the driver and the time it takes him.

b Show that the travelling time can be reduced if the driver does not always have to take a **direct** route between restaurants.   *(AQA)*

4 The values in the table give the shortest distances, in miles, between pairs of villages.

	J	K	L	M	N
J	–	2	5	6	8
K	2	–	3	4	7
L	5	3	–	5	9
M	6	4	5	–	8
N	8	7	9	8	–

a Use Prim's algorithm, starting at J, to obtain a Minimum Spanning Tree for the network represented by the table. State the order in which vertices are added to the tree.

b Draw your Minimum Spanning Tree.

c Hence find an upper bound for the Travelling Salesman Problem.

d By initially removing K, find a lower bound for the Travelling Salesman Problem.

e Find a Travelling Salesman route with a length that is greater than your lower bound and less than your upper bound. State the route and give its length.   *(OCR)*

5 Amy, Bea, Cara and Di are four friends. The lengths of the paths between their houses, measured in km, are given in the table.

	A	B	C	D
A	0	3.6	2.2	2.3
B	3.6	0	1.2	1.0
C	2.2	1.2	0	1.9
D	2.3	1.0	1.9	0

Amy wants to visit each of her friends and return to her own house using the shortest route possible. She decides to use the following algorithm.

```
She will start at her own house.
At each stage she moves to a friend's house that she
has not yet visited; she always chooses the nearest
such house.
She repeats this until all three friends have been
visited.
She then returns directly to her own house.
```

a Give the formal name of this algorithm.
b Write down the route that this algorithm gives for Amy, and find the length of this route.   *(OCR)*

Applications and Extensions

Other constraints
The algorithm used for TSP assumes that the only relevant information is the distance between vertices. Below are some other factors which may actually have to be taken into account. Try investigating real-world situations and consider how to deal with these extra factors (or others which you may discover in your particular example).

a Availability
The algorithm used for TSP assumes that the vertices of a network can be visited in any order. In practice, this is often not possible. For example, a student designing a tour of six universities they hope to apply to might be limited by the dates of open days.

b Travel time and accommodation
A salesperson planning a trip of several days would have to consider where they would be able to spend the night, and how long they would have to spend with each client. This might be affected by the number of clients they had in each town.

Summary

- The **Travelling Salesperson Problem** is that of finding a route which visits every vertex once, returning to the starting point. We usually aim to minimise the length of this route.

- In a complete graph, this will be a **Hamiltonian Cycle**.

- In the **Practical Problem**, the graph will not be complete. It is generally preferable to convert this to the **Classical Problem** by connecting every edge to every other edge by the shortest route available in the network.

- The **Nearest Neighbour algorithm** is an heuristic algorithm which generally gives a good approximation to the solution.

- An **upper bound** is a solution, but it is anticipated that a better (smaller) solution exists. It is usually found by the Nearest Neighbour algorithm, though there are other approaches such as doubling the Minimum Spanning Tree.

- Trial and improvement methods, such as shortcuts and vertex interchange can be used to improve an upper bound.

- A **lower bound** is not a solution (unless it is the optimum solution), but gives a value below which a solution cannot exist.

- There are some practical problems, based on scheduling, which can be represented by a network and whose solution has the same conditions as TSP and therefore can be solved using the same techniques.

8 Critical Path Analysis

8.1 Formulation and Notation

There are many instances in daily life where the accomplishment of a task requires a number of activities to be undertaken. Where there is the possibility for some of these activities to occur simultaneously, it is possible to analyse the relative importance of each one in ensuring that the overall task is completed in the minimum time, and to calculate that minimum time.

Unfortunately, there are two notations recognised and used commercially and for examination specifications; activity on arc and activity on node. This chapter uses activity on arc as its basis, but where appropriate, examples are repeated using activity on node so the reader can choose which method they wish to study.

Example

As a birthday surprise, Paula and Martin decide to renovate their mother's overgrown garden, replacing the rough lawn with a patio of pots which she can reach without having to bend down. They want to complete the task in a weekend whilst she is away. They want to know how long it will take to complete it, and whether they need to get any extra helpers in to get it done in time.

The following table lists the activities involved in the project, together with the time each activity takes, the number of people required to complete it, and any activities which have to be completed before the current one can be done.

Activity Name	Activity	Preceding Activities	Time (hours)	No. people required
A	Clear Garden	–	5	2
B	Measure Area	–	1	2
C	Design Patio	B	2	1
D	Choose Fencing	B	1	1
E	Buy pots and plants	A, C	3	2
F	Plant all pots	E	1	1
G	Purchase Slabs	C	1	1
H	Construct Garden	C, D, G	6	2

Represent the activities as a network.

Solution 1 – Activity on Arc (Edge)

Our activities have been defined, and we are going to put these on the edges of our network. Our vertices will be events, which indicate that preceding activities have all been completed, and that the following ones may begin. Events are usually numbered, with the convention that every activity finishes at an event of higher number than it starts.

Algorithm to draw network

1 Create an event 'Start' and put all activities which have no precedents coming out from it (do not put finish events on).

2 Choose an activity for which all preceding activities are already in the network and add it (you will need to put finish events on existing activities, but do not put one on the activity you are adding). Use dummies as necessary.

3 If there are more activities to add, repeat step 2.

4 Terminate all 'loose' activities in a single completion event. You may well then need to re-draw the network to make it look tidy.

We draw a start vertex and connect the activities A and B to it.

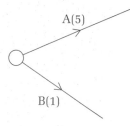

Now that B has finished, we can add C and D. We do this by putting an event at the end of B and then placing the new edges on.

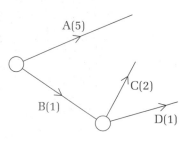

With both A and C now finished, we can add E by connecting it to an event we now place on A and C.

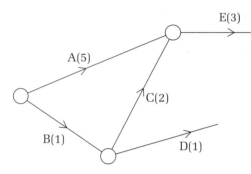

F can now follow E.

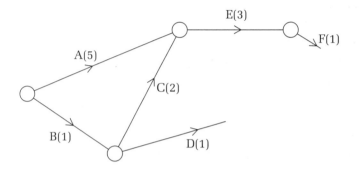

G can follow C but the completion of C is at an event which also concludes A which is not a required precedent for G. We therefore terminate C earlier, putting in a new event and restore the link to the original event with a dummy activity, drawn as a dotted line.

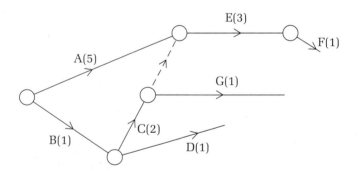

H is dependent on C, D and G, but since G is already dependent on C, this is a redundant piece of information. We draw D and G together at an event to add H, and finally add the terminal event to complete the network.

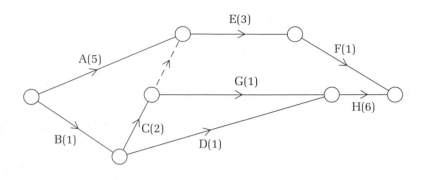

Dummy activities

A dummy is an activity of duration 0, used to force the correct logic. There are two cases where it is used – the one which occurred in the example above, and the other when two activities would otherwise link the same pair of vertices, i.e.

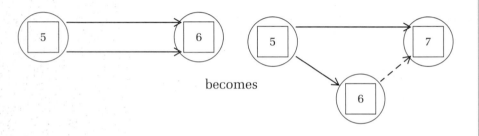

becomes

Solution 2 – Activity on Node (vertex)

Our activities have been defined, and we are going to put these on the vertices of our network. Our edges will be showing the preceding activities, with the first activity being called start, and the last one finish.

We draw our start, and the activities A and B which have no precedents, and join them.

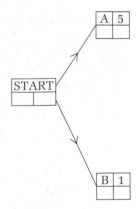

The reason for using the boxes shown is explained in Section 8.2.

We can now add C and D, each connected back to B, their preceding activity.

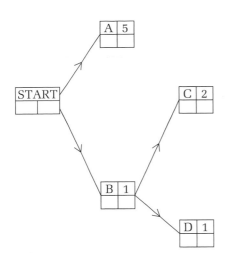

We add E by drawing edges from A and C, and F follows E. G follows C, H is connected back to D and G, and we add a finish to draw together the end of tasks F and H.

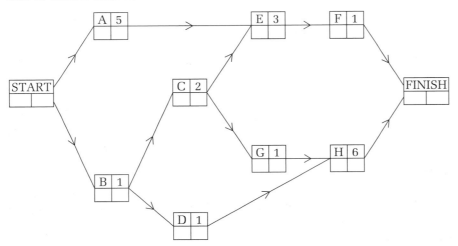

8.1 Formulation and Notation

Exercise

Technique

Each section of this chapter introduces a further stage in the process of analysing a complex project. The questions in this exercise represent the start of the process, and will be gradually completed through the chapter.

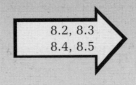

8.2, 8.3
8.4, 8.5

You may find it helpful to start each of the questions in this exercise on a new piece of paper, so that you can complete them as you work through the chapter.

Solution

Our first attempt at creating a schedule looks like this:

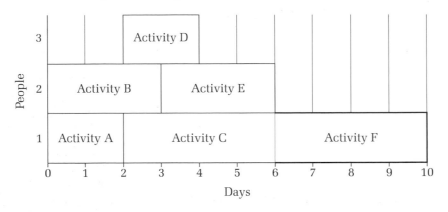

We have assigned all the critical activities to one person. A second person can do activities B and E, but since D could start whilst B is still in progress, we require a third person for this task.

However, on closer examination of the cascade chart, it can be seen that activity E has 4 days float and can therefore be delayed. Furthermore, activity D has 3 days float. By delaying D by one day, and E by 2 days, we can move E sufficiently far through the schedule to allow activity D to be done by person 2.

Our schedule is now as follows:

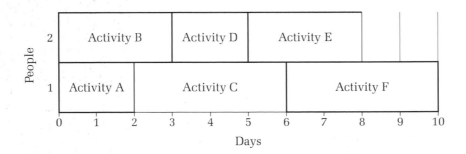

Example 2

Draw a resource histogram for the garden example used throughout this chapter and use this to analyse the number of people required to complete the project in the minimum time.

Solution

To construct a resource histogram, we are really only concerned with the number of people required, rather than the individual activities. The activities have been included below to assist the reader in identifying the source of each section.

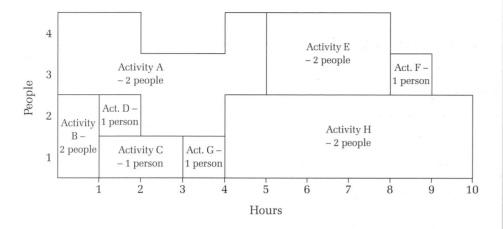

As there is only 1 hour when we need two people, and 6 hours when we need four people, it will not be possible to complete the project in 10 hours with less than four people.

8.5 Scheduling and Resources

Exercise

Technique

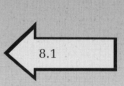

1 – 4

Draw up a schedule for questions 1 to 4 in Exercise 8.1, assuming that each activity only requires one person, and hence find the minimum number of people needed to complete the project in the minimum time.

The following tables show how many people are required for each of the activities in questions 5 and 6 of Exercise 8.1. Use this information to construct a resource histogram, and hence find the minimum number of people needed to complete the project in the minimum time.

5

Activity	People required
A	1
B	2
C	2
D	1
E	3
F	1
G	2
H	1
I	1
J	2
K	2

6

Activity	People required
A	1
B	1
C	2
D	2
E	1
F	3
G	2
H	1
I	2
J	1
K	1

8.6 Crashing a Network

We have looked at the calculation of float times, and how this allows some flexibility in the scheduling of those tasks which have non-zero float. However, there are cases when adjusting the timings of a task has a significant effect. In such cases either the overall project time or the activities forming the critical path, or possibly both, change. This is known as **crashing** the network.

Example

Paula and Martin have enlisted two more friends to help so that they can manage the 10 hour schedule (see the resource histogram in Section 8.5, Example 2). However, they decide that they want to try and finish earlier on the Sunday afternoon, so they ask Alex to help with activity H, the construction of the garden. Since there are now three people, this now has a revised duration of $(6 \times 2) \div 3 = 4$ hours. What effect does this have on the critical path and completion time?

Solution

We can use the same network since the precedences have not changed. However, activity H is now of duration 4 and this leads to a revised calculation for the earliest finish time at the end of the project of 9 hours. This then affects the latest starting times when performing the backward pass and gives the following solutions (activity on arc and node):

This assumes that the two people for 6 hours quoted in the original problem equated to 12 person-hours to share between 3 people in the revised problem.

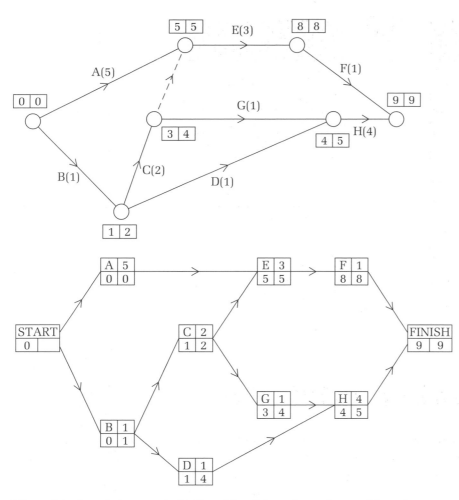

The critical path is now A, E, F and is of duration 9 hours. Therefore, although we have saved 2 hours on activity H, it has not saved 2 hours overall, but has crashed the network, generating a new solution.

8.6 Crashing a Network

Exercise

Technique

The tables below give information about which activities in each project are now to be done by more people. In each case, calculate the effect this has on the critical path and completion time.

1

Activity	Number of people now available
H	3

2

Activity	Number of people now available
G	2

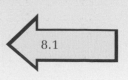
8.1

3

Activity	Number of people now available
A	2
E	2

4

Activity	Number of people now available
A	3

5

Activity	Number of people now available
B	4

6

Activity	Number of people now available
A	2
H	2
J	2

Consolidation

Exercise A

1 For these networks find:

a the early and late times for each activity

b the critical path

c the total float on each activity.

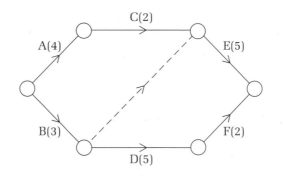

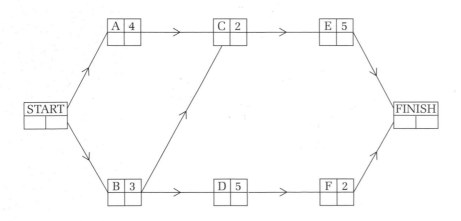

2 The table shows the six activities in a project, together with their durations, precedences and the number of people required for each activity.

Activity	Duration (days)	Preceded by	People required
A	3	–	2
B	2	–	1
C	1	A, B	3
D	5	B	2
E	4	B, C	1
F	5	D, E	2

Draw an activity network to represent these activities and their precedences.

In addition to the precedences shown in the table, activity E must not start until at least 2 days after activity B has finished.

a Determine the earliest and latest starting times for each activity, for completion of the project in the minimum time.

b Identify the critical activities, and state the minimum time for the completion of the project, assuming that there are sufficient people available.

c Find the least number of people required for the project to be completed in the minimum time, explaining your reasoning.

d By how many days must the project over-run if the least possible number of people are used? Justify your answer.

(OCR)

3 A project is modelled by the activity networks.

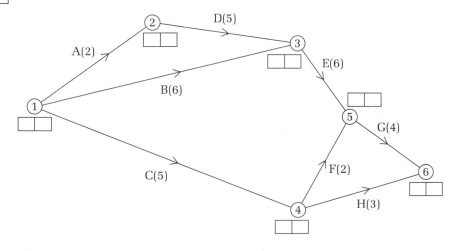

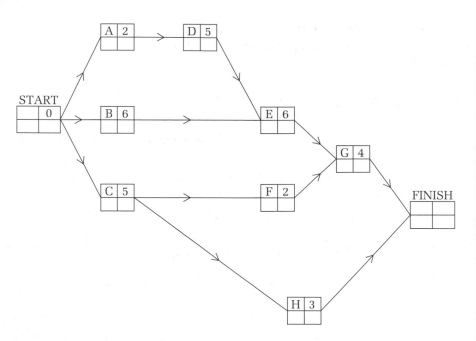

a Determine the critical activities and the length of the critical path.

b Obtain the total floats for the non-critical activities.

c Draw a cascade (Gantt) chart showing the information found in parts **a** and **b**.

d Given that each activity requires one worker, draw up a schedule to determine the minimum number of workers required to complete the project in the critical time. State the minimum number of workers.

(EDEXCEL modified)

4 The table shows the activities included in a project, their durations, and their immediate predecessors.

Activity	A	B	C	D	E	F	G	H
Duration (days)	3	1	1	4	5	2	2	2
Immediate predecessors	–	–	B	A	A, C	B	F	D, E

a Draw an activity network for the project.

b Perform a forward and backward pass on your activity network. Give the minimum completion time and the activities forming the critical path.

c Draw up a cascade chart for this project.

d The number of people needed for each activity is as follows:

Activity	A	B	C	D	E	F	G	H
People	3	2	2	2	3	1	1	4

Activities are to be scheduled, some later than their earliest possible time, so that at most five people are needed at any one time, whilst the project is still completed in the minimum time.

What are the new scheduled start times for activities D, F and G?

(AQA modified)

5 The process of constructing a chest of drawers from a kit consists of the following tasks, some of which cannot be done until others are completed. The time which each task takes, in hours, is also given.

Task	Time needed	Must follow
A assemble sides and back	2	–
B assemble the drawers	3	–
C fit the drawers	1	A, B
D fit the top	$1\frac{1}{2}$	A
E clear up the packaging	$\frac{1}{2}$	A, B
F varnish and polish	2	C, D

Construct an activity network for this project, where each undotted arc represents one of the tasks.

a Perform a forward and backward pass on your activity network in order to calculate all the early and late event times.
b State the minimum completion time and critical tasks for the construction.
c Find the independent float of task E and state its possible range of starting times.
d Each task is done by one person. Draw a cascade chart to illustrate a schedule which allows the whole construction to be completed in the minimum time by two people.
e If task B is replaced by three tasks of one hour each and an unlimited number of helpers is available, explain how that will affect the minimum completion time.

(AQA modified)

Exercise B

1 For the following networks find:

a the early and late times for each activity
b the critical path
c the total, interfering and independent float on each activity.

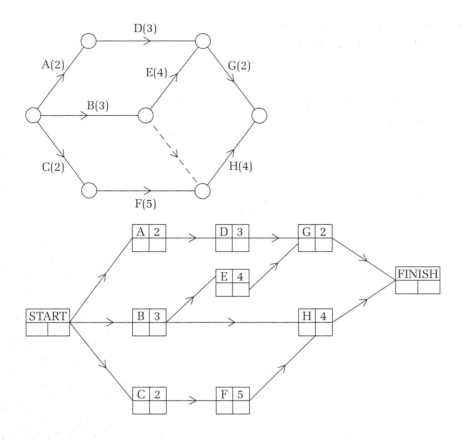

2 A workshop uses the project plan outlined below for repairing a washing machine.

Activity	Duration (minutes)	Immediate predecessor
A Assemble tools and spares	20	–
B Remove rear panel	2	A
C Prepare pump and new hoses	15	A
D Disconnect old pump and hoses	10	B
E Remove drum	15	D
F Lubricate and adjust motor	15	D
G Fit new bearings	10	E
H Replace drum	8	G
I Replace drive belt	1	F, H
J Fit new pump and hoses	12	C, D
K Replace rear panel	2	I, J

a Construct an activity network for this task.
b Analyse your network to find, and indicate clearly, the critical path.
c In each of the following cases find the minimum time required to complete the project and describe any change in the critical path.

   i   Activity C takes 15 minutes longer than expected.

   ii Activity F takes 15 minutes longer than expected.

(AQA)

3   The table shows the activities involved in completing a project, together with their durations. For each activity, any other activities which must be completed before the activity can begin are shown under the heading 'Immediate predecessors'.

Activity	Duration (weeks)	Immediate predecessors
A	3	–
B	5	–
C	2	A, B
D	6	B
E	5	C, D
F	2	D
G	7	C

  a Draw an activity network for the project.

  b Using an appropriate algorithm, find the critical path and the project duration.

  c If the duration of each activity is increased by a week, by how much will the project completion be delayed?

(AEB)

4   A village bypass is to be constructed. The table shows the tasks involved, their duration in weeks, and their immediate predecessors, i.e. tasks which must be completed before the given task can begin.

Task	Duration (weeks)	Immediate Predecessors
A Complete survey	6	–
B Purchase land	20	A
C Supply materials	8	–
D Provide machinery	4	–
E Excavate cuttings	7	B, D
F Build bridges and embankments	9	B, C, D
G Lay drains	7	E, F
H Lay hardcore	4	G
I Lay bitumen	2	H
J Install road furniture	9	E, F

a Produce an activity network for this project.

b Given that the bypass is to be completed as soon as possible, find the earliest and latest starting time for each task. Give the fastest completion time and the critical path.

c Each of the tasks E, F, G and J can be speeded up at extra cost. The maximum number of weeks by which each task can be shortened and the extra cost per week of shortening the task are shown in the table below.

Task	E	F	G	J
Maximum number of weeks by which task may be shortened	3	3	1	3
Extra cost per week of shortening task (£000's)	50	20	10	30

What is the new shortest time for the bypass to be completed? Which activities will need to be hurried-up to achieve this and by how much? What will be the total extra cost?

(AEB)

5 A project involves six tasks as follows.

Task	Duration (mins)	Immediate predecessors
A	15	–
B	20	–
C	10	A, B
D	6	A
E	25	B, D
F	23	C

a Draw an activity network for the project.

b By labelling your network with earliest and latest times, find the minimum duration of the project, the critical path, and the float time for each non-critical task.

An extra condition is now imposed: task A may not begin until task B has been under way for at least 6 minutes.

c Draw a new network to take account of this condition, and say what difference it makes to the completion time and to the critical path.

(AEB)

Activities and Extensions

Activity Numbering
Numbering activities in a sensible order can help in constructing activity networks. Research algorithms used for numbering activities.

Applications
Investigate real life situations where CPA can be applied. You could use it to plan out a joint piece of coursework.

Formulating as an LP
Try formulating a CPA problem as a Linear Programme. It is a directed network, in which you need to find the maximum length route. If you have access to an appropriate computer package, you could use this method to check your solutions to some of the questions in this chapter.

Summary

- **Critical Path Analysis** consists of a set of activities required to complete a task.

- The activities will have associated **durations** and **precedences** – other activities which must be completed first.

- Activities can be represented by **edges** (**activity on arc**) or by **vertices** (**activity on node**).

- A dummy activity has duration zero and is added either to enforce the correct logic of precedences, or to prevent parallel activities.

- Earliest and latest times for events/activities are calculated by carrying out first a forward, then a backward pass.

- The **critical path** is those activities whose timing is critical if the project is to be completed in the minimum possible time. Their latest finish time minus their earliest start time will be equal to their duration.

- **Float** is a measure of the amount of time by which an activity can be delayed or extended.

- An activity can have **independent** float which does not affect other activities or **interfering** float which, if used, can affect the availability of float on other activities. Adding these together gives the **total** float.

- A **cascade** or **Gantt** chart sets out each activity as a horizontal bar above a time line with dependencies (precedences) identified.

- A **resource schedule** considers the resources (often number of workers) required at a given time. These are shown on a **resource histogram**.

- **Resource levelling** is the process of using float time to adjust the timings of the activities so that the resource histogram has a flatter, smoother shape, with a reduced maximum requirement for resources.

- If the duration of one or more events is changed sufficiently to change either the overall project time or the activities forming the critical path, it is said to be **crashing** the network.

9 Linear Programming

What you need to know

- How to re-arrange linear equations
- How to draw straight line graphs
- How to shade the unwanted side of an inequality
- How to solve simultaneous equations

Review

1 Write the equation $y = 4 - 3x$ in the form $ax + by = c$

2 Draw the straight lines represented by $3x + 2y = 6$ and $3x + y = 4$ on the same axes.

3 By shading out the unwanted areas, show on your graph the region which satisfies both $3x + 2y \leqslant 6$ and $3x + y \leqslant 4$.

4 Solve the following pairs of simultaneous equations:

a $2x + 3y = 8$
  $5x + 1y = 7$

b $5x - 3y = 14$
  $2x + y = 10$

Hint: Remember how to find the axis intercepts by putting y, then x, equal to zero.

9.1 Variables, Constraints and Graphs

Variables are a vital part of any algebraic problem solving. By a **variable**, we mean that it can take various values within our problem. In Linear Programming, variables represent the items whose quantities we control. For graphical solutions, we can only have two variables (one on each axis).

A **constraint** is an equation, involving one or more of our variables, which limits or controls the values it can take. In this chapter, almost all our constraints will be inequalities, although in other types of linear programming, equalities also occur quite frequently. For example, $x \leqslant 6$ limits the values x can take, whilst $x + y = 6$ means that as x increases, y will have to decrease to compensate.

Programming is about a set of pre-determined rules leading to a solution, a sort of recipe. This is Linear Programming because the governing rules are straight lines.

The technique of Linear Programming (LP) originated in the USA in the 1940s for solving economic and business problems.

Variables normally represent real quantities and can therefore not be negative. We therefore introduce **non-negativity constraints** e.g. $x \geqslant 0$

These equations and inequalities can then be drawn on a graph. By shading out those areas which do not apply, we are left with an unshaded **feasible region** – those points on the graph which satisfy all our constraints. Even a very small region will have an infinite number of points, but in many problems we are only interested in whole numbers (the set of points with integer co-ordinates).

Example

Horsey Weavers make small wool rugs in a workshop behind their cottage. There are two parts to the process – spinning the yarn and weaving the rug. A fireside rug takes 2 hours to spin the yarn and 1 hour to weave. A bedroom rug takes $\frac{1}{2}$ hour to spin the yarn and 2 hours to weave. They work for 7 hours a day and have one spinning wheel and one loom. What are the daily production options?

Solution

The **variables** will be the two types of rug. We need to give our variables simple letter names. We could use f and b for **f**ireside and **b**edroom but it is often easier to use x and y because that fits in with the graph we are going to draw. So we define them as:

Let x be the number of **fireside** rugs made.
Let y be the number of **bedroom** rugs made.

The **constraints** in this case are the limitations on equipment and time – the 'difficulties' that the weavers would encounter if they tried to make too many rugs, or too many of a particular type. They are the limited amount of available time on each of the wheel and the loom, so we write an inequality for each.

Spinning Wheel: $2x + \frac{1}{2}y \leqslant 7$
This represents the fact that each x (fireside rug) takes 2 hours and each y (bedroom rug) takes $\frac{1}{2}$ hour on the wheel and there are only 7 hours available.

Loom: $x + 2y \leqslant 7$
This represents the fact that each x (fireside rug) takes 1 hour to weave and each y (bedroom rug) takes 2 hours to weave and there are 7 hours available.

So, for example, if they make 3 fireside rugs and 1 bedroom rug, represented by $\{x = 3, y = 1\}$ then the spinning wheel time is $2 \times 3 + \frac{1}{2} \times 1 = 6\frac{1}{2}$ hours and the loom time is $1 \times 3 + 2 \times 1 = 5$ hours.

Notice that the constraints are written as 'less than or equal to' because the 7 hours is only a limit – it is acceptable for the equipment to be idle part of the time.

We also need the non-negativity constraints $x \geqslant 0$, $y \geqslant 0$.

Thus our problem is defined by the four constraints:

$2x + \frac{1}{2}y \leqslant 7$

$x + 2y \leqslant 7$

$x \geqslant 0$

$y \geqslant 0$

Our constraints can now be drawn on a graph. It is best to draw the equalities $2x + \frac{1}{2}y = 7$ and $x + 2y = 7$ first and then shade out the unwanted side.

$2x + \frac{1}{2}y = 7$: when $x = 0$, $y = 14$ so plot $(0, 14)$ and when $y = 0$, $x = 3\frac{1}{2}$ so plot $(3\frac{1}{2}, 0)$ and join up these points. Shade out the side above/to the right of the line.

$x + 2y = 7$: when $x = 0$, $y = 3\frac{1}{2}$ so plot $(0, 3\frac{1}{2})$ and when $y = 0$, $x = 7$ so plot $(7, 0)$ and join up these points. Shade out the side above/to the right of the line.

Also, the non-negativity constraints $x \geqslant 0$, $y \geqslant 0$ mean that we only need the quadrant shown below.

$\leqslant$ constraints will always require you to keep the lower left (x, y both small/negative) and shade out the upper right (large/positive).

The feasible region is the unshaded region in the middle of the graph. All points contained in the feasibile region and on its boundary meet all of the constraints. However, in the context of this question we would want to restrict ourselves to integer points.

9.1 Variables, Constraints and Graphs

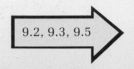

9.2, 9.3, 9.5

We will continue to use and extend these questions throughout the chapter – make sure you keep your solutions handy.

Exercise

Technique

1 Draw the graph represented by the constraints

$x + y \leqslant 5,$
$2x + y \leqslant 8$
$x, y \geqslant 0$

2 Draw the graph represented by the constraints

$2x + 3y \leqslant 12, 5x + 2y \leqslant 10 \ (x, y \geqslant 0)$

3 Draw the graph represented by the constraints $4x + 3y \leqslant 16, x \leqslant 2 \ (x, y \geqslant 0)$

4 Draw the graph represented by the constraints $x + y \geqslant 7, 2x + y \leqslant 10$

Contextual

For questions **1** to **4**, choose and define appropriate variables and write down the constraints.

1 A school librarian is ordering new books. He has a total budget of £100. He must order at least 3 books on discrete mathematics, and at least 3 books on pure mathematics. Discrete books cost £12, pure books cost £15.

2 A teacher is organising a trip. They have booked a 53 seater coach. There must be one teacher for every 10 students.

3 A potter can make either mugs, or cups and saucers. A mug needs 150 g of clay, and needs 120 cm^2 in the kiln. A cup and saucer set needs 100 g of clay, and takes up 180 cm^2 in the kiln. The kiln measures 75 cm by 125 cm. The potter has 12 kg of clay.

4 A gardener grows radishes and lettuces on a plot 2 m wide. A 10 cm strip is needed for a row of radishes and a 50 cm strip is needed for a row of lettuces. She uses a seed dispenser that has to be filled twice to sow a row of radish seed and once for a row of lettuces, and she only has time to fill the dispenser at most 22 times. Write down two constraints representing the plot width and the dispenser filling. Draw a graph to show the feasible region.

Choose to work either entirely in cm or entirely in m.

9.2 Optimisation

There is normally a purpose or **objective** to linear programming problems. In many cases is it about costs and profits, and **the objective function** is an expression involving our variables, which is to be either maximised or minimised. This **objective function** is sometimes referred to as the **profit function**.

Example

Horsey Weavers sell their rugs at a local craft centre. Having deducted the cost of materials, the fireside rugs give a net profit of £6 each, whilst the bedroom ones make £9 because they sell for a better price. Which production option gives the best potential profit?

Solution

The profit function is $6x + 9y$ so our objective is to maximise the profit P, where

$P = 6x + 9y$

Clearly one method of solution would be to evaluate the profit at each possible point in the feasible region, and choose the best (largest). However, this could be a very large number of points, particularly if they are not limited to integers. We therefore need to find a method of identifying the best profit without considering every point. There are in fact two approaches which are useful.

Method 1: Tour of vertices
It can be proved that, in two dimensions, a tour from vertex to vertex will lead to the optimum solution.

```
Select a start vertex — usually (0, 0) — and evaluate
the profit.
Repeat
  Calculate the profit at an adjacent vertex.
  If it is greater, make that the current vertex
until no adjacent vertex has greater profit
```

(0, 0)   profit = 0
$(0, 3\frac{1}{2})$ profit = $31\frac{1}{2}$
(3, 2)   profit = 36
$(3\frac{1}{2}, 0)$ profit = 21 [so do not move to this vertex]

Maximum profit = $6 \times 3 + 9 \times 2 = 36$
We could also have gone the other way round [(0, 0), $(3\frac{1}{2}, 0)$, (3, 2), $(0, 3\frac{1}{2})$ – reject and return to (3, 2)]

Any set of constraints will always generate a convex shape (that is, all corners point outwards). A set of parallel lines with gradient equal to the profit function and with the first one passing through the point of least profit, will pass through the other vertices in order round each side, giving increased profit, until the maximum is reached.

Method 2: Profit Line

Draw a line through the origin, parallel to the gradient of the profit function.

$P = 6x + 9y \Rightarrow y = \frac{1}{9}(-6x + P)$ so gradient is $\frac{1}{9}(-6) = \frac{-2}{3}$

Move this line up the y-axis until it is just leaving the feasible region – the point of exit is the optimum value.

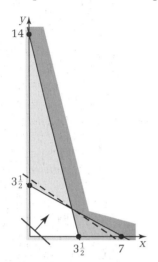

Thus again the maximum profit $= 6 \times 3 + 9 \times 2 = 36$

Efficiency and choice of method:

Method 1 requires that the co-ordinates of each vertex are known. Whilst it may be possible to read these off an accurately drawn graph, many will be fractions not corresponding to exact lines on your graph paper. It is then necessary to solve simultaneously the equations of the two constraints intersecting at that point (treating them as equalities).

Method 2 can often be approximated from a sketch graph, but it will still be necessary to calculate and evaluate likely solution points in order to verify them. A consideration of gradients will also help since the optimum point will lie at the intersection of constraints whose gradients are the closest above and below the gradient of the profit line.

It is fortunate that the optimum point has integer coordinates, as required by our context. The method for ensuring we obtain integer solutions is covered in Section 9.3.

You can use a graphical calculator to draw constraints and profit lines, but remember when looking for solutions that most fractions will be shown as a decimal approximation.
You can also solve simultaneous equations on many graphical calculators.

9.2 Optimisation

Exercise

Technique

1 **a** Draw the graph represented by the constraints

$2x + y \leqslant 16$, $2x + 3y \leqslant 24$, $y \leqslant 6$, $x, y \geqslant 0$

b If the Profit function is $P = x + y$, evaluate the profit at the vertices and find the optimum solution. Draw a line parallel to the profit function, passing through this optimum solution.

c Repeat **b** for the profit function $P = x + 2y$

2 – **4** use the graphs you plotted for technique section of Exercise 9.1 questions **2** – **4**

9.1

2 Find the optimum solution if the Profit function is

a $P = x + y$
b $P = 3x + y$

3 Find the optimum solution if the Profit function is

a $P = x + y$
b $P = 2x + y$

4 Find the optimum solution if the Profit function is

a $P = x + y$
b $P = 3x + 2y$

9.3 Integer Solutions

In our example of Horsey Weavers, the co-ordinates of the intersection of the two constraints were integers. However, this is often not the case. In such situations, the integer points within the feasible region must be considered to find the one with the best profit.

Example

Maximise $3x + 2y$
subject to $2x + y \leqslant 8$
            $2x + 3y \leqslant 11$
            $x, y \geqslant 0$ with x and y integer.

Solution

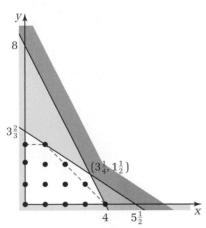

The integer feasible points have been marked with a dot.

Maximum profit occurs at $(3\frac{1}{4}, 1\frac{1}{2})$ which is not integer.

The dotted line on the diagram indicates the boundary of the integer feasible region and the dots mark the integer points. As before we have the choice of methods (tour of vertices or profit line) to find the optimum solution.

Tour of vertices

$(0, 0)$ profit $= 0$
$(4, 0)$ profit $= 12$
$(1, 3)$ profit $= 9$

return to previous optimum integer solution is $x = 4, y = 0$ with profit 12.

Merely truncating the real solution, which in this case gives (3, 1) does not necessarily give the optimum solution. In fact, the optimum can be a considerable distance from the real solution.

9.3 Integer Solutions

Exercise

Technique

1 Using the graph from Exercise 9.1 question 2 for
$2x + 3y \leqslant 12$, $5x + 2y \leqslant 10$ $(x, y \geqslant 0)$
find the maximum profit if

  a $P = 2x + 4y$
  b $P = 2x + 8y$

9.1

2 Maximise $5x + 6y$ subject to $x + y \leqslant 6$
                                                  $2x + 3y \leqslant 14$

3 Maximise $x + y$ subject to $x + 2y \leqslant 8$
                                                  $3x + 2y \leqslant 15$

Contextual

Questions **1** to **4** refer to the contextual questions in Exercise 9.1.

9.1

1 The librarian wants to buy the maximum number of books.

  a   Write down the profit function.
  b   Find the optimum solution.

2 The teacher wants to take as many students as possible.

  a   Write down the profit function.
  b   Find the optimum solution.

3 Mugs sell for £5, cup and saucer sets for £7.50. The potter wants to maximise their income.

a Write down the profit function.
b Find the optimum solution.

4 One row of radishes will produce a profit of 50p; one row of lettuces will produce a profit of 75p. The gardener wishes to maximise her profit.

a Write down the profit function.
b Find the optimum solution.

9.4 Multiple Solutions

There are two cases when multiple solutions occur. The following examples demonstrate these.

Example 1

Maximise $9x + 6y$ subject to
$$x + 3y \leqslant 15$$
$$3x + 2y \leqslant 17$$
$$2x + y \leqslant 11$$
$$x, y \geqslant 0$$

Solution

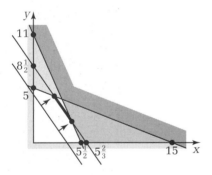

Since the profit line is parallel to the second constraint, all points on that line between $(3, 4)$ and $(5, 1)$ have an equal profit of 51 and are optimum solutions. This could be written as $3 \leqslant x \leqslant 5$, $y = \frac{(17-3x)}{2}$

Example 2

Maximise $3x + 3y$ subject to
$$5x + 2y \leqslant 18$$
$$2x + 7y \leqslant 18$$
$$x, y \geqslant 0$$

Solution

Maximum profit occurs at approximately $(2.90, 1.74)$. Truncated would give an integer solution of $(2, 1)$. Increasing x, we consider $(3, 1)$ which satisfies the constraints, and (4, 1) which does not. Increasing y, we consider (2, 2) which satisfies the constraints [it lies on the second constraint], and (2, 3) which therefore does not. We have therefore found two possible optimum points – (3, 1) and (2, 2). In this question, both give the same profit of 12 so they are both optimum solutions.

9.4 Multiple Solutions

Exercise

Technique

1 Maximise $8x + 6y$ subject to $3x + 5y \leqslant 30$
$4x + 3y \leqslant 24$

2 Maximise $x + y$ subject to $3x + 2y \leqslant 17$
$4x + 1y \leqslant 15$

and where x and y and integers

9.5 Slack Variables and Interpretation

Our constraints have been given in terms of our variables being less than or equal to a specified value. At any point not lying directly on the constraint line, we are therefore under-using the constraint – if we consider that constraint in isolation, there is the option to increase one or more of our variables without exceeding the limitation of that constraint. We call this under-use **slack**, and can introduce a variable to represent it. By doing so our constraint becomes an equality.

$2x + y \leqslant 16$ becomes $2x + y + s = 16$.

The following tables gives some possible values for s

x	y	s
0	0	16
3	4	6
5	$2\frac{1}{2}$	$3\frac{1}{2}$
6	4	0

If there is slack in a constraint at the optimal solution, it means that the constraint value (right hand side) can be reduced without changing the solution.

Example

Taking the Horsey Weavers problem from page 140, calculate and interpret the slack in the solution at the point (3, 1)

Solution

We start by re-writing the constraints to include slack variables:

$2x + \frac{1}{2}y \leqslant 7$ becomes $2x + \frac{1}{2}y + s_1 = 7$
$x + 2y \leqslant 7$ becomes $x + 2y + s_2 = 7$

At the point (3, 1):

$s_1 = 7 - 2x - \frac{1}{2}y = 7 - 6 - \frac{1}{2} = \frac{1}{2}$
$s_2 = 7 - x - 2y = 7 - 3 - 2 = 2$

We could express the co-ordinates of (3, 1) in terms of all variables in the form (x, y, s_1, s_2) and hence it would become $(3, 1, \frac{1}{2}, 2)$

This means that there is $\frac{1}{2}$ hour of slack time on the spinning wheel and 2 hours slack on the loom. Therefore the availability of the wheel could be reduced by up to $\frac{1}{2}$ hour and the loom by up to 2 hours without this particular solution being affected (i.e. the point (3, 1) would remain a feasible solution).

It is good practice to write the constraints out with spacing so that each variable is in a different column – the benefit will become apparent in Chapter 10.

9.5 Slack Variables and Interpretation

Exercise

Contextual

1 Use slack variables to convert each constraint in the following problem into an equality.
Maximise $x + y$
Subject to $3x + 2y \leqslant 18$
$2x + y \leqslant 10$
Find the value of the slack variables at each of the vertices of the feasible region.

2 – **3**

Rewrite the constraints for the contextual questions in Exercise 9.1, questions 3–4 using slack variables to convert each constraint into an equality. Find the values of the slack variables at each of the vertices of the feasible region.

9.1

4 **a** Sketch the feasible region given by the constraints

$$5x + 5y \leqslant 1000$$
$$10x + 5y \leqslant 1500$$
$$140x + 100y \leqslant 24\,000$$
$$x, y \geqslant 0$$

b Use slack variables to rewrite each constraint as an equality.

c Find the values of all five variables (x, y and the three slack variables) at each vertex of the feasible region.

9.6 Minimisation Problems

Many real problems are about minimising costs rather than maximising profit. These can be solved in the same manner, with the following differences:

● The feasible region is usually infinite.

● The origin is not feasible, so a vertex on one of the axes is usually taken as a starting point for a tour of vertices.

● The cost line starts towards the top right of the graph, and moves towards the origin to find the lowest cost.

Example

Minimise $3x + 2y$ subject to $2x + 3y \geqslant 15$
$4x + 2y \geqslant 17$

Solution

If an integer solution is required, we use the methods of Section 9.3. This gives the solution (3, 3), with cost 15.

The optimum real solution is evaluated to be $(2\frac{5}{8}, 3\frac{1}{4})$ which gives a cost of $14\frac{3}{8}$.

9.6 Minimisation Problems

Exercise

Technique

1 Minimise $x + 2y$ subject to $4x + 5y \geqslant 40$
$8x + 3y \geqslant 48$

2 Minimise $x + y$ subject to $3x + 5y \geqslant 30$
$3x + 2y \geqslant 24$

a when x and y can take any values

b when x and y must be integers.

3 A diamond company has two mines. The first costs £15 000 a day to operate, and will produce in one day 1 kg of jewel grade diamonds, 2 kg of medium grade, and 5 kg of industrial grade. The second mine costs £22 000 a day, and produces in one day 4 kg of jewel grade diamonds, 1 kg of medium grade, and 6 kg of industrial grade. The company must produce at least 8 kg of jewel grade, 8 kg of medium grade and 30 kg of industrial grade diamonds each month. How many days should it operate each mine to meet this quota as cheaply as possible if

a it can use a mine for only part of a day

b it must use each mine for a whole number of days?

Consolidation

Exercise A

1 A manufacturing company has a production plan in which at least 500 units are to be produced each week. The company employs two categories of employee: category A and category B. Category A employees are paid £265 per week. They each produce 13 units per week. Category B employees are paid £205 per week and each produce 10 units per week. Company policy is to have at least 45 employees producing these units.

a Write down a linear programme to find the optimal mix of employees at the cheapest cost.

b Use a graphical approach to solve your linear programming problem, ignoring for the moment the fact that the solution to the problem must be integer.

c The best **integer** solution to the problem incurs a weekly pay bill of £10 235. Find this solution.

d Compare and contrast for the linear problem in part **b** and the integer problem in part **c**, the solutions and their associated costs.

(AEB)

2 A company producing dining chairs and tables requires a production plan for the next month. The company has £10 000 budgeted to buy materials. Chairs each require £20 of materials and tables £100. Tables each need 15 hours of work from craftsmen and chairs each need 4 hours. There are 1950 hours of craftsman time available per month. The company sells chairs at £80 each and tables at £350. A production plan is required which maximises potential income.

a Formulate the problem as a linear programming problem.
b Use a graphical method to solve the problem.

Had the simplex method been used, slack variables would have been needed.

c State what those slack variables would have represented and give their values at the solution.
d Comment on any practical difficulty there may be with your solution to this problem.

(AQA)

The Simplex Method is dealt with in Chapter 10, and makes extensive use of slack variables.

3 The Elves toy company makes toy trains and dolls' prams, which use the same wheels and logo stickers.
Each train requires 8 wheels and 2 logo stickers.
Each pram requires 8 wheels and 3 logo stickers.
The company has 7200 wheels and 2200 logo stickers available.
The company is to make at least 300 of each type of toy and at least 800 toys in total.
The company sells each train for £20 and each pram for £25.
The company makes and sells x trains and y prams.
The company needs to find its minimum and maximum total income, £T.

a Formulate the company's situation as a linear programming problem.
b Draw a suitable diagram to enable the problem to be solved graphically, indicating the feasible region and the direction of the objective line.
c Use your diagram to find the company's minimum and maximum total income, £T.

(AQA)

4 A recycling company makes three grades of recycled paper.
Let a be the number of boxes of grade 1 paper, b be the number of boxes of grade 2 paper and c be the number of boxes of grade 3 paper that the company makes during a day.
The table below shows how much recycled newspaper and how much non-recycled paper it takes to make one box of each grade of paper.

	Recycled newspaper	Non-recycled newspaper
One box of grade 1 paper	10 kg	90 kg
One box of grade 2 paper	25 kg	60 kg
One box of grade 3 paper	80 kg	0 kg

The company has 785 kg of recycled newspaper and 540 kg of non-recycled newspaper.

a Write down two inequalities that must be satisfied by the variables, other than that they must be non-negative.

b What other restriction applies to a, b and c?

Each box of grade 1 paper sold gives a profit of £70, each box of grade 2 paper sold gives a profit of £120 and each box of grade 3 paper sold gives a profit of £180. The company wants to maximise the daily profit from the sale of the paper.

c Write down the objective function for this problem, assuming that the company can sell all the boxes of paper that they make.

(OCR)

5 Mr Baker is making cakes and fruit loaves for sale at a charity cake stall. Each cake requires 200 g of flour and 125 g of fruit. Each fruit loaf requires 200 g of flour and 50 g of fruit. He has 2800 g of flour and 1000 g of fruit available.
Let the number of cakes that he makes be x and the number of fruit loaves he makes be y.

a Show that these constraints can be modelled by the inequalities

$x + y \leqslant 14$ and $5x + 2y \leqslant 40$

Each cake takes 50 minutes to cook and each fruit loaf takes 30 minutes to cook. There are 8 hours of cooking time available.

b Obtain a further inequality, other than $x \geqslant 0$, $y \geqslant 0$ which models this time constraint.

c On graph paper illustrate these three inequalities indicating clearly the feasible region.

It is decided to sell the cakes for £3.50 each and the fruit loaves for £1.50 each. Assuming that Mr Baker sells all that he makes,

d write down an expression for the amount of money P, in pounds, raised by the sale of Mr Baker's products.

e Explaining your method clearly, determine how many cakes and how many fruit loaves Mr Baker should make to maximise P.

f Write down the greatest value of P.

(EDEXCEL)

Investigate ways of applying the techniques in this chapter to guide investment.

Hint: you may find it helpful to give different 'risk values' to different types of share.

Three Dimensions

Many linear programming problems have far more than two variables. If they can be expressed in three variables, they can still be solved 'visually' using 3-dimensional axes. The feasible region becomes a convex polyhedron, with each constraint becoming the equation of a plane, a face of the polyhedron. Try setting up and solving some.

Summary

- The choices to be made will be defined as a set of **variables**.

- Variables are usually defined to be positive only.

- A linear programming problem will be a constrained optimisation – that is a **maximisation** or a **minimisation** of an objective function of the variables, subject to some constraints (limitations or restrictions) on those variables.

- A graph can be drawn with the unwanted side of each constraint shaded out. This will leave a **feasible region** unshaded.

- The optimum (real) solution occurs at a vertex of the feasible region.

- Some problems require an integer solution: if the optimum vertex does not have integer co-ordinates, an alternative (nearby) point must be found.

- **Slack variables** are used to transform an inequality into an equality.

- The value of a slack variable at a point is a measure of the amount by which that constraint can be altered without the solution at that point becoming invalid (but will only represent an absolute amount if the constraint has not been scaled to simplify it).

10 The Simplex Method

What you need to know

- How to formulate a problem as a Linear Programme
- How to add slack variables to the constraints

Review

1 A company can make two kinds of soft toys: teddy bears and dragons. Each bear needs 200 g of stuffing, and each dragon needs 300 g of stuffing. A bear takes 12 minutes to make; a dragon takes half an hour. Each week the company can purchase a maximum of 100 kg of stuffing. Due to severe overproduction last year, there is no shortage of bear and dragon 'skins' to stuff. The company employs 20 workers, each working for 8 hours each day. (Breaks are not included in the 8 hours.) The profit on a bear is £3; the profit on a dragon is £5.

a Formulate this as an LP problem. Let x represent the number of bears made each week, and y represent the number of dragons made each week.

b Use slack variables to convert your constraints from part **a** as equalities.

c Solve this problem graphically.

d Calculate the value of your slack variables at each vertex of the feasible region, and explain what these values mean in relation to the problem.

10.1 The Simplex Algorithm

The Simplex algorithm gives a methodical approach to the algebraic solution of linear programming problems. In its simplest form, it requires a problem to be expressed as a maximisation, subject to a set of constraints which are equalities following the addition, where necessary, of slack variables.

The algorithm contains some specific terminology which will be explained in the example which follows.

> ## Simplex Algorithm
>
> **1** Represent the problem in a tableau.
>
> **2** Use the objective row to find the pivot column.
>
> **3** Use the ratio test to find the pivot element.
>
> **4** Divide through the pivot row by the pivot element.
>
> **5** Add/subtract multiples of the transformed pivot row to/from the other rows to create zeros in the pivot column.
>
> **6** Repeat steps 2 to 5 until there are no negatives in the objective row.
>
> **7** Set basic variables (with columns containing a 1 and 0s) to corresponding right-hand-side values, and non-basic variables to zero.

Example 1

Solve the following linear programming problem by using the Simplex algorithm.

Maximise $4x + 5y$ subject to

$$3x + 2y \leqslant 18$$
$$2x + 4y \leqslant 24$$
$$2y \leqslant 11$$

Solution

Step 1 – the tableau.

We set out all our variables and constraints in a table, each row representing an equation, and each column a variable. The columns include the profit variable P, and the 'right-hand-side' value of the equations. We must therefore re-write our profit equation so that all the variables are on the left side, $P - 4x - 5y = 0$, and convert our inequalities to equalities by adding slack variables:

$$3x + 2y + s_1 \qquad\quad = 18$$
$$2x + 4y \quad\; + s_2 \qquad = 24$$
$$2y \qquad\;\; + s_3 = 11$$

We put all our equations into the table; conventionally the profit goes first, giving us the following table (known as a Simplex Tableau). It is also useful to add a column for row number and later to use it to indicate the calculations that have been done.

P	x	y	s_1	s_2	s_3	RHS	Notes
1	−4	−5	0	0	0	0	R1
0	3	2	1	0	0	18	R2
0	2	4	0	1	0	24	R3
0	0	2	0	0	1	11	R4

Note that the variables whose columns are zeros except a single one, take the value in the RHS corresponding to their 1, and all other variables take the value zero. Thus the above table represents $P = 0$ (because the RHS is 0), $x = 0$, $y = 0$, $s_1 = 18$, $s_2 = 24$, $s_3 = 11$.

Step 2 – the pivot column

We have to choose one of the variables to operate on. We can choose any variable in the objective row whose coefficient is *negative*, but it is usual to pick the one with largest magnitude, and the priority is to increase original rather than slack variables.

So, we pick y and highlight the column.

This is equivalent to choosing which way round the feasible region to start your vertex tour in Chapter 9.

P	x	y	s_1	s_2	s_3	RHS	Notes
1	−4	−5	0	0	0	0	R1
0	3	2	1	0	0	18	R2
0	2	4	0	1	0	24	R3
0	0	2	0	0	1	11	R4

Step 3 – the ratio test

This involves dividing each RHS value by the corresponding element in the pivot column, ignoring any which give a negative ratio, or require division by zero.

$18 \div 2 = 9$

$24 \div 4 = 6$

$11 \div 2 = 5.5$ – smallest

We select the row with the smallest positive ratio, making this the pivot row; the element of that row in the pivot column becomes the pivot element.

P	x	y	s_1	s_2	s_3	RHS	Notes
1	−4	−5	0	0	0	0	R1
0	3	2	1	0	0	18	R2
0	2	4	0	1	0	24	R3
0	0	2	0	0	1	11	R4

Step 4 – divide through

We divide each value in the pivot row by the pivot element.

P	x	y	s_1	s_2	s_3	RHS	Notes
1	−4	−5	0	0	0	0	R1
0	3	2	1	0	0	18	R2
0	2	4	0	1	0	24	R3
0	0	1	0	0	0.5	5.5	R8 = R4 ÷ 2

Step 5 – row operations

Now add/subtract multiples of the pivot row to/from each of the other rows, so that the pivot column becomes zero in all but the pivot row. It is useful to note at the side how this was achieved in case you need to check your working later.

P	x	y	s_1	s_2	s_3	RHS	Notes
1	−4	0	0	0	2.5	27.5	R5 = R1 + 5 × R8
0	3	0	1	0	−1	7	R6 = R1 − 2 × R8
0	2	0	0	1	−2	2	R7 = R3 − 4 × R8
0	0	1	0	0	0.5	5.5	R8

We have now finished the first iteration and have produced a new tableau. This represents the solution $x = 0$, $y = 5.5$, with profit of 27.5.

We now have to repeat the process, and this time choose to increase x since it is the only negative coefficient left. The ratio test gives $\frac{7}{3}$, 1 and a division by zero, so the second ratio is the smallest.

Our highlighted tableau is therefore as follows:

P	x	y	s_1	s_2	s_3	RHS	Notes
1	−4	0	0	0	2.5	27.5	R5
0	3	0	1	0	−1	7	R6
0	2	0	0	1	−2	2	R7
0	0	1	0	0	0.5	5.5	R8

We divide through the pivot row by the pivot element of 2, and use this to set the remainder of the x column to zero.

P	x	y	s_1	s_2	s_3	RHS	Notes
1	0	0	0	2	−1.5	31.5	R9 = R5 + 4 × R11
0	0	0	1	−1.5	2	4	R10 = R6 − 3 × R11
0	1	0	0	0.5	−1	1	R11 = R7 ÷ 2
0	0	1	0	0	0.5	5.5	R12 = R8

We now have an improved solution of $x = 1$, $y = 5.5$ with profit of 31.5. However, since there is still a negative in the profit row (on the slack variable s_3) we can perform another iteration.

We highlight the s_3 column, and perform the ratio test, giving 2, −1 and 11, so we pick the first constraint as being the smallest positive.

P	x	y	s_1	s_2	s_3	RHS	Notes
1	0	0	0	2	−1.5	31.5	R9
0	**0**	**0**	**1**	**−1.5**	**2**	**4**	**R10**
0	1	0	0	0.5	−1	1	R11
0	0	1	0	0	0.5	5.5	R12

P	x	y	s_1	s_2	s_3	RHS	Notes
1	0	0	0.75	0.875	0	34.5	R13 = R9 + 1.5 × R14
0	0	0	0.5	−0.75	1	2	R14 = R10 ÷ 2
0	1	0	0.5	−0.25	0	3	R15 = R11 + R14
0	0	1	−0.25	0.375	0	4.5	R16 = R12 − 0.5 × R14

This represents the solution $x = 3$, $y = 4.5$, profit = 34.5, and there is slack in the third constraint of 2 units.

Example 2

Minimise $x - y - z$ subject to $4x - 2y + z \geqslant -2$
$2x + 4y + 4z \leqslant 7$

Solution

We must first write our objective and constraints in the standard format.

Since the objective is to minimise $P = x - y - z$, we make $Q = -P$, and maximise $Q = -x + y + z$, which then becomes $Q + x - y - z = 0$.

The first constraint needs a surplus variable to be subtracted from it to form an equality:

$4x - 2y + z - s_1 = -2$

Minimisation is negative maximisation and this approach is also used elsewhere in this book. The alternative is to minimise by decreasing positive values in the objective fun~

The second constraint needs a slack variable, as before.

$$2x + 4y + 4z + s_2 = 7$$

The initial tableau is then as follows:

Q	x	y	z	s_1	s_2	RHS	Notes
1	1	−1	−1	0	0	0	R1
0	4	−2	1	−1	0	−2	R2
0	2	4	4	0	1	7	R3

Choosing to increase y (we could also have chosen z), $\frac{-2}{-2} = 1$ and $\frac{7}{4} = 1.75$ so the former is the smallest positive ratio and becomes our pivot row.

Our second tableau is therefore

Q	x	y	z	s_1	s_2	RHS	Notes
1	−1	0	$-\frac{3}{2}$	$\frac{1}{2}$	0	1	R4 = R1 + R4
0	−2	1	$-\frac{1}{2}$	$\frac{1}{2}$	0	1	R5 = R2 ÷ −2
0	10	0	6	−2	1	3	R6 = R3 − 4 × R5

Working with improper fractions is often clearer than decimals.

We now choose to increase z (could also have chosen x), and the 3rd row is the only one with a positive ratio so this is our pivot row.

Q	x	y	z	s_1	s_2	RHS	Notes
1	$\frac{3}{2}$	0	0	0	$\frac{1}{4}$	$\frac{7}{4}$	R7 = R4 + $\frac{3}{2}$R9
0	$-\frac{5}{3}$	1	0	$\frac{1}{3}$	$\frac{1}{12}$	$\frac{5}{4}$	R8 = R5 + $\frac{1}{2}$R9
0	$\frac{5}{3}$	0	1	$-\frac{1}{3}$	$\frac{1}{6}$	$\frac{1}{2}$	R9 = R6 ÷ 6

This tableau is optimal and gives us the following solution:

$Q = 1\frac{3}{4}$, which means that $P = -1\frac{3}{4}$

when $x = 0$, $y = 1\frac{1}{4}$, $z = \frac{1}{2}$

10.1 The Simplex Algorithm

Exercise

Technique

Use the Simplex algorithm to solve the following Linear Programming problems.

1 | Maximise $5x + 6y$ subject to $x + y \leqslant 6$
$$2x + 3y \leqslant 14$$

2 | Maximise $x + y$ subject to $x + 2y \leqslant 8$
$$3x + 2y \leqslant 15$$

3 | Maximise $x + 2y + z$ subject to $x + y + z \leqslant 15$
$$2x + y + z \leqslant 20$$
$$3x + 2y - z \leqslant 10$$

4 | Maximise $8x + 6y$ subject to $3x + 5y \leqslant 30$
$$4x + 3y \leqslant 24$$

5 | Maximise $x + y$ subject to $3x + 2y \leqslant 17$
$$4x + y \leqslant 15$$

6 | Minimise $5x - 3y - 5z$ subject to $-2x - y + 3z \leqslant 2$
$$-x + y + z \leqslant 3$$

10.2 The Two Stage Algorithm – Artificial Variables

When the initial simplex tableau is set up, it corresponds to the solution where all the original variables are zero (equivalent to a graphical solution starting from the origin). However, in many problems, this is not a feasible solution and we need to adapt the algorithm.

The two-stage simplex algorithm requires us to introduce artificial variables, and to solve the associated problem to find a feasible solution. This can then be used as a starting point for the main algorithm.

Example

We will use again the example from Section 10.1, but with an additional constraint that $x + y$ must be at least 1.

Maximise $\quad 4x + 5y \quad$ subject to $\quad 3x + 2y \leqslant 18$
$$2x + 4y \leqslant 24$$
$$2y \leqslant 11$$
$$x + y \geqslant 1$$

Solution

Since our additional constraint is a 'greater than' inequality, we first need to introduce a surplus variable, s_4, to give the equation

$$x + y - s_4 = 1$$

However, since $x = y = 0$ will not satisfy this equation (because it would require s_4 to be negative, and we only allow our variables to be positive or zero), we also add an artificial variable a, giving

$$x + y - s_4 + a = 1$$

Our initial aim is to remove the artificial variable, so our objective is to minimise its sum. We therefore write $Q = -a$ (the sum of the artificial variables), and then maximise Q as before.

We first write a in terms of the other variables and move all variables to the left side giving the equation:

$$Q - x - y + s_4 = -1$$

Our tableau needs this equation included, and we must therefore now have columns for Q, a and s_4 as well as rows for this and the additional constraint.

Q	P	x	y	s_1	s_2	s_3	s_4	a	RHS	Notes
1	0	−1	−1	0	0	0	1	0	−1	R1
0	1	−4	−5	0	0	0	0	0	0	R2
0	0	3	2	1	0	0	0	0	18	R3
0	0	2	4	0	1	0	0	0	24	R4
0	0	0	2	0	0	1	0	0	11	R5
0	0	1	1	0	0	0	−1	1	1	R6

A slack variable was added to a '$\leqslant$' constraint to take up the slack. In the same way, a surplus variable is subtracted from a '$\geqslant$' constraint to remove the surplus.

Although we have a new objective function in terms of Q, we must retain the original for P in the tableau too.

In choosing our pivot column, we have an arbitrary choice, and for this example will choose x.

The ratio test gives $\frac{0}{-4}$ (negative), $\frac{18}{3} = 6$, $\frac{24}{2} = 12$, $\frac{11}{0}$ which is undefined and $\frac{1}{1} = 1$. We choose the smallest which is the last one as our pivot element.

Q	P	x	y	s_1	s_2	s_3	s_4	a	RHS	Notes
1	0	−1	−1	0	0	0	1	0	−1	R1
0	1	−4	−5	0	0	0	0	0	0	R2
0	0	3	2	1	0	0	0	0	18	R3
0	0	2	4	0	1	0	0	0	24	R4
0	0	0	2	0	0	1	0	0	11	R5
0	0	1	1	0	0	0	−1	1	1	R6

We now apply the simplex algorithm to produce a revised table.

Q	P	x	y	s_1	s_2	s_3	s_4	a	RHS	Notes
1	0	0	0	0	0	0	0	1	0	R7 = R1 + R12
0	1	0	−1	0	0	0	−4	4	4	R8 = R2 + 4 × R12
0	0	0	−1	1	0	0	3	−3	15	R9 = R3 − 3 × R12
0	0	0	2	0	1	0	2	−2	22	R10 = R4 − 2 × R12
0	0	0	2	0	0	1	0	0	11	R11 = R5
0	0	1	1	0	0	0	−1	1	1	R12 = R6

We notice that the column for the artificial variable a is not a 'zero with a single one' column, so a currently has the value 0 and with a positive coefficient in the first row it is not available to be increased either. We also note that the sum of the artificial variables Q is 0 and we can therefore eliminate these from our tableau since they are playing no part in our solution.

Q	P	x	y	s_1	s_2	s_3	s_4	a	RHS	Notes
1	0	0	0	0	0	0	0	1	0	R7
0	1	0	−1	0	0	0	−4	4	4	R8
0	0	0	−1	1	0	0	3	−3	15	R9
0	0	0	2	0	1	0	2	−2	22	R10
0	0	0	2	0	0	1	0	0	11	R11
0	0	1	1	0	0	0	−1	1	1	R12

This leaves a smaller, simplified tableau representing the solution $x = 1$, $y = 0$ with profit 4, which can then be improved in the normal way.

P	x	y	s_1	s_2	s_3	s_4	RHS	Notes
1	0	−1	0	0	0	−4	4	
0	0	−1	1	0	0	3	15	
0	0	2	0	1	0	2	22	
0	0	2	0	0	1	0	11	
0	1	1	0	0	0	−1	1	

Activity

Continue the Simplex algorithm on the above tableau and show that the solution is the same as that found in the example in Section 10.1.

10.2 The Two Stage Algorithm – Artificial Variables

Exercise

Technique

Use the Simplex algorithm to solve the following Linear Programming problems.

1 Maximise $x + y$ subject to $x + 2y \leqslant 8$
$3x + 2y \geqslant 12$

2 Maximise $x + y$ subject to $x + 2y \geqslant 8$
$3x + 2y \geqslant 12$
$2x + 3y \leqslant 15$

3 Maximise $5x + 2y$ subject to $x + 2y \geqslant 8$
$3x + 2y \leqslant 12$
$2x + 3y \geqslant 15$

10.3 The Big-M method

This is essentially the same as the Two Stage Simplex algorithm, but rather than introducing a new objective function to reduce the artificial variables, subtracts a large multiple of them from the existing function.

Example

Solve the problem in Section 10.2 using the Big-M method.

Solution

We need to set up the equations with slack, surplus and artificial variables as before, so our constraints become

$$3x + 2y + s_1 \qquad\qquad = 18$$
$$2x + 4y \quad + s_2 \qquad\qquad = 24$$
$$2y \qquad + s_3 \qquad = 11$$
$$x + \ y \qquad\qquad - s_4 + a = 1$$

We now need to subtract a large multiple (M) of the artificial variable from the objective function, so it becomes

Maximise $4x + 5y - Ma$

M is always positive.

However, we need to re-write this so that it does not contain the artificial variable so we rearrange the final constraint and substitute in.

$$a = 1 - x - y + s_4$$

Maximise $4x + 5y - M(1 - x - y + s_4) = (4 + M)x + (5 + M)y - Ms_4 - M$

Putting all this into the tableau in the usual way:

P	x	y	s_1	s_2	s_3	s_4	a	RHS	Notes
1	$-(4 + M)$	$-(5 + M)$	0	0	0	M	0	$-M$	R1
0	3	2	1	0	0	0	0	18	R2
0	2	4	0	1	0	0	0	24	R3
0	0	2	0	0	1	0	0	11	R4
0	1	1	0	0	0	-1	1	1	R5

We arbitrarily choose to increase y. Ratio test gives $\frac{18}{2} = 9$, $\frac{24}{4} = 6$, $\frac{11}{2} = 5.5$, $\frac{1}{1} = 1$ so the pivot row is the last row.

P	x	y	s_1	s_2	s_3	s_4	a	RHS	Notes
1	1	0	0	0	0	−5	5 + M	5	R6 = R1 + (5 + M) × R10
0	1	0	1	0	0	2	−2	16	R7 = R2 − 2 × R10
0	−2	0	0	1	0	4	−4	20	R8 = R3 − 4 × R10
0	−2	0	0	0	1	2	−2	9	R9 = R4 − 2 × R10
0	1	1	0	0	0	−1	1	1	R10 = R5 ÷ 1

We now increase s_4, with the ratio test giving row 9 as the minimum positive ratio.

P	x	y	s_1	s_2	s_3	s_4	a	RHS	Notes
1	−4	0	0	0	2.5	0	M	27.5	R11 = R6 + 5 × R14
0	3	0	1	0	−1	0	0	7	R12 = R7 − 2 × R14
0	2	0	0	1	−2	0	0	2	R13 = R8 − 4 × R14
0	−1	0	0	0	0.5	1	−1	4.5	R14 = R9 ÷ 2
0	0	1	0	0	0.5	0	0	5.5	R15 = R10 + R14

We now increase x, with row 13 giving the smallest positive ratio.

P	x	y	s_1	s_2	s_3	s_4	a	RHS	Notes
1	0	0	0	2	−1.5	0	M	31.5	R16 = R11 + 4 × R18
0	0	0	1	−1.5	2	0	0	4	R17 = R12 − 3 × R18
0	1	0	0	0.5	−1	0	0	1	R18 = R13 ÷ 2
0	0	0	0	0.5	−0.5	1	−1	5.5	R19 = R14 + R18
0	0	1	0	0	0.5	0	0	5.5	R20 = R15

There is still another variable to increase, s_3, with Row 17 giving the smallest positive ratio.

P	x	y	s_1	s_2	s_3	s_4	a	RHS	Notes
1	0	0	0.75	0.875	0	0	M	34.5	R21 = R16 + 1.5 × R22
0	0	0	0.5	−0.75	1	0	0	2	R22 = R17 ÷ 2
0	1	0	0.5	−0.25	0	0	0	3	R23 = R18 + R22
0	0	0	0.25	0.125	0	1	−1	6.5	R24 = R19 + R22 ÷ 2
0	0	1	−0.25	0.375	0	0	0	4.5	R25 = R20 − R22 ÷ 2

We now have a solution: $x = 3$, $y = 4.5$, with a profit of 34.5 as before.

10.3 The Big-M method

Exercise

Technique

Use the Big-M method to solve the problems in Exercise 10.2.

Consolidation

Exercise A

1 Solve the following LP problems using the Simplex algorithm

    a   Maximise $3x + 2y$ **b**   Maximise $3x + 2y$
          subject to $2x + 3y \leqslant 24$ subject to $2x + 3y \leqslant 24$
                         $8x + 3y \leqslant 48$ $7x + 3y \leqslant 42$

2 Solve the following LP problem using both two-stage Simplex and the Big-M method.

    Minimise $3x + 2y$ subject to $2x + 3y \geqslant 24$
                                               $7x + 3y \geqslant 42$

3 A craftworker makes three types of wooden animals for sale in wildlife parks. Each animal has to be carved and then sanded.

Each Lion takes 2 hours to carve and 25 minutes to sand.
Each Giraffe takes $2\frac{1}{2}$ hours to carve and 20 minutes to sand.
Each Elephant takes $1\frac{1}{2}$ hours to carve and 30 minutes to sand.

Each day the craftworker wishes to spend at most 8 hours carving and 2 hours sanding.
Let x be the number of Lions, y the number of Giraffes and z the number of Elephants he produces each day.
The craftworker makes a profit of £14 on each Lion, £12 on each Giraffe and £13 on each Elephant.

    a   Model this as a Linear Programming problem, simplifying your expressions so that they have integer coefficients.

It is decided to use the Simplex Algorithm to solve this problem.

b Explaining the purpose of r and s, show that the initial tableau can be written as:

P	x	y	z	r	s	
1	−14	−12	−13	0	0	0
0	4	5	3	1	0	16
0	5	4	6	0	1	24

c Choosing to increase x first, work out the next complete tableau, where the x column includes two zeros.

d Explain what this first iteration means in practical terms.

(EDEXCEL)

4 Three products, X, Y and Z are to be manufactured. They all require resources A, B, C and D which are in limited supply. The table summarises these requirements in suitable units per item produced.

	A	B	C	D
X	2	0	2	4
Y	5	2	4	3
Z	4	1	2	2
Availability	60	10	70	180

Profits are £3 per item of X produced, £2 per item of Y and £5 per item of Z.

a Formulate a Linear Programming problem to maximise profit within the constraints imposed by resource availability.

b Use the Simplex algorithm to solve the problem.

c An extra constraint is imposed by a contract to supply at least 5 items of Y. Show how to incorporate this constraint into an initial tableau using a surplus and an additional variable.

d Explain how to use either two-stage Simplex or the Big-M method to move to a feasible solution to the modified problem. You should show the initial tableau, including the objective function(s), and explain briefly how to proceed. You are not required to do the iterations.

(AQA)

5 Consider the Linear Programming problem:

Maximise $P = 2x + y$ subject to
$$x + y \leqslant 7$$
$$x + 2y \leqslant 10$$
$$2x + 3y \leqslant 16$$
$$x \geqslant 0 \text{ and } y \geqslant 0$$

a   By introducing slack variables, represent the problem as an initial Simplex tableau.

b   Perform **one** iteration of the Simplex algorithm, choosing to pivot first on an element chosen from the x-column.

c   State the values of x, y and P resulting from the iteration in part **c**.

d   Explain how you know whether or not the optimal solution has been achieved.

(OCR)

Exercise B

1   Solve the following LP problems using the Simplex algorithm

    a   Maximise $x + y$ subject to $4x + 3y \leqslant 24$

                                              $5x + 7y \leqslant 35$

    b   Maximise $2x + 3y$ subject to $2x + 5y \leqslant 20$

                                              $3x + y \leqslant 17$

2   Solve the following LP problem using both two-stage Simplex and the Big-M method.

    Minimise $5x + 3y$ subject to $2x + 5y \geqslant 20$

                                              $3x + y \geqslant 17$

3   In a particular factory three types of product, A, B and C are made. The number of each of the products made is x, y and z respectively and P is the profit in pounds. There are two machines involved in making the products which have only a limited time available. These time limitations produce two constraints.

In the process of using the Simplex algorithm the following tableau is obtained, where r and s are slack variables.

P	x	y	z	r	s	
1	$\frac{3}{2}$	0	0	$\frac{3}{4}$	0	840
0	$\frac{1}{3}$	0	1	-8	1	75
0	$\frac{2}{11}$	1	0	$\frac{17}{11}$	0	56

a   Give the reason why this tableau can be seen to be optimal (final).

b   By writing out the profit equation, or otherwise, explain why a further increase in profit is not possible under these constraints.

c   From this tableau deduce

    i   the maximum profit

    ii   the optimum number of type A, B and C that should be produced to maximise the profit.

(EDEXCEL)

4 Consider the Linear Programming problem:

Maximise $P = x + 3y$ subject to $2x + 3y \leqslant 8$
$x + 6y \leqslant 10$
$x \geqslant 0$ and $y \geqslant 0$

a By adding slack variables, represent this problem as an initial Simplex tableau.

b Carry out **two** iterations of the Simplex algorithm.

c State the values of x, y and P resulting from each iteration in part **b**.

(OCR)

5 A Linear Programming problem is specified as:

Maximise $P = 6x + 4y$ subject to $x + 2y \leqslant 14$
$x + y \leqslant 8$
$2x + y \leqslant 11$
$3x + y \leqslant 15$
$x \geqslant 0, y \geqslant 0$

a Solve this problem graphically.

b At an intermediate stage in the application of the Simplex method the tableau is as follows.

P	x	y	s_1	s_2	s_3	s_4	RHS
1	0	0	0	0	6	−2	36
0	0	0	1	0	−5	3	4
0	0	0	0	1	−2	1	1
0	0	1	0	0	3	−2	3
0	1	0	0	0	−1	1	4

   i   To what point on your graph from part **a** does this correspond, and what is the value of the objective function?

   ii   Express P in terms of s_3 and s_4. Explain why your expression shows that the solution is not optimal.

c i   Give the values of the slack variables at the optimum point.

   ii   For each inequality say what information is given by the value of its slack variable at the optimum point.

(AQA)

Applications and Extensions

Using Software

Most realistic LP problems involve a large number of variables. The Simplex algorithm can deal with any number of variables, but doing the calculations by hand makes the process excessively time consuming.

Commercial software is available to do the hard work – if you have access to such software you could use it to check your answers to the exercises.

Wider uses

In quite a number of chapters in this book, the Applications and Extensions section gives the relationship between those problems and Linear Programming. Try to solve some of them, either using software, or by the Simplex algorithm.

Post-optimal Analysis

It is often both interesting and useful to undertake some further analysis once the solution has been found. What if my constraint was relaxed/tightened (change the constant)? What if my objective function changed? By how much could these things change without changing the optimal solution?

Summary

- The **Simplex** algorithm allows the solution of Linear Programming problems without restriction on the number of variables.

- All variables must be positive, and all constraints are made equalities by the addition of **slack** or **surplus variables**.

- A **tableau** or matrix of values is formed to represent the objective function and the constraints.

- A tableau has been optimised when all the coefficients in the objective row are non-negative.

- Columns of the tableau containing all zeros except for a single one are the basic variables. The current value of a basic variable can be found in the right-hand column, in the row corresponding to the 1. All other (non-basic) variables are zero.

- Minimisation problems can be solved as maximisations of minus the objective function.

- If the origin is not a feasible solution of the initial problem, artificial quantities must be introduced and either the two-stage algorithm, or the Big-M method must be used.

11 Matchings

What you need to know

- The language and notation of graphs

- The definition of a bipartite graph

- The definition of a complete graph

Review

1 State which of the following graphs are bipartite.

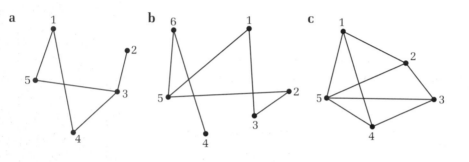

2 State which of the following bipartite graphs are complete.

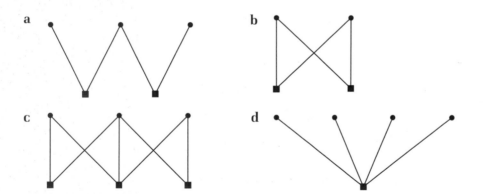

11.1 Modelling with Bipartite Graphs

There are a number of problems which, when modelled using a graph, form a **Bipartite Graph**. In many of these cases, the requirement is to pair off, or match, vertices between the two sets within the graph.

Example

Avril has been sent some catalogues for new books for the library. She and her colleagues are going to go through one catalogue each, looking for suitable books to add to their collection. The catalogues are: Paperback Fiction, Science and Education, Especially for Children and Home and Garden.

Avril knows about paperbacks and children's books.
Bryan knows the science and gardening sections.
Cheryl usually deals with education and children's books.
David knows about the paperbacks and science sections.

Model this as a Bipartite Graph and suggest which catalogue Avril should give to each person so that everyone gets a catalogue they know something about.

Solution

Our graph is formed from the two groups – people and catalogues – with an edge representing the relationship '*person knows about this subject area*'.

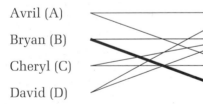

It is apparent from the graph that Bryan should take the Home and Garden catalogue.

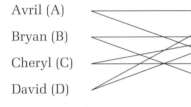

We mark this with a thick line, and say that this is part of our matching.

A possible solution is now for Avril to keep (F), and to give Cheryl (E) and to give David (S).

This gives the **complete** matching:

However, this is not a **unique** solution.

It is not always possible to find a **complete** matching in which every vertex is connected. In such cases we seek the **maximum** matching – one which connects as many vertices as possible.

Activity

Find the other solution.

11.1 Modelling with Bipartite Graphs

Exercise

Technique

For each of the bipartite graphs below, find a best possible matching.

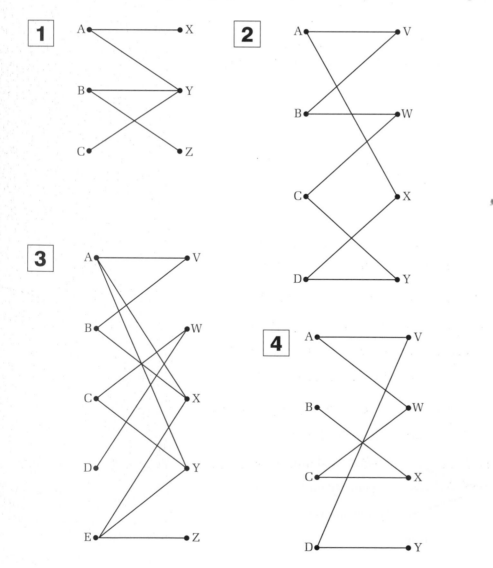

11.2 Maximum Matching Algorithm

In our example above, we noticed that one vertex on our graph could only be matched in one way, selected it and thus simplified the remaining problem. In larger graphs, we need a method for finding the best matching. The maximum matching algorithm is an 'improvement' algorithm.

Maximum Matching Algorithm

1 Find an initial matching (which could be the 'empty' matching with no edges).

2 Search for an alternative path which allows the matching to be improved, and, if found, incorporate it into the current matching.

3 If the matching is complete, or a path could not be found, stop, otherwise repeat step 2.

However, this needs the algorithm for finding an alternating path expanded. The following example works through this, and the algorithm is given at the end.

Example

We repeat the problem set in Section 11.1, Example 1, seeking a complete matching by using the algorithm.

Solution

A common initial matching is to allocate each vertex on the left side to the first available vertex on the right side, omitting any which cannot be done.

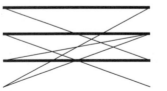

Avril (A)	Paperback Fiction (F)
Bryan (B)	Science and Education (S)
Cheryl (C)	Especially for Children (E)
David (D)	Home and Garden (H)

We pick a vertex which is not currently in our matching, say David (it does not matter which side of the graph this vertex is on).

We note that D is connected to F and S and that one of these edges would be needed to include it in our matching.

However, if we are giving one of these catalogues to David, we can no longer give it to the person in the current matching, so that edge would need to be removed from the matching.

A could now be connected to E, or B could be connected to H.

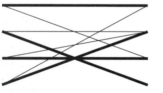

Whilst it would be possible to continue the chain beyond E, there is no need to because we have a **breakthrough** at H. A breakthrough means that we have found a vertex not currently in the matching.

Our alternating path is D + S − B + H. We add the edges DS and BH to our matching, and remove the edge SB. This gives us a new matching:

Avril (A)   Paperback Fiction (F)

Bryan (B)   Science and Education (S)

Cheryl (C)   Especially for Children (E)

David (D)   Home and Garden (H)

which is complete and so we have finished.

Note: If a matching is not complete, the process is repeated, but it is essential that the method of finding an alternating path is started again as the graph has now changed and any other paths already found may no longer be valid.

Alternating Path Algorithm

1 Choose a vertex which is not in the current matching — this forms the start of your alternating path

2 If your current vertex connects to one which is currently unmatched you have a breakthrough. If not, then any edge which connects your current vertex to one in the current matching can be added to your path, followed by the associated edge from the current matching. Make the end of your path the current vertex.

Repeat this stage until either a breakthrough is reached, or until there are no more vertices to add to your path.

3 If you have a breakthrough, then the path can be incorporated into your matching.

If you cannot reach a breakthrough, the matching cannot be improved, and you must revert to the original edges.

11.2 Alternating Path Algorithm

Exercise

Technique

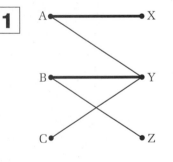

For each of the bipartite graphs below, use the alternating path algorithm to find a maximum matching, taking the edges shown in bold as your initial matching.

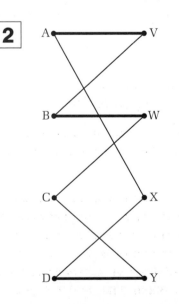

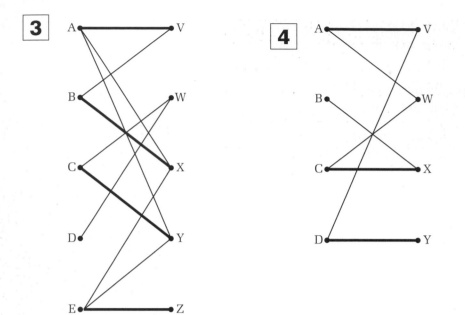

5 – **8** For each of the following tables

a draw a bipartite graph to represent those preferences

b using the initial allocation in the table as a starting point, apply the alternating path algorithm to find an optimum matching.

5

Person	Preferences		Person	Initial matching
X	A, C		X	C
Y	A, B		Y	B
Z	B, C		Z	

6

Person	Preferences		Person	Initial matching
W	A, B		W	A
X	B, C		X	B
Y	C, D		Y	C
Z	A		Z	

7

Person	Preferences		Person	Initial matching
W	B, D		W	B
X	A, B		X	A
Y	B, C, D		Y	C
Z	A, C		Z	

8

Person	Preferences		Person	Initial matching
V	A, C		V	C
W	B, D		W	B
X	A, E		X	A
Y	B, C		Y	
Z	D, E		Z	E

Consolidation

Exercise A

1 A group of five pupils have to colour in some pictures. There are five coloured crayons available, Orange (O), Red (R), Yellow (Y), Green (G) and Purple (P). The five pupils have each told their teacher of their first and second choice of coloured crayons.

Pupil	First choice	Second choice
Alison (A)	Orange	Yellow
Brian (B)	Orange	Red
Carly (C)	Yellow	Purple
Danny (D)	Red	Purple
Emma (E)	Purple	Green

a Show this information on a bipartite graph.

b Initially the teacher gives pupils A, C, D and E their first choice of crayons.
Demonstrate, by using an algorithm from this initial matching, how the teacher can give each pupil either their first or second choice of coloured crayons. *(AQA)*

2 Alex likes ready-salted and salt-and-vinegar crisps, Bill likes prawn-cocktail and salt-and-vinegar crisps, while Charles prefers ready-salted and salt-and-vinegar crisps.

a Show this information on a bipartite graph.

b Just one of each of these crisps is available. Alex chooses the ready-salted bag and Bill chooses the salt-and-vinegar bag. Charles is then disappointed. Demonstrate, by using an algorithm to find an alternating path from this initial matching, how these selections could be made so that each has a bag of crisps to their own liking. *(AQA)*

3 A manager has five workers, Mr Ahmed, Miss Brown, Ms Clough, Mr Dingle and Mrs Evans. To finish an urgent order he needs each of them to work overtime, one on each evening, in the next week. The workers are only available on the following evenings:

Mr Ahmed (A) – Monday and Wednesday
Miss Brown (B) – Monday, Wednesday and Friday
Ms Clough (C) – Monday
Mr Dingle (D) – Tuesday, Wednesday and Thursday
Mrs Evans (E) – Wednesday and Thursday

The manager initially suggests that A might work on Monday, B on Wednesday and D on Thursday.

a Draw a bipartite graph to model the availability of the five workers. Indicate, in a distinctive way, the manager's initial suggestion.
b Obtain an alternating path, starting at C, and use this to improve the initial matching.
c Find another alternating path and hence obtain a complete matching.

(EDEXCEL)

4 A college wishes to staff classes in French (F), German (G), Italian (I), Russian (R) and Spanish (S). Five language teachers are available – Mr Ali (A), Mrs Brown (B), Ms Corrie (C), Dr Donald (D) and Miss Eares (E). The languages they can teach are shown in the table.

Mr Ali (A)	French and German
Mrs Brown (B)	French and Italian
Ms Corrie (C)	Russian
Dr Donald (D)	Russian and Spanish
Miss Eares (E)	French and Spanish

The three most senior teachers were allowed to choose their preferences. Their choices were:

Mr Ali (A) – French (F)
Dr Donald (D) – Russian (R)
Miss Eares (E) – Spanish (S)

a Draw a bipartite graph to show the information in the table. Indicate the above choices in a distinctive way.
b Using your answer to part **a** as the initial matching, apply the maximum matching algorithm to obtain a complete matching. Alternating paths and the final matching should be stated.

(EDEXCEL)

Some exam boards refer to the alternating path algorithm as the maximum matching algorithm.

5 Five packs of sandwiches have been prepared for lunch, one each of egg, cheese, ham, tuna and salmon. Five people have been invited for lunch and the sandwiches which they like are given in the table.

Mr Large	egg, cheese
Mrs Moore	egg, tuna, salmon
Ms Nice	cheese, ham
Mr Oliver	cheese, tuna, salmon
Miss Patel	ham, tuna, salmon

a Draw a bipartite graph to model this situation.

The host allocates the egg sandwich to Mr Large, the cheese to Ms Nice, the tuna to Mr Oliver and the salmon to Miss Patel.

b Indicate this initial matching in a distinctive way on your bipartite graph.

c Starting from this matching use the maximum matching algorithm to find a complete matching. Indicate clearly how the algorithm has been applied.   *(EDEXCEL)*

Exercise B

1 Granny has bought Christmas presents for her five grandchildren.

The teddy bear is suitable for Cathy, Daniel or Elvis; the book is suitable for Annie or Ben; the football is suitable for Daniel or Elvis; the moneybox is suitable for Annie or Daniel; the drum is suitable for Cathy or Elvis.

Draw a bipartite graph, G, to show which present is suitable for which grandchild.

Granny decides to give Annie the book, Cathy the teddy bear, Daniel the moneybox and Elvis the drum. This leaves Ben without a present, since the football is not suitable for him.

a Show the incomplete matching, M, that describes which present Granny has decided to give to each child.

b Use a matching algorithm to construct an alternating path for M in G, and hence find a maximal matching between the presents and the grandchildren.   *(OCR)*

2 The student guild has four officers: the president, vice-president, secretary and treasurer.

On the first day of term, an officer of the student guild is needed at each of four meetings: the board meeting, the curriculum meeting, the finance meeting and the new students meeting.

- The board meeting must be attended by either the president or the vice-president.

- The curriculum meeting must be attended by either the vice-president or the secretary.

- The finance meeting must be attended by either the treasurer or the vice-president.

- The new students meeting must be attended by either the president or the secretary.

The president decides to go to the new students meeting, the vice-president decides to go to the finance meeting, and the secretary decides to go to the curriculum meeting.

a Draw a bipartite graph, G, showing which officers may attend which meetings, and use it to show the incomplete matching, M, described above.

b Use a matching algorithm to construct an alternating path for M in G, explaining your method carefully, and hence obtain a complete matching between the officers and the meetings. *(OCR)*

3 Julie is planning her homework schedule.

She works at a burger bar on Friday evenings and all day on Saturdays and Sundays (including the evenings). On Tuesday evenings she always plays badminton. This means that Julie does no homework on Fridays, Saturdays, Sundays and Tuesdays.

Julie is studying computing, discrete mathematics and economics. She has homework for each of these subjects every week. Julie never does the homework for more than one subject on any one evening.

- Her computing homework is always set on Tuesdays and is due in on Friday.

- Her discrete mathematics homework is always set on Thursdays and is due in the next Thursday.

- Her economics homework is always set on Wednesdays and is due in on Tuesday.

Julie uses the following homework schedule: she always does discrete mathematics and economics homeworks on the evenings of the days that they are set.

a Draw a bipartite graph, G, showing which homeworks could be done on which evenings, and show the incomplete matching, M, that describes the homework schedule that Julie uses now.

b Use a matching algorithm to construct an alternating path for M in G, and hence find a maximal matching between the subjects and the evenings. *(OCR)*

4 Four children are choosing sandwiches. The four sandwiches available are one bacon, one cheese, one egg and one fish-paste sandwich. Each child must get one of the four sandwiches, and each sandwich must be given to one child.

Jemma would like bacon or cheese, Kay would like cheese or egg, Luke would like cheese or fish-paste, and Matthew would like bacon or fish-paste.

a Draw a bipartite graph, G, showing which children would like which sandwiches.

b Jemma chooses bacon, Kay chooses cheese and Luke chooses fish-paste.
Show this incomplete matching, M, on your graph, G.

c Use a matching algorithm to construct an alternating path for M in G, explaining your method carefully, and hence obtain a complete matching between the children and your sandwiches. *(OCR)*

5 Snow White has knitted hats for six of her dwarf friends – the dwarf called Grumpy didn't want one. The hats are different colours, and each of the six dwarfs wants a hat in one of the colours of his favourite football team.

The table shows which colours each dwarf likes.

Dwarf	Colours liked
Bashful	blue, white
Doc	red, yellow
Dopey	red, white
Happy	green, yellow
Sleepy	blue, maroon
Sneezy	maroon

a Draw a bipartite graph, G, showing which dwarfs could be given which hats.

Snow White has given Bashful the blue hat, Doc the red hat, Dopey the white hat, Happy the yellow hat and Sleepy the maroon hat. Sneezy ends up without a hat and the green hat is left over.

b Show this incomplete matching, M, on your graph, G.
c Use a matching algorithm to construct an alternating path for M in G, and hence find a maximal matching between the dwarfs and the hats.
(OCR)

Applications and Extensions

Multi-task Matching

The examples and exercises in this chapter have produced one-to-one matchings, based on preferences and possibilities. Another possible situation is described below.

Delegates to a conference are asked to name at least three sessions that they would like to attend. The organisers then allocate each delegate to two sessions, bearing in mind the preferences of the delegates and the maximum capacity of the rooms in which the sessions are scheduled.

Try setting up such a problem, and modifying the algorithm in this chapter to produce a solution.

Formulating as a Linear Programme

As a constrained optimisation (LP), the object of a matching is to maximise the number of edges used, subject to the constraint that no vertex can be associated with more than one used edge.

Each edge becomes an **indicator variable** (taking either the value 1 to show that the edge is used in the matching, or 0 if it is not) and each vertex generates a constraint. The objective is to maximise the sum of the variables.

In the library example show that Avril's problem can be written as

Maximise $AF + AE + BS + BH + CS + CE + DF + DS$
subject to
$$AF + AE \leqslant 1$$
$$BS + BH \leqslant 1$$
$$CS + CE \leqslant 1$$
$$DF + DS \leqslant 1$$
$$AF + DF \leqslant 1$$
$$AE + CE \leqslant 1$$
$$BS + CS + DS \leqslant 1$$
$$BH \leqslant 1$$

If you have access to a Linear Programming computer package, run this programme. What does the objective function value of 4 tell you?

Try setting up and solving some other matchings as Linear Programmes.

Summary

- Where there are two distinct groups of items with a relationship linking them, they can be modelled using a **bipartite graph**.

- A **matching** is a set of edges on the bipartite graph chosen so that no vertex is connected to more than one edge.

- For a bipartite graph with groups of size m and n ($m \geqslant n$), a matching will contain as most n edges.

- A **complete matching** is a matching which includes every vertex in the bipartite graph (and therefore requires $m = n$).

- A **maximum matching** for a given problem is a matching which uses the most edges possible.

- An **alternating path** is a sequence of edges which are alternatively *not in* and *in* our current matching, starting and finishing at vertices which are not currently connected by the matching.

- A matching can be improved by modifying it with an alternating path (replacing some existing edges with currently unused ones).

12 Allocation and Transportation

12.1 Minimum Cost Allocations

An allocation is about finding an assignment, or matching, but unlike the problems considered in Chapter 11, each potential pairing has an associated cost. The mathematical problem to be solved is not of whether a matching exists (the bipartite graph is usually a complete graph), but of how to achieve this with minimum cost.

Example 1

Barsett Taxis have a number of vehicles, each operated by an owner-driver. On a particular morning, they have four bookings to collect travellers for the 7:30 am train. The following table shows the time it will take each driver to get from their home to each of the four hotels. The manager wants to minimise the time taken in order to reduce his salary costs.

	Azure	Baron	Coral	Domus
Jim	5	3	4	2
Ken	8	3	5	5
Laura	2	5	3	6
Mike	3	6	9	5

Since the journey from the hotel to the station is not affected by who the driver is, we only need consider the time taken to get to the hotel.

Solution

There are many possible matchings. For example:

	A	B	C	D
J	5	3	4	2
K	8	3	5	5
L	2	5	3	6
M	3	6	9	5

has total 'cost' of 23 minutes.

We could employ an heuristic algorithm, such as choosing matchings in ascending order of cost: L–A, J–D, K–B leaving M–C. Although we have chosen smallest wherever possible, it has forced us to select the largest for the final pairing.

We reduce names to their first letter for clarity.

188

By reducing the cost in a row or column by a fixed amount, we are not changing the cost differences between the possible matchings.

We reduce each row by its smallest value:

	A	B	C	D	*Min value*
J	3	1	2	0	*2*
K	5	0	2	2	*3*
L	0	3	1	4	*2*
M	0	3	6	2	*3*

and then repeat the exercise for the columns

	A	B	C	D
J	3	1	1	0
K	5	0	1	2
L	0	3	0	4
M	0	3	5	2
Min	*0*	*0*	*1*	*0*

The shaded cells represent a complete matching and, since they are all zero, are of minimum cost. By adding up the minimum values we have used in our reduction, we get 2 + 3 + 2 + 3 + 1 = 11 so this is our minimum cost. Jim goes to the Domus, Ken goes to the Baron, Laura goes to the Coral and Mike goes to the Azure hotel, and they have to be paid for a total of 11 minutes driving.

Example 2

The following morning, the same four travellers need collecting, but a 5th driver, Nina is now available. Does this change the optimum allocation?

Solution

Our initial matrix is not square so we augment it by adding a dummy column. This is set to equal values so that it does not influence the other choices: this can be any non-zero value but the largest value in the matrix is often chosen.

	A	B	C	D	Dummy
J	5	3	4	2	9
K	8	3	5	5	9
L	2	5	3	6	9
M	3	6	9	5	9
N	4	2	8	3	9

We now proceed as before, first reducing the rows

	A	B	C	D	Dummy	*Min value*
J	3	1	2	0	7	*2*
K	5	0	2	2	6	*3*
L	0	3	1	4	7	*2*
M	0	3	6	2	6	*3*
N	2	0	6	1	7	*2*

and then the columns

	A	B	C	D	Dummy
J	3	1	1	0	1
K	5	0	1	2	0
L	0	3	0	4	1
M	0	3	5	2	0
N	2	0	5	1	1
Min	*0*	*0*	*1*	*0*	*6*

There is now a zero matching as follows:
Jim–Domus, Laura–Coral, Mike–Azure, Nina–Baron
whilst Ken is not used.

This has a cost of 2 + 3 + 2 + 3 + 2 + 1 + 6 − 9 = 10

The subtracted 9 is the cost of the dummy assignment.

12.1 Minimum Cost Allocations

Exercise

Technique

In each of the questions below, you must allocate a person (indicated by letters A to D) to a room (indicated by letters V to Z) while minimising the total costs.

1

	A	B	C	D
V	1	8	12	9
W	9	5	2	8
X	10	12	6	6
Y	10	3	12	14

2

	A	B	C	D
V	2	3	3	9
W	8	4	7	9
X	10	8	3	3
Y	10	6	3	9

3

	A	B	C	D
V	5	7	11	3
W	14	14	6	7
X	10	4	8	9
Y	6	14	15	9

4

	A	B	C	D
V	18	11	24	2
W	7	14	2	8
X	1	11	4	5
Y	3	2	15	9
Z	7	9	7	5

5

	A	B	C	D
V	9	15	7	20
W	8	16	24	14
X	5	1	4	4
Y	8	6	23	9
Z	2	5	6	3

12.2 The Hungarian Algorithm

The Hungarian Algorithm extends the method used in the previous section, to enable further manipulations if a zero matching is not found after the initial column and row reductions.

The algorithm takes its name from the Hungarian mathematician Konig, on whose theorem it is based.

Hungarian Algorithm

1 Ensure that the matrix of costs is square by adding rows/columns if necessary, and reduce it by both row and column subtractions.

2 Find a way of shading rows and columns so that all zeros are shaded, using as few lines of shading as possible. If the number of lines is equal to the dimension of the matrix, go to step 4.

3 Select the minimum unshaded element

- subtract this value from all unshaded elements

- double this value, and add to all elements covered by two lines.
  Go back to step 2.

4 There is an optimal matching using only pairings represented by a zero in the current matrix. Select this matching, and find its cost from the original table of costs.

Example 1

The following week, Barsett Taxis have the same five drivers available, and there is now a fifth traveller, staying at the Eaton hotel. Use the Hungarian algorithm to minimise the travelling time.

	Azure	Baron	Coral	Domus	Eaton
Jim	5	3	4	2	6
Ken	8	3	5	5	4
Laura	2	5	3	6	8
Mike	3	6	9	5	3
Nina	4	2	8	3	6

Solution

We choose the minimum value in each row, and subtract it from every element in that row.

	A	B	C	D	E	*Min value*
J	3	1	2	0	4	*2*
K	5	0	2	2	1	*3*
L	0	3	1	4	6	*2*
M	0	3	6	2	0	*3*
N	2	0	6	1	4	*2*

We then repeat for the columns.

	A	B	C	D	E
J	3	1	1	0	4
K	5	0	1	2	1
L	0	3	0	4	6
M	0	3	5	2	0
N	2	0	5	1	4
Min	*0*	*0*	*1*	*0*	*0*

If at this point, we could find a matching which only used the cells containing 0, we would have found our optimal solution. However, for the above matrix, this is not possible and so we need to apply a further step in the algorithm. We have to find a way of shading rows and columns such that all the zeros are shaded, using as few rows/columns as possible.

	A	B	C	D	E
J	3	1	1	0	4
K	5	0	1	2	1
L	0	3	0	4	6
M	0	3	5	2	0
N	2	0	5	1	4

The above is a (not unique) way of using only four and it cannot be done in less. We pick the smallest element not shaded (= 1), subtract this from each unshaded value, and add double it to each value on a shaded intersection.

	A	B	C	D	E
J	2	1	0	0	3
K	4	0	0	2	0
L	0	5	0	6	6
M	0	5	5	4	0
N	1	0	4	1	3

There is now a complete matching using zeros:
J–D, K–E, L–C, M–A, N–B so we have a solution. By referring to the original matrix, we can calculate the total cost as 2 + 4 + 3 + 3 + 2 = 14 minutes.

Example 2 – Maximisation

A farmer has four fields, and needs to grow each of four different crops. Due to the size, location and soil characteristics, each field creates a different yield on each crop. The following table shows the anticipated profit (in £1000) for each pairing of crop to field. Maximise the expected total profit.

	Field P	Field Q	Field R	Field S
Crop A	2	3	1	5
Crop B	4	2	3	2
Crop C	1	2	3	1
Crop D	3	4	6	4

Solution

First we have to change the problem to a minimisation one, by negating all the values.

	Field P	Field Q	Field R	Field S
Crop A	−2	−3	−1	−5
Crop B	−4	−2	−3	−2
Crop C	−1	−2	−3	−1
Crop D	−3	−4	−6	−4

We now start our row reduction, the smallest value in each row being the most negative.

	Field P	Field Q	Field R	Field S	*Min value*
Crop A	3	2	4	0	*−5*
Crop B	0	2	1	2	*−4*
Crop C	2	1	0	2	*−3*
Crop D	3	2	0	2	*−6*

These two steps are equivalent to subtracting each value from the largest in its row.

Then the column reduction

	Field P	Field Q	Field R	Field S
Crop A	3	1	4	0
Crop B	0	1	1	2
Crop C	2	0	0	2
Crop D	3	1	0	2
Min	*0*	*1*	*0*	*0*

The shaded cells give a complete matching using only zero cells, so we have found the optimal solution. Referring back to the original table, this will give the farmer a profit of 5 + 4 + 2 + 6 = 17, so £17 000.

12.2 The Hungarian Algorithm

Exercise

Technique

In each of the questions below, use the Hungarian algorithm to allocate a person (indicated by letters A to F) to a task (indicated by letters V to Z) while minimising the total costs. Each person must be given a separate task; not all the people have to be used, but all the tasks must be done. In each case, you should aim to find the minimum cost allocation.

1

	V	W	X	Y	Z
A	6	1	9	4	4
B	7	13	24	5	7
C	11	1	4	8	4
D	1	15	6	4	9
E	14	3	24	9	9

2

	V	W	X	Y	Z
A	12	17	16	9	1
B	1	13	20	8	3
C	2	9	14	3	8
D	2	8	8	3	6
E	9	14	17	3	7

3

	V	W	X	Y	Z
A	14	18	23	20	17
B	1	4	25	5	12
C	21	20	6	2	10
D	19	14	25	11	7
E	8	6	21	18	17

4

	V	W	X	Y
A	7	12	9	23
B	12	9	12	4
C	4	13	14	18
D	9	10	6	6
E	1	20	25	7

5

	V	W	X	Y	Z
A	23	30	25	24	7
B	34	20	31	28	4
C	35	20	35	13	16
D	22	26	1	19	12
E	19	35	22	4	16
F	32	9	13	12	27

In each of the questions below, you must allocate a worker (indicated by letters A to E) to a task (indicated by letters V to Z) in order to maximise total income. All the workers must be used, and each must be given a different task.

6

	V	W	X	Y
A	5	7	11	3
B	14	14	6	7
C	10	4	8	9
D	6	14	15	9

7

	V	W	X	Y
A	7	15	14	8
B	7	4	12	15
C	7	12	14	5
D	12	13	4	13

8

	V	W	X	Y	Z
A	18	14	11	12	15
B	5	2	10	5	9
C	2	20	8	19	8
D	14	19	16	8	18
E	20	9	7	15	5

12.3 Transportation Problems

These look at first sight like an allocation problem. However, they are different in that each item to be paired is not a single element, but a source or destination with associated quantities. In this section, we consider two heuristic approaches to solving such problems.

Example 1 – North West Corner

During the autumn, Plumstead Orchards guarantee to deliver freshly pressed apple juice to four wholesalers each week. They have three farms spread across the area, each with its own apple press.

The requirements are the casks per week ordered by each wholesaler and the capacity is the litres per week produced by each farm. A courier company charges per 50 litre cask, and the costs of transportation are given in the following table.

	Wholesaler				Production capacity
	W	X	Y	Z	
Farm A	2	3	2	4	20
Farm B	3	2	5	2	50
Farm C	4	2	3	3	30
Requirements	20	30	25	25	100

Use the North-West corner algorithm to find a delivery pattern.

Solution

Using the North-West corner algorithm, we aim to utilise the capacity of the top-left most pairing.

	W	X	Y	Z	
A	2 (20)	3	2	4	20
B	3	2	5	2	50
C	4	2	3	3	30
	20	30	25	25	100

By supplying W with 20 casks from A, we have both satisfied the demand, and used all the capacity.

	W	X	Y	Z	
A	2 (20)	3	2	4	20
B	3	2 (30)	5	2	50
C	4	2	3	3	30
	20	30	25	25	100

By supplying X with 30 from B, we satisfy the demand of X, but have not fully utilised the capacity of B. Therefore we now consider supplying Y from B as well.

	W	X	Y	Z	
A	2 (20)	3	2	4	20
B	3	2 (30)	5 (20)	2	50
C	4	2	3	3	30
	20	30	25	25	100

We have a capacity of 20 which can be delivered to Y, leaving Y with a further requirement of 5.

This can be supplied from C, leaving 25 at C to supply Z. The final delivery pattern is therefore

	W	X	Y	Z	
A	2 (20)	3	2	4	20
B	3	2 (30)	5 (20)	2	50
C	4	2	3 (5)	3 (25)	30
	20	30	25	25	100

with a cost of $(2 \times 20) + (2 \times 30) + (5 \times 20) + (3 \times 5) + (3 \times 25) = £290$

Example 2 – Lowest Cost

We use the same example again, but this time choose our pairings by selecting the cheapest transportation cost available.

Solution

There are four pairings whose transportation costs are 2. We can choose arbitrarily, say A to Y.

	W	X	Y	Z	
A	2	3	2 (20)	4	20
B	3	2	5	2	50
C	4	2	3	3	30
	20	30	25	25	100

We now choose arbitrarily from the remaining 2s, say B to Z.

	W	X	Y	Z	
A	2	3	2 (20)	4	20
B	3	2	5	2 (25)	50
C	4	2	3	3	30
	20	30	25	25	100

Then say B to X, which uses the remaining capacity from B.

This is a Greedy algorithm which produces a feasible, but not necessarily optimum solution.

	W	X	Y	Z	
A	2	3	2 (20)	4	20
B	3	2 (25)	5	2 (25)	50
C	4	2	3	3	30
	20	30	25	25	100

There is still a cost of 2 left, on C to X, so we allocate 5 units to this, and then 5 to Y, and then the remaining 20 from C will go to W.

	W	X	Y	Z	
A	2	3	2 (20)	4	20
B	3	2 (25)	5	2 (25)	50
C	4 (20)	2 (5)	3 (5)	3	30
	20	30	25	25	100

Total cost = $(2 \times 20) + (2 \times 25) + (2 \times 25) + (4 \times 20) + (2 \times 5) + (3 \times 5) = £245$

12.3 Transportation Problems

Exercise

Contextual

In the following exercises, the tables give information about the supply, demand and transportation costs of sacks of organic potatoes between farms and shops. Use the North-West corner algorithm to find a possible delivery pattern.

1

	Shop				
	A	B	C	D	Supply
Farm V	3	2	3	1	50
Farm W	5	4	3	3	50
Farm X	1	2	6	2	80
Demand	30	60	50	40	

2

	Shop				
	A	B	C	D	Supply
Farm V	2	2	3	3	70
Farm W	1	4	3	3	30
Farm X	1	5	2	2	70
Demand	50	20	40	60	

3

	Shop				
	A	B	C	D	Supply
Farm V	7	1	5	7	80
Farm W	3	4	2	3	30
Farm X	5	3	4	2	90
Demand	50	50	50	50	

4

	Shop				
	A	B	C	D	Supply
Farm V	4	1	5	4	40
Farm W	3	2	4	2	30
Farm X	2	3	2	1	20
Farm Y	5	1	4	5	60
Demand	50	30	40	30	

5

	Shop				
	A	B	C	D	Supply
Farm V	5	2	3	2	40
Farm W	5	3	5	4	40
Farm X	1	4	5	1	40
Shop Y	2	1	3	4	60
Demand	60	30	40	50	

In the following exercises, use the lowest cost method from example 2.

6

	Shop				
	A	B	C	D	Supply
Farm V	7	2	4	10	40
Farm W	8	1	3	12	40
Farm X	6	5	9	11	40
Demand	30	30	30	30	

7

	Shop				
	A	B	C	D	Supply
Farm V	14	15	22	8	50
Farm W	16	12	17	12	60
Farm X	24	21	11	10	70
Demand	60	50	30	40	

8

	Shop				
	A	B	C	D	Supply
Farm V	2	3	1	4	40
Farm W	2	8	4	3	30
Farm X	15	5	3	7	20
Farm Y	8	7	6	6	60
Demand	50	30	40	30	

12.4 Testing for Optimality

Methods such as the North-West corner provide a feasible, but not necessarily optimum solution to our problem. We need to test our solution to see whether or not it can be improved.

It is important for the method described below that the number of cells used in our feasible solution is one less than the total number of rows and columns in the table. If this is not the case then our current solution is **degenerate** and needs to be modified before proceeding further.

Example 1

In the previous section Example 2 found the following feasible solution to the Plumstead Orchards problem:

	W	X	Y	Z
A	2	3	2 (20)	4
B	3	2 (25)	5	2 (25)
C	4 (20)	2 (5)	3 (5)	3

Test this solution for optimality.

Solution

This feasible solution uses six cells. The total number of rows + columns is seven so the solution is not degenerate.

For those cells which currently form part of our solution we share the transportation cost between the supply (rows) and the demand (columns), which we do by allocating an arbitrary value to one cell and calculating the values for all the others *relative to this value*.

The simplest choice is to allocate the value zero to the first demand cost, D_W. Then, since cell CW = 4, the corresponding supply cost, S_C, must equal 4. This then means that $D_X = -2$ and $D_Y = -1$ to satisfy CX and CY.

	W	X	Y	Z	Supply cost S_j
A	2	3	2	4	
B	3	2	5	2	
C	4	2	3	3	4
Demand Cost D_i	0	−2	−1		

We now know that $S_A = 3$ and $S_B = 4$ to satisfy AY and XB, and that $D_Z = -2$ to satisfy BZ, giving us the following table.

	W	X	Y	Z	Supply cost S_j
A	2	3	2	4	3
B	3	2	5	2	4
C	4	2	3	3	4
Demand Cost D_i	0	-2	-1	-2	

The next step is to calculate the total relative cost for each of the currently unused cells. We do this by subtracting the supply and demand costs from the current cell cost. These results have been circled in the following table.

	W	X	Y	Z	Supply cost
A	2 (-1)	3 (2)	2	4 (3)	3
B	3 (-1)	2	5 (2)	2	4
C	4	2	3	3 (1)	4
Demand Cost	0	-2	-1	-2	

Beware of subtracting negatives such as cell BY where
$5 - 4 - (-1) = 2.$

The cells AW and BW contain negative values. This means that these cells have lower relative costs than cells that we are currently using and that the solution **can be improved** by utilising at least one of them.

Note that if the table contains zero relative costs, but no negatives, this represents the existence of alternative solutions of equal cost.

Example 2

Test for optimality the solution found in Example 1 of the previous section to the Plumstead Orchards problem:

	W	X	Y	Z
A	2 (20)	3	2	4
B	3	2 (30)	5 (20)	2
C	4	2	3 (5)	3 (25)

Solution

The number of cells currently used is 5, which is two less than the total number of rows and columns, so the solution is **degenerate**.

All unused cells have a quantity of 0 casks associated with them. We choose one of these cells to become part of our solution, still with quantity 0. The problem has arisen through cell AW satisfying supply and demand simultaneously, so it is best to choose the extra cell as being in either row A or column W. The best choices would be AX or AZ as both of these columns only have one cell currently used in them. We will choose AX.

We then proceed as in Example 1, by assigning relative values to the supply and demand costs to give the following table

	W	X	Y	Z	Supply cost
A	2	3	2	4	2
B	3	2	5	2	1
C	4	2	3	3	−1
Demand cost	0	1	4	4	

and then calculating the total relative cost for each of the currently unused cells.

	W	X	Y	Z	Supply cost
A	2	3	2 ④(−4)	4 (−2)	2
B	3 ②	2	5	2 (−3)	1
C	4 ⑤	2 ②	3	3	−1
Demand cost	0	1	4	4	

The cells AY, AZ and BZ contain negative values. This means that those cells have lower relative costs than cells that we are currently using. Unlike Example 1, this only means that there **may** be a possible improvement because we added a zero cell to our solution to remove the degeneracy.

It is possible that the method will reassign the zero and it will be necessary to try making a different zero cell part of the solution.

12.4 Testing for Optimality

Exercise

Technique

1 – 8

Test for optimality the solution to each of the problems in exercise 12.3

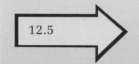

12.5 Improving a Solution

Once the potential to improve a solution has been shown (negative relative costs from the previous section) we need to identify a pattern of adjustments that can be made.

Method

1 Start from a cell with a negative relative cost, and assign it N units.

2 Move to a used cell in the current row and reduce it by N units.

3 Move to a used cell in the current column and increase it by N units.

4 Move to a used cell in the current row and reduce it by N units.

5 If the current cell is not in the same column as the first cell used, repeat steps 3 and 4.

6 Choose N to be the largest possible value such that none of the cells containing it become negative, and adjust the values in these cells accordingly.

Example

Example 1 of the previous section identified AW and BW as potential improvements for the following table.

	W	X	Y	Z	
A	2	3	2 (20)	4	20
B	3	2 (25)	5	2 (25)	50
C	4 (20)	2 (5)	3 (5)	3	30
	20	30	25	25	100

Find a better solution and test it for optimality.

Solution

Following the method given above:

Step 1: Assign the value N to cell AW.

Step 2: Subtract N from cell AY.

Step 3: Add N to cell CY.

Step 4: Subtract N from cell CW.

Step 5: since we are in column W where we began, we stop.

This gives the following table.

	W	X	Y	Z	
A	2 (N)	3	2 (20 − N)	4	20
B	3	2 (25)	5	2 (25)	50
C	4 (20 − N)	2 (5)	3 (5 + N)	3	30
	20	30	25	25	100

The cells which determine the value of N are AY and CW since they will go negative if N > 20.

Step 6: Choose N = 20 and adjust the table accordingly.

This gives a new assignment as follows

	W	X	Y	Z	
A	2 (20)	3	2	4	20
B	3	2 (25)	5	2 (25)	50
C	4	2 (5)	3 (25)	3	30
	20	30	25	25	100

which has cost $(2 \times 20) + (2 \times 25) + (2 \times 5) + (3 \times 25) + (2 \times 25) = £225$

This solution is degenerate so we make the cell AZ (arbitrarily) part of the solution. Calculating the relative costs as in the previous section of the chapter gives the following table.

	W	X	Y	Z	
A	2	3 ⟨−1⟩	2 ⟨−3⟩	4	2
B	3 ⟨3⟩	2	5 ⟨2⟩	2	0
C	4 ⟨4⟩	2	3	3 ⟨1⟩	0
	0	2	3	2	

The algorithm does not guarantee that this is an optimum solution.

Although this contains negative values which would suggest the existence of a better solution, the application of the above algorithm for finding an improvement will require us to reduce the allocation in cell AZ which cannot be done because it is already zero. This is therefore the optimum solution.

12.5 Improving a Solution

Exercise

Technique

1 – 8

For those questions in Exercise 12.4 which were not optimal, find an optimal solution.

Consolidation

Exercise A

1 Four coaches are to be allocated, one each, to train four rowing crews. They have an initial training session with each crew who are then timed over a fixed course with the following results.

		Crews			
		P	Q	R	S
Coach	Bert	85	88	93	84
	Carl	88	87	88	84
	Debby	82	83	81	81
	Elaine	84	98	85	81

Use the Hungarian algorithm to suggest how to assign one coach to each crew by choosing the allocation which would minimise the total time achieved by this assignment in the initial training session. *(AQA)*

2 A large room in a hotel is to be prepared for a wedding reception. The tasks that need to be carried out are:

I   clean the room
II   arrange the tables and chairs
III set the places
IV   arrange the decorations

The tasks need to be carried out consecutively and the room must be prepared in the *least possible time*. The tasks are to be assigned to four teams of workers A, B, C and D. Each team must carry out only one task. The table below shows the times, in minutes, that each team takes to carry out each task.

	A	B	C	D
I	17	24	19	18
II	12	23	16	15
III	16	24	21	18
IV	12	24	18	14

a Use the Hungarian algorithm to determine which team should be assigned to each task. You must make your method clear and show

   (i)   the state of the table after each stage of the algorithm

   (ii) the final allocation.

b Obtain the minimum total time for the room to be prepared.

(EDEXCEL)

3 Five children are playing a game of hide-and-seek. Annie, Benny, Connie and Danny each choose a hiding place and Edward has to try and find them. Two or more children may not share a hiding place.

The scores in the table below show how many minutes it will take Edward to find each child in each hiding place.

		Hiding place			
		Trunk room	**Under stairs**	**Veranda**	**Wardrobe**
	Annie	5	4	6	6
	Benny	4	5	4	6
Child	**Connie**	7	5	4	7
	Danny	3	4	3	4

a Use the Hungarian algorithm to pair the children to the hiding places so that the total time that Edward takes is minimised.

b Find the total time that Edward takes, according to the table, using the pairing from part **a**.

c Explain how you would modify the table so that you could use the Hungarian algorithm to pair the children to the hiding places so that the total time that Edward takes is maximised. *(You do not need to apply the algorithm.)* (OCR)

4 Simon is planning a four day break. He wants to spend one day at the art gallery, one day at the beach, one day at the castle and one day at the exhibition.

The cost, in £, for Simon to visit each of these places on each of the four days of his holiday is given in the table below.

	Art Gallery	Beach	Castle	Exhibition
Wednesday	5.00	1.50	4.50	6.30
Thursday	4.50	1.20	5.00	6.00
Friday	5.00	1.50	5.00	6.00
Saturday	6.00	1.50	5.50	7.00

a Use the Hungarian algorithm to pair the four places with the four days so as to minimise Simon's total cost.

b Give the minimum total cost. (OCR)

5 The following table gives information about the supply, demand and transportation costs of sacks of organic potatoes between farms and shops.

	Farm A	Farm B	Farm C	Farm D	Demand
Shop A	6	7	5	9	40
Shop B	8	3	16	4	30
Shop C	13	15	12	3	20
Shop D	11	14	2	12	60
Supply	50	30	40	30	

a Use the North-West corner algorithm to find a possible delivery pattern.

b Test your solution for optimality, and if it is not optimal find a better solution.

Exercise B

1

	Warehouse			
	W_1	W_2	W_3	Availabilities
F_1	7	8	6	4
F_2	9	2	4	3
F_3	5	6	3	8
Requirements	2	9	4	

A manufacturer has three factories F_1, F_2, F_3 and three warehouses W_1, W_2, W_3. The table shows the cost C_{ij}, in appropriate units, of sending one unit of product from factory F_i to warehouse W_j. Also shown in the table are the number of units at each factory F_i and the number of units required at each warehouse W_j. The total number of units available is equal to the total number of units required.

a Use the North-West corner rule to obtain a possible pattern of distribution and find its cost.
b Calculate shadow costs R_i and K_j for this pattern and hence obtain improvement indices I_{ij} for each route.
c Using your answer to part **b** explain why the pattern is optimal.

(EDEXCEL)

"Shadow costs" and "Improvement indices" are terms used by EDEXCEL to refer to processes used in this chapter for finding relative costs.

2 Four workers are to be allocated to four jobs. The cost, in £ thousands, of using each worker for each job is given in the table below.

	Job			
	Building	Carpentry	Drainage	Electrics
Jenny	4	3	2	7
Kenny	3	2	3	4
Lenny	6	3	4	5
Penny	7	7	7	6

a Use the Hungarian algorithm to pair the four workers with the four jobs to minimise the total cost.
b Give the minimum total cost. *(OCR)*

3 A relay team consists of four runners, A, B, C and D, each of whom runs one leg of the race. The best training times, in seconds, for each of the runners over each of the legs are given in the table.

	1st leg	2nd leg	3rd leg	4th leg
A	47	45	45	43
B	48	44	45	44
C	46	45	44	43
D	50	47	46	44

Use the Hungarian algorithm to decide which runner should be allocated to which leg of the race. *(OCR)*

4 Granny is on holiday and wants to send postcards to her five grandchildren. She has chosen six postcards and has given each card a score to show how suitable it is for each grandchild. A high score means that a card is more suitable.

		Card					
		Maps	Puppies	Railway	Seaside	Teddies	Views
Grandchild	Arnie	5	0	4	1	0	3
	Beth	3	1	0	1	0	3
	Cyril	0	3	2	3	2	1
	Des	3	2	2	3	2	2
	Erin	1	2	3	3	1	2

a The Hungarian algorithm finds the allocation with minimum total cost. Show how Granny's problem can be converted into a minimisation problem.

b The Hungarian algorithm requires the matrix to be square. Explain how to represent Granny's problem as a square matrix.

c Use the Hungarian algorithm, **reducing columns first**, to pair the cards to the grandchildren in the most appropriate way. *(OCR)*

5 The following table gives information about the supply, demand and transportation costs of sacks of organic potatoes between farms and shops.

a Use the lowest cost algorithm to find a possible delivery pattern.

b Test your solution for optimality, and if it is not optimal find a better solution.

	Farm A	Farm B	Farm C	Farm D	Demand
Shop A	6	7	5	9	40
Shop B	8	3	16	4	30
Shop C	13	15	12	13	20
Shop D	11	14	2	12	60
Supply	50	30	40	30	

Applications and Extensions

Knapsack
In the knapsack problem you have a number of items of differing value and size, and a limited space in which to pack them. The aim is to maximise the value of what you pack. Extend this to several packing cases and solve using the methods of this chapter.

Linear Programming
Formulate Allocation and Transportation problems as linear programmes. What is your objective? What are your constraints?

Summary

- Allocation problems are matchings where each possible pairing has an associated cost or weight. The optimum solution is a minimum cost complete matching.

- The allocation matrix can be reduced by row and column minimums: the position of the resulting zeros indicates a possible matching.

- The **Hungarian algorithm** performs additions and subtractions on the matrix to improve the matching.

- **Transportation** problems involve both cost (weight) and supply and demand (quantity) in the assignment. The objective is to apportion delivery so that the cost is minimised whilst satisfying the demand.

- The **North-West corner** method makes the initial allocation in the top-left of the matrix, then works right and down as columns and rows become satisfied.

- By calculating relative demand and supply costs for the existing solution, and comparing these to the relative costs of unused assignments, improvements can be identified.

13 Network Flow

What you need to know

● The language and notation of graphs

● How to draw a network from a table

Review

1 Use the following tables to construct networks.

a

	A	B	C	D
A		3	4	
B	3		5	2
C	4	5		2
D		2	2	

b

	S	A	B	C	D	T
S		4	3			
A			2	6		
B		2		5		
C					4	1
D						2
T						

13.1 Formulation and Notation

There are many examples in real life where we have a network through which there are a variety of routes from a starting point to an end point. In this chapter, we investigate problems where the objective is to optimise the use of each route.

Example 1

Fossilfuel Ltd has opened a new oil well with a high capacity for extraction. The oil needs to be piped to their existing refinery. They have laid new pipelines to their two existing pumping stations (labelled A and B) to utilise spare capacity in their existing pipelines from these on to the refinery. The following table gives the capacity in barrels/second of each connection.

Connection from	Well	Well	A	B	A	B
to	A	B	B	A	Refinery	Refinery
Capacity	3	4	2	2	4	2

Model this as a network.

Solution

We call the starting point the **source** and the end point the **sink**, and label them S and T respectively. We add the other vertices and join them according to the connections shown, putting the capacities on. In this example, the edge between A and B appears to be bi-directional, that is it can carry a flow of two in either direction. It can therefore be modelled as a single edge. Notice that, even if it was actually two separate edges, we would never use both at the same time since this would be counter-productive and have a cancelling effect. By default, the edges connected to the source and sink will be uni-directional since nothing can arrive at the source, or leave the sink.

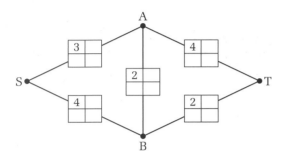

You will notice that we have used four boxes for each edge – these will be used in the next section when we consider the flow in each edge.

Example 2

There are two gas processing plants, providing gas via a network of pipes, to three distribution centres. The following table gives the cross-sectional area of each pipe in 100 cm^2 units, proportional to its capacity. Model this as a network.

	Junc A	Junc B	Junc C	Junc D	Junc E	Dist 1	Dist 2	Dist 3
Plant 1	5	3						
Plant 2		4	5					
Junc A				4				
Junc B				3	4			
Junc C					2			2
Junc D						3	4	
Junc E							2	5

Solution

We create a super source, S, and a super sink, T. S is connected to P1 and P2, and D1, D2 and D3 are all connected to T. The capacity of each of these additional five edges is arbitrary, provided that it is sufficiently large so as not to restrict the flow elsewhere in the network. The simplest way is to use the sum of the capacities of the edges leading from P1 as the capacity of the edge into it from S i.e. $5 + 3 = 8$. Likewise, since the greatest flow that can arrive at D2 is 6, we set the edge from D2 to T to have capacity 6. This gives the following network:

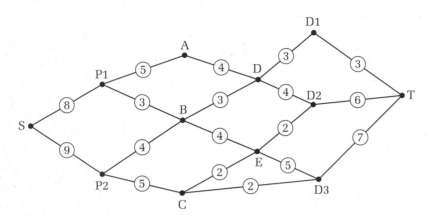

13.1 Formulation and Notation

Exercise

Technique

The following tables give information about possible flows in a network. For each table, draw the associated network. Note that each link can be used in either direction (but only in one direction at any given time). In each case the starting point is labelled **S**, and the end point **T**.

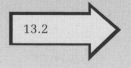

13.2

1

Edge	S–A	S–C	A–C	A–B	A–D	C–D	B–D	B–T	D–T
Capacity	5	7	3	6	4	2	8	3	9

2

Edge	S–A	S–C	S–D	A–B	A–C	C–D	B–C	B–T	C–T	D–T
Capacity	4	3	2	3	5	6	2	4	3	3

3

Edge	S–A	S–C	A–D	A–B	C–D	C–B	B–E	B–T	E–T	D–T
Capacity	5	6	4	3	6	5	1	4	2	3

4

Edge	S–A	S–C	S–D	A–B	A–C	C–D	B–T	C–T	D–T
Capacity	5	4	3	5	6	4	4	2	3

5

Edge	S–A	S–D	A–D	A–B	A–E	D–B	D–E	B–E	B–C
Capacity	7	8	2	5	3	2	4	3	8

...

	B–F	E–C	E–F	C–F	C–T	F–T
...	2	1	2	6	8	7

13.2 Solutions

We can usually find a feasible solution quite easily, and for simple networks can improve this to find the optimal solution by inspection.

Example

Suggest a possible flow pattern for Fossilfuel Ltd (see Example 1 in Section 13.1), and improve it to give the optimal solution.

Solution

The most obvious flow is along the edges of the network – that is the routes S–A–T and S–B–T. Since the route S–A–T has capacities of 3 and 4, we are constrained by the lower and can therefore pump 3 litres/second along that route. Similarly, for the route S–B–T, the capacities are 4 and 2, so we can pump 2 litres/second along that route. This is represented on the following diagram.

Notice that the flow in to each vertex equals the flow out from it (except of course for the source and sink). It is impossible to gain or lose oil at a pumping station.

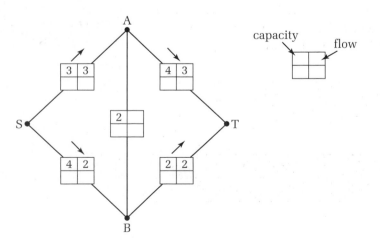

However, there is still some spare capacity in the network. In particular, the pipe S–B has capacity for another 2 litres/second, B–A has an unused capacity of 2 litres/second, and A–T has a spare capacity of 1 litre/second. We can add an additional flow of 1 litre/second along the route S–B–A–T, giving a total flow of 6 litres/second for the entire network. (Note that the path S–B–A–T is known as a **flow augmenting path**, and will be discussed in more detail in Section 13.4.)

This is shown on the following diagram.

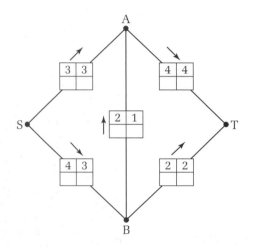

The arrows show the direction of flow.

This is the best we can do, so our maximum flow is 6 litres/second.

13.2 Solutions

Exercise

Technique

| 1 | – | 5 |

Find a feasible flow for each for your networks in Exercise 13.1.

Find a feasible flow for each of the networks below.

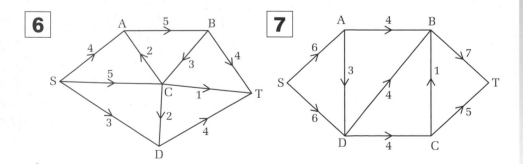

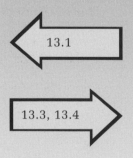

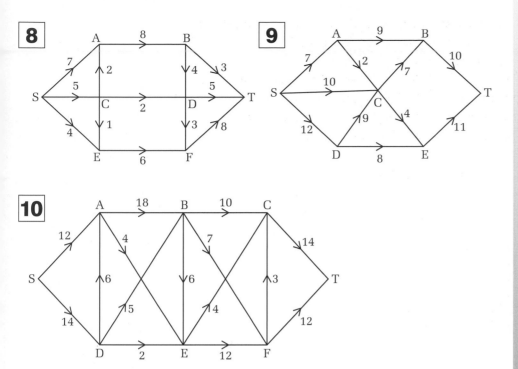

13.3 Cuts and Optimality

A **cut** divides a network into two distinct parts such that the source and sink are separated, and always crosses edges, never through a vertex. There are two measurements which we can take across a chosen cut – the capacity and flow. If we can find a flow which equals a cut, we have found an optimal solution (since any larger flow would exceed the capacity).

The **Max flow/Min cut theorem** states that the maximum flow obtainable in a network will be equal to the minimum cut available in that network. The minimum cut is sometimes referred to as a bottleneck since it is the point of most restriction in the flow.

Example 1

Using the network for Fossilfuel Ltd, find the capacity of each possible cut in the network, and show that the smallest of these is equal to the optimal solution found above.

Solution

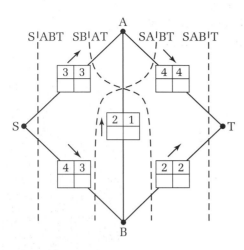

Cut	S | ABT	SA | BT	SB | AT	SAB | T
Capacity	7	10	7	6
Flow	6	6	6	6

The minimum cut is 6, and this corresponds to the flow of 6 found, so this flow is optimal.

Example 2

Find the capacity and flow across each possible cut in the following network. Note that the edge BA is directed (one-way).

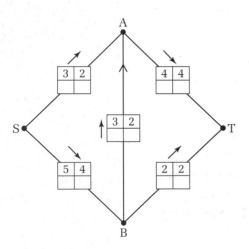

Solution

Cut	S | ABT	SA | BT	SB | AT	SAB | T
Capacity	8	9	8	6
Flow	6	6	6	6

For the cut SA | BT, the flow from B to A is going the wrong way (T to S) across the cut so we must count it as negative, and the net flow is 4−2 + 4 = 6. However, when considering the capacity of that cut, the best we can do on the edge AB is not to use it, so we count it as zero, and our capacity is 4 + 0 + 5 = 9.

13.3 Cuts and Optimality

Exercise

Technique

| 1 | – | 10 |

By finding a minimum cut, state the optimal flow through each of the networks from Exercise 13.2.

13.2

13.4 The Labelling Algorithm

Although we have a test for optimality, and indeed a way of finding what our optimal solution should be, for networks of any significant size, we need an algorithm for finding the optimal flow pattern.

When drawing our networks, we have allowed four boxes on each edge. The two that we have not used yet are the potential flow, and the potential back flow.

Each edge needs to have a notional direction of flow (obvious for directed edges, otherwise an arbitrary choice). Potential is the amount by which the flow could be increased in the positive direction, whilst back-flow is the amount by which it can be reduced. This latter quantity includes, for bi-directional edges, the amount by which it could flow in the opposite direction.

Flow Augmenting Algorithm

1 Find a feasible flow (could be null) and label all edges accordingly.

---

2 Find a path from S to T such that there is potential flow along each edge in the path in the direction S to T.

3 Increase the flow along that path by the smallest potential flow in the path.

4 Repeat steps 2 and 3 until no more paths can be found.

Example 1

Find flow augmenting paths to maximise the flow in this network, which already has existing flows of 4 along SABT and 3 along SCT.

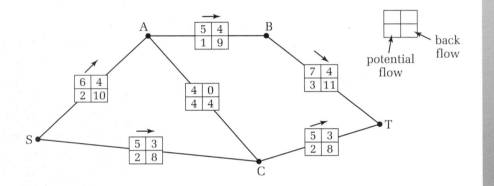

Solution

There is a flow augmenting path S–A–C–T. The potential to increase is {2, 4, 2} so we select the minimum of 2 and add this flow, giving the following.

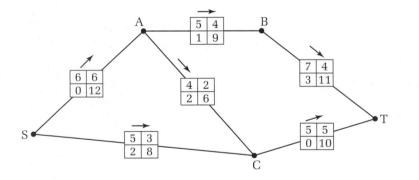

The edge SA is at maximum capacity, but there is spare capacity on SC of 2. Similarly, CT is full, but the route C–A–B–T has capacity so our path is S–C–A–B–T, with capacities {2, 6, 1, 3} and we can therefore augment with a flow of 1 along this path.

The potential along CA is 6 because it is a back flow against the current direction.

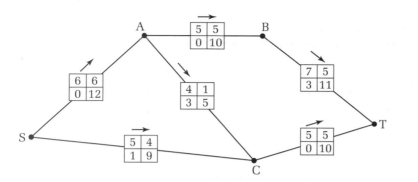

We now have a total flow of 10, and the cut SAC│BT has a capacity of 10. Therefore the max flow/min cut theorem is satisfied and we have an optimum solution.

Example 2

The following network represents some water pipes which during winter must have a minimum flow maintained to stop them freezing. There is currently a flow of 4 along SA and BT, and 2 along each of SB, AB and AT. Calculate the potential and backflows. What is the range of the total flow?

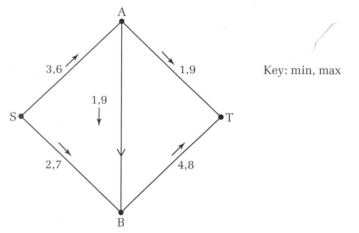

Key: min, max

Solution

The minimum flow has been written in brackets after the maximum. The potential flow is the maximum flow minus the current flow, and the backflow is the current flow minus the minimum flow.

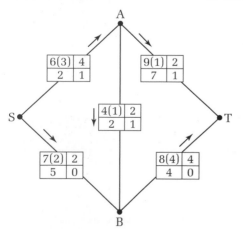

The flow could be increased by 2 along S-A-T, and by 4 along S-B-T. This would give a total flow of 12.

The flow could be decreased along S-A-T by 1, giving a total flow of 5.

Therefore the range is from 5 to 12.

13.4 The Labelling Algorithm

Exercise

Technique

1 – 10

◀ 13.2

Starting with the feasible flows you found in Exercise 13.2, use the labelling algorithm to find an optimal flow for each of the networks.

Consolidation

Exercise A

1

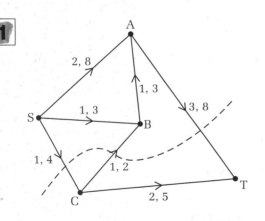

a Find the maximum value of the cut through arcs AT, BC and SC in the network shown in the diagram above (minimum and maximum flows along arcs are marked).

b Draw the network with flow equal to the value of the cut found in part **a** which uses the maximum capacity of arc BA. Explain why this flow is a maximum.

c A new arc is added to the network from B to T with maximum flow of 3 and no minimum flow. By considering a flow augmentation (i.e. labelling procedure) of the flow in part **b**, find the maximum flow of the new network and draw the network with the new solution.

(AQA)

2 The network shows a system of pipes. The numbers represent the capacities of the pipes.

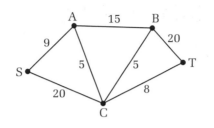

a By marking flows in pipes on a copy of the diagram, show that it is possible to achieve a flow of 27 units from S to T.

b Give a cut with a capacity of 27 units. Say what this shows about the flow of 27 units.

c If there must be a flow of at least 2 from A to C in AC, what will the maximum flow be from S to T, and what flow will be needed in SC to achieve that maximum?

(AQA)

3 A manufacturing company has two factories F_1 and F_2 and wishes to transport its products to three warehouses W_1, W_2 and W_3. The capacities of the possible routes, in lorry loads per day, are shown below.

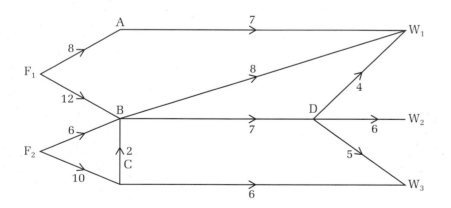

a On a copy of the diagram add a supersource F and a supersink W to obtain a single-source, single-sink capacitated network. State the capacities of the arcs you have added.

b Use the labelling procedure to obtain a maximal flow through the network.

c Interpret your final flow pattern giving
  i the number of lorry loads leaving F_1 and F_2,
  ii the number of lorry loads reaching W_1, W_2 and W_3,
  iii the number of lorry loads passing through B each day.

(EDEXCEL)

4 The diagram represents a
system of pipes. The weights
show the (directed)
maximum capacity for each
pipe in litres/minute.

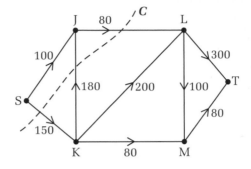

a Calculate the capacity of the cut marked **C** in the diagram.
b Draw a diagram showing a flow from S to T of 230 litres per minute in which each of the pipes JL, KM and MT is carrying its full capacity.
c Explain what can be deduced from parts **a** and **b** about flows through this network.

(OCR)

5 The diagram below shows a system of pipes and the upper and lower capacities of each pipe, in litres/second.

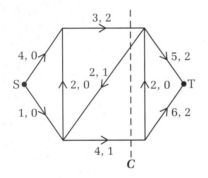

a Work out the capacity of the cut **C**, marked on the diagram.
b Describe a flow from S to T with value 2 less than the capacity of cut **C**.
c What can you deduce from the results of parts **a** and **b**?

(OCR)

Exercise B

1 The diagram below shows a system of telephone cables and the maximum number of telephone lines, in thousands, that each cable can carry.

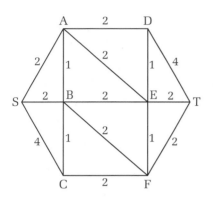

a Draw a diagram showing how S and T can be joined by 5000 lines.

b Augment your answer to part **a**, using a labelling procedure and showing your working clearly, to find the maximum number of lines that the system can carry between S and T.

c Use the maximum flow/minimum cut theorem to verify that the answer you found in part **b** is maximal.

(OCR)

2 The diagram below shows a network of routes through a forest that is being used for a cadet training exercise. The cadets start at S and finish at T.

The weights on the arcs show the minimum and maximum numbers of cadets who may be on each route at any one time during the exercise. The cadets run through the forest at a steady pace.

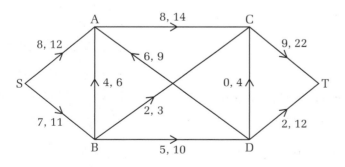

a By considering possible flows through vertex B, explain why the constraints on arc DA can never be satisfied.

The maximum number of cadets who may be on arc SB at any one time is increased from 11 to 21.

b By considering possible flows through vertex A, explain why the constraints on arc AC can never be satisfied.

As well as the previous change, the minimum number of cadets who may be on arc SA at any one time is decreased from 8 to 0. There is now a feasible flow from S to T.

c Calculate the capacity of the cut that partitions the vertices into the two sets {S, A, B} and {C, D, T}. Show all your working.

(OCR)

3 The diagram below shows a system of corridors and the maximum number of people that can move along the corridor (in either direction) each minute. When the fire bell rings all the people in the three rooms S_1, S_2 and S_3 must move along the corridors to one of the two fire assembly points T_1 or T_2.

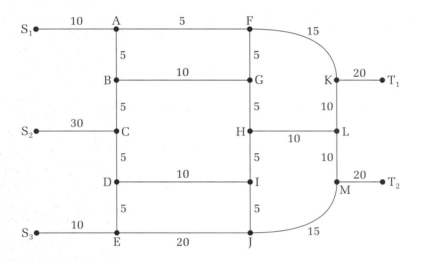

a Modify the network so that it has a single source, S, and a single sink, T.

b A cut, **C**, separates the vertices of the diagram into the two sets X and Y, where X = {S_1, S_2, S_3, A, B, C, D} and Y = {E, F, G, H, I, J, K, L, M, T_1 and T_2}. Ignoring the rest of the network, calculate the maximum number of people per minute who can cross **C** from X to Y.

c Give a flow in which exactly 25 people per minute move from S to T.

d i Find a flow in which the maximum number of people per minute can move from S to T.

ii Use the maximum flow/minimum cut theorem to show that the flow in **i** is maximal.

(OCR)

4 The diagram below shows a capacitated network. The numbers on the arcs indicate the capacities of the arcs.

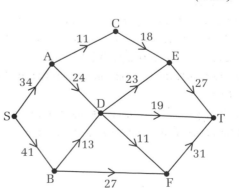

a   State the maximum flow along SADT for this network.

The table below gives a feasible flow of value 70 through the same network.

Start vertex	S	S	A	A	B	B	C	D	D	E	D	F
End vertex	A	B	C	D	F	D	E	E	F	T	T	T
Flow	30	40	11	19	27	x	11	y	z	20	19	31

b   Explaining your reasoning carefully, work out the value of the flows x, y and z.

c   Explain why 70 is not a maximum flow.

d   Using the flows in the table as your initial flow pattern, use the labelling procedure to find the maximum flow through this network. You should list each flow augmenting route you use together with its flow.

e   Draw a network (or modify your existing network) to show the maximum flow.

f   Verify your answer using the maximum flow-minimum cut theorem, listing the arcs that your minimum cut passes through.

(EDEXCEL modified)

5   The diagram below shows a capacitated, directed network. The number on each arc indicates the capacity of that arc.

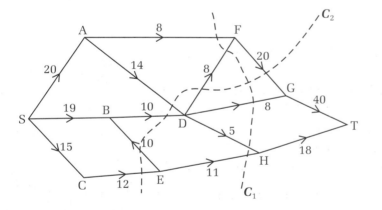

a   calculate the values of cuts C_1 and C_2.

Given that one of these cuts is a minimum cut:

b   State the maximum flow.

c   Deduce the flow along GT, making your reasoning clear.

d   By considering the flow into D, deduce that there are only two possible integer values for the flow along SA.

e   For each of the two values found in part **d**, draw a complete maximum flow pattern.

f   Given that the flow along each arc must be an integer, determine the number of other maximum flow patterns. Give a reason for your answer.

Applications and Extensions

Emergency Evacuation

Try using the techniques learned in this chapter to find the best way of evacuating a building during a fire alarm.

Roads

How do you design a road network to maximise traffic flow?
What causes bottlenecks?

Formulating as a Linear Programme

The task of finding a maximum flow through a network can be defined thus:

Maximise the flow across a cut, subject to the conditions that no edge can have a flow greater than its capacity, and the flow into each intermediate vertex is equal to the flow out from that vertex.

For all our variables to remain positive, we need to replace all undirected edges (other than those connected to the source or sink) with two directed edges, one in each direction.

The Fossilfuel problem from Section 13.1 then becomes

Maximise SA + SB, subject to

SA $\leqslant$ 3, SB $\leqslant$ 4, AT $\leqslant$ 4, BT $\leqslant$ 2, AB $\leqslant$ 2, BA $\leqslant$ 2 and
SA + BA = AB + AT, SB + AB = BA + BT.

Try writing some of the other problems from this chapter as Linear Programmes and, if you have access to it, solve them with an appropriate computer package.

Summary

- Network flow problems are about finding the maximum flow through a network, where each edge has a maximum capacity.

- The start vertex is called the **source**, and the end point the **sink**. If there is more than one source they are linked to form a **super-source**. Similarly with the sink.

- A **cut** is a partition of the network into two sub-graphs. A cut has a capacity and flow equal to the sum of the capacities and flows across it (taking care with edges whose flow is from the sub-graph containing the sink to the sub-graph containing the source).

- A **bottleneck** is a minimum cut.

- The **Max flow/Min cut** theorem states that if a flow and a cut can be found to be equal on a network, then the flow is at its maximum.

- A **flow augmenting path** is a sequence of edges, each with spare capacity, leading from S to T. By adding flow along this path, the total flow through the network can be increased.

- The **flow augmenting algorithm** is a methodical approach, using potential and back flow, to find and implement flow augmenting paths.

14 Dynamic Programming

14.1 Principles and Notation

Dynamic Programming is an approach to problem solving rather than a class of problems in its own right, though certain types of problems lend themselves to its methods. It breaks up a **multistage** problem (one which can be seen as a consecutive sequence of tasks or decisions) into a series of smaller problems which can be solved and combined to produce the optimum solution to the larger problem. In this chapter we only consider **deterministic** problems – those for which the values are fixed and known.

The method starts from the final **stage** and works back one stage at a time, finding the optimum route from each **state** (possibility) at that stage. Provided that each stage is independent of the decisions taken at the previous stage, we are always making the best possible decision for each state, and thus are guaranteed to find the optimum solution to the whole task.

Bellman's principle says that:

an optimal sequence of decisions has the property that whatever the initial state and decision are, the remaining decisions must constitute an optimal decision sequence with regard to the state resulting from the first decision.

In other words, if you know the best decision(s) at each stage (called the **sub-optimal strategy**), you will reach the optimum solution for the entire task.

Example 1

Stage and state variables are defined for each vertex in the following network in the form (**stage, state**).

- The stage variable is defined as being the maximum number of edges from the start.

- The state variable is used to differentiate the different possible choices at this stage.

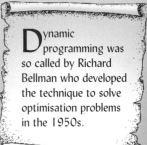

Dynamic programming was so called by Richard Bellman who developed the technique to solve optimisation problems in the 1950s.

This is a recursive definition – each stage defined in terms of the previous one.

Shortest path problems can be solved by Dynamic Programming provided that the network is directed.

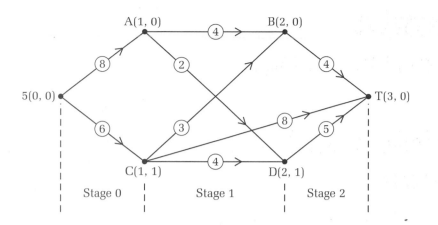

Use Dynamic Programming to find the shortest path from S to T.

Solution

Stage 3
Since there is only one vertex at this stage, with nothing leading from it, there is no decision to be made and we move back to stage 2.

Stage 2
We look at each of the stage 2 vertices in turn, recording the cost (value) of reaching the final stage via each available action (in this case only one for each state). We then record the best (minimum) distance for each.

State	Action	Value	Current Minimum
B (2, 0)	1 (edge BT)	4	4
D (2, 1)	1 (edge DT)	5	5

Stage 1
For each of the stage 1 vertices, we repeat the previous step, calculating the value for each possible action, and identifying the minimum for each state.

State	Action	Value	Current Minimum
A (1, 0)	1 (edge AB)	4 + 4 = 8	
	2 (edge AD)	2 + 5 = 7	7 via D
C (1, 1)	1 (edge CB)	3 + 4 = 7	7 via B
	2 (edge CT)	8	
	3 (edge CD)	4 + 5 = 9	

The numbering of the actions is sometimes referred to as the decision variable, the variable which takes the reference value of the decision.

Each of the minima identified in the final column represents the sub-optimal strategy for that stage and state. So, for any route passing through A, we should then go via D, whilst for any route passing through C we should then go via B.

Stage 0

Repeating the process again for the single stage 0 vertex gives the following table:

State	Action	Value	Current Minimum
S (0, 0)	1 (edge SA)	8 + 7 = 15	
	2 (edge SC)	6 + 7 = 13	13 via C

Our shortest path is therefore of length 13. The route can be found by following back through the stages;
at stage 0 we selected the second action which was the edge SC,
at stage 1, from C, we selected the first action which was the edge CB,
at stage 2, from B, we only had one action which was the edge BT.
Our shortest path is therefore S−C−B−T.

Example 2

Barsett coachlines, operating between Alton to Flordon, have been contracted to operate an additional bus each evening on that route. All routes operate via either Barton or Caldon, and either Denton or Elton. The overall income is unlikely to be affected by the route, but the operating costs vary. In addition the council have offered to subsidise the route from Caldon to Denton so that it would make a profit of £2 per day. The following network models the problem (all costs in £/day): use Dynamic Programming to find the best route for the company to operate.

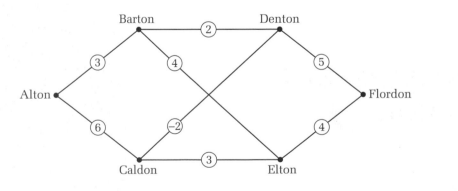

Dynamic Programming assumes a movement across the graph so the arrows on the edges are often omitted.

Solution

Stage	State	Action	Value	Current Minimum
2	D (2, 0)	1 DF	5	5
	E (2, 1)	2 EF	4	4
1	B (1, 0)	1 BD	2 + 5 = 7	7 via D
		2 BE	4 + 4 = 8	
	C (1, 1)	1 CD	−2 + 5 = 3	3 via D
		2 CE	3 + 4 = 7	
0	A (0, 0)	1 AB	3 + 7 = 10	
		2 AC	6 + 3 = 9	9 via C

The company should choose the route Alton–Caldon–Denton–Flordon, with a resultant cost of £9.

Comparison with other approaches

The principle of a greedy algorithm is that of always making the best possible choice. The difference between this and Dynamic Programming is that a greedy algorithm requires a single choice to be made, whereas Dynamic Programming will generally hold a number of possible choices at each stage. However, this in turn is better than complete enumeration because dynamic programming eliminates those decisions which can be shown to definitely not be part of an optimum solution.

Activity

If you are familiar with Dijkstra's algorithm for finding a shortest path, use this on the problem in Example 2 and explain why dynamic programming is better.

14.1 Principles and Notation

Exercise

Technique

For each of the following networks, use Dynamic Programming to find the shortest path from S to T.

Dynamic Programming can be used to solve TSP (see Chapter 7). However, although it is quicker – $O(n^2 2^n)$ rather than $O(n!)$, it requires the storage of a very large number of intermediate values and is thus quite unwieldy to use.

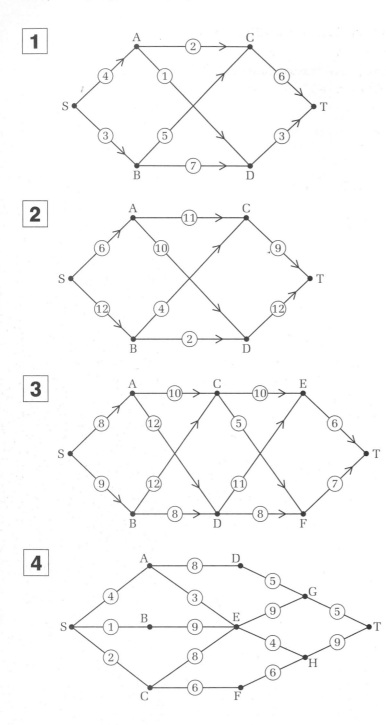

14.2 Common Applications

Dynamic Programming can be applied to a wide variety of problem solving. The following examples consider two of these.

Example 1 – Maximin

A heavy freight train needs to run between the docks and a distribution terminal. Each part of the railway network is classified on a scale of 1 to

Maximin problems seek to maximise the minimum value, whilst **minimax** problems require the minimisation of the maximum value.

10 (1 is the lightest, 10 the heaviest): this is the highest classification of train that can operate on it. The following network gives the classifications of the potential routes. Use Dynamic Programming to find the maximum classification that the freight train can be loaded to.

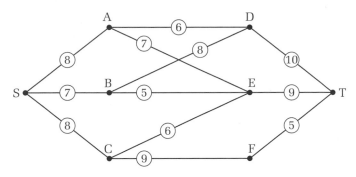

Solution

We assign stage and stage variables to each vertex as in Section 14.1, number from left and top from zero. Then, working from the right, we complete the following table. Since each route is constrained by its smallest classification, our value is the minimum of those on the route we are considering. However, since our objective is to find a route with high classification, we identify the maximum for each state as the sub-optimal strategy.

Stage	State	Action	Minimum choice	Value	Route Max
2	0	DT		10	10
	1	ET		9	9
	2	FT		5	5
1	0	AD	Min (6, 10) = 6	6	
		AE	Min (7, 9) = 7	7	7
	1	BD	Min (8, 10) = 8	8	8
		BE	Min (5, 9) = 5	5	
	2	CE	Min (6, 9) = 6	6	6
		CF	Min (9, 5) = 5	5	
0	0	SA	Min (8, 7) = 7	7	
		SB	Min (7, 8) = 7	7	7
		SC	Min (8, 6) = 6	6	

The sub-optimal strategy at stage 0 is 7. Therefore the highest classification that the freight train can be assigned is 7, and there is then a choice of suitable routes that it can take: S–A–E–T or S–B–D–T

Example 2 – A 'Knapsack' problem

Sue only has 1000 cm^2 of shelf space in her conservatory to over-winter her tender plants. She checks the space required by each plant, and assigns it a value based on frost risk and cost/difficulty of replacing it if it is not adequately protected.

Species	Number of pots	Space required for each pot (cm²)	Value
Geranium	2	500	5
Fuschia	1	300	4
Begonia	4	100	1

Formulate this as a Dynamic Programming problem and suggest which plants Sue should bring in.

Solution

We assign each type of plant to a stage in our process.
Stage 3: Geranium

Space available at stage 3	Decision (number stored)	Value
0–400	0	0
500–900	1	5
1000	2	10

Stage 2: Fuschia
We do not yet know how much space will be available for the plants at stage 2, so we must consider what we would do under each possible scenario (though a few have been grouped together where there is no different choice at stage 2 for the different values).

Space available at stage 2	Decision (Fushcia, Geranium)	Value
0–200	(0, 0)	⓪
300–400	(0, 0)	0
	(1, 0)	④
500–700	(0, 0)	0
	(1, 0)	4
	(0, 1)	⑤
800–900	(0, 0)	0
	(1, 0)	4
	(0, 1)	5
	(1, 1)	⑨
1000	(0, 0)	0
	(1, 1)	0
	(0, 1)	5
	(0, 2)	⑩

The decision pairs (a, b) are found by considering all possible pairings, subject to the space constraint.

In the later states, all possible options have been listed, but some are clearly not going to be part of an optimum solution. – e.g. (1, 0) will always be better than (0, 0).

The circled value in each state is the optimum value for that state – to be used in the next stage.

Stage 1: Begonia

We now have to decide how many Begonias to bring in. As this is the first stage, there is only 1 state – that of having 1000 cm^2 of shelving available. We consider each possible decision against the optimum available if we make that decision.

Space available at stage 1	Decision	Value	Space left	Sub-optimal strategy at stage 2	Total value
1000	0	0	1000	(0, 2)	0 + 10 = 10
	1	1	900	(1, 1)	1 + 9 = 10
	2	2	800	(1, 1)	**2 + 9 = 11**
	3	3	700	(1, 0)(0, 1)	3 + 5 = 8
	4	4	600	(1, 0)(0, 1)	4 + 5 = 9

E.g. if we choose one Begonia, that will leave 900 cm^2 for which we already know the optimum is one Fuschia and one Geranium, with joint value 9, giving total value 10.

So Sue's best plan is to bring in two Begonias, one Fuschia and one Geranium, with total 'value' of 11.

14.2 Common Applications

Exercise

Technique

For each of the networks in Exercise 14.1, use Dynamic Programming to find:

a the minimax route from S to T
b the maximin route from S to T.

Consolidation

Exercise A

1 Use Dynamic Programming to find the shortest path from S to T on the network below.

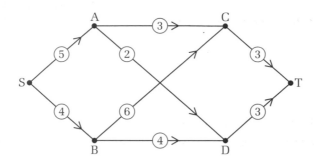

2 For the network below, find

  a the maximin route

  b the minimax route.

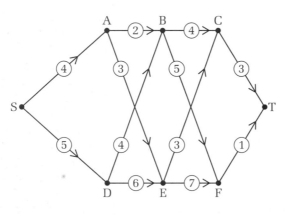

3 At the beginning of each month an advertising manager must choose one of three adverts: the previous advert; the current advert; a new advert. She therefore has three options.

A: use the previous advert

B: use the current advert

C: run a new advert

The possible choices are shown in the network below together with (stage, state) variables at the vertices and the expected profits, in thousands of pounds, on the arcs.

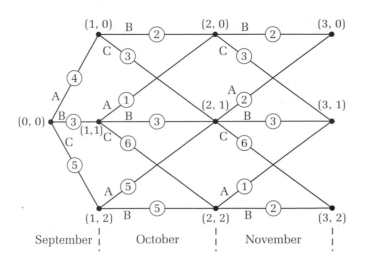

September | October | November

The manager wants to maximise her profits for the three month period.

Use dynamic programming to find the sequence of decisions giving the
maximum profits.

(EDEXCEL)

4 A theatre company intends to perform three plays, A, B and C during a
particular season. The order in which they perform the plays is a matter
of choice. However, because of the need to construct and dismantle
scenery, the running cost for each play depends on which, if any, plays
have preceded it. The costs in thousands of pounds are given in the table
below.

Play Number	Previous Play(s)	Cost (£000's)		
		A	B	C
1	—	11	9	7
2	A	—	10	9
	B	14	—	10
	C	12	12	—
3	A and B	—	—	12
	A and C	—	13	—
	B and C	14	—	—

Use Dynamic Programming, together with a clearly labelled network, to
determine an order of plays that minimises the total cost for the season.

(AQA)

5 The Rolling Pebbles are choosing which venues to include on a short
tour.

on day 1 they will play at one of A, B and C;
on day 2 they will play at one of D, E and F;
on day 3 they will play at one of G, H and I;

they return home on day 4.

The following diagram shows the venues, labelled using (stage, state).
The weights on the edges show the expected profit (in £10 000) from
playing at each venue.
Use Dynamic Programming, working backwards from day 4, to find
which venues should be played on which day to maximise the total
profit.

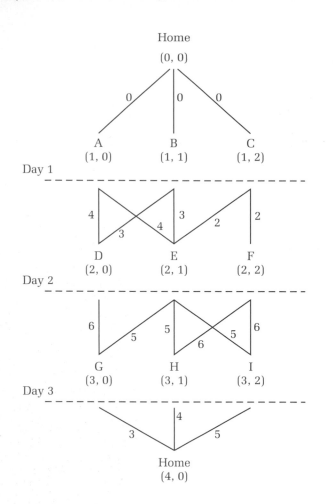

(OCR)

Exercise B

1 Use Dynamic Programming to find the shortest path from S to T on the network below.

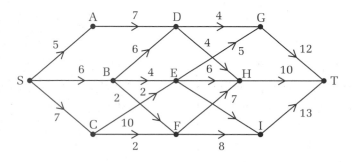

2 For the network below, find

a the maximin route

b the minimax route.

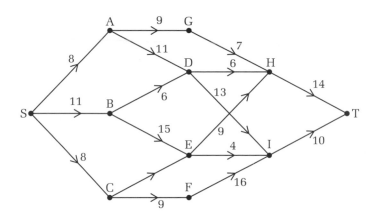

3 The diagram below shows a network with (stage, state) variables at the vertices and costs on the arcs.

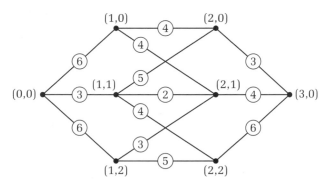

It is required to find the route from (0, 0) to (3, 0) for which the minimum cost is a maximum (the maximin route).

The table below gives a Dynamic Programming tabulation showing stages, states and actions, together with columns for working out the route minimum at each stage and for indicating the current maximin (sub-optimal maximin).

Copy and complete the table and hence find the maximin route.

Stage	State	Action	Route minimum	Current maximin
2	0	0		
	1	0		
	2	0		
1	0	0		
		1		
	1	0		
		1		
		2		
	2	1		
		2		
0	0	0		
	1	1		
	2	2		

(OCR)

4 Jim is playing a space adventure game. He has found the alien headquarters and now has four turns to escape from the planet, or else perish. On each turn, Jim must play one of three tactics. He can attack, run away or dodge the aliens. The number of energy pods used up during the turn is shown in Table 1.

Table 1.

Tactic	Energy pods used
Attack	2
Run away	1
Dodge	0

The number of squares that Jim travels with each of these tactics is shown in Table 2.

Table 2.

	Energy pods remaining at start of turn				
	5	4	3	2	1
Attack	6	7	6	4	–
Run away	5	4	4	3	1
Dodge	1	2	1	1	0

Jim currently has five energy pods, and needs to maximise the number of squares that he travels in the four turns that he has left. He should finish the game with no energy pods remaining, but he needs at least one energy pod at the start of each of his four turns.

a Draw up a network showing Jim's remaining options, labelling the vertices with (stage, state) variables, where stage = number of turns left and state = number of energy pods left, and the edges with the number of squares travelled with each action.

b Use Dynamic Programming to find Jim's optimum strategy.

(OCR)

5 The diagram shows a network with costs on the arcs. Set up a Dynamic Programming tabulation, working backwards, to find the route with the minimum total cost.

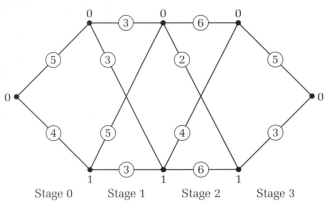

(OCR)

Applications and Extensions

Work from previous chapters

Dynamic programming is a technique for solving problems, rather than a new type of problem. Try applying this technique to the problems you have met elsewhere in this textbook.

For example, you could use this technique on the Knapsack Problem (from the Applications and Extensions section of Chapter 12).

The margin note on page 233 suggests that Dynamic Programming can be used to solve TSP problems. Try doing this on a small network of 4 or 5 vertices.

Summary

- Dynamic Programming is an approach to problem solving which requires the task to be divided into a number of independent stages.

- The method requires the stages to be analysed in turn from the end to the start, retaining only those options which could lead to an optimum solution from that stage.

- **Stage** and **state** variables are used to identify each phase and the options available within it.

- A **sub-optimal strategy** is a solution which is optimal for the sub-problem of getting from the current position to the end.

15 Game Theory

What you need to know

- How to draw the graphs of linear functions

- How to formulate a linear programming problem

Review

1 On the same axes, sketch the graphs of

  a $f(p) = 3 - p$
  b $f(p) = 2p + 4$
  c $f(p) = 5 - 3p$

2 Andy is playing a board game with his nephew, Charlie, and niece, Seren. The game involves moving a counter along one of three routes. Andy knows that if he chooses route A, he will score 12 points, Charlie will score 9 and Seren will score 17. If he chooses route B, he will score 21 points, Charlie will score 16 and Seren will score 15. If he chooses route C, he will score 19 points, Charlie will score 14 and Seren will score 6.

  a Represent this information in a table.

Andy knows that if he beats the children too easily, they will be upset, but they will also complain if he doesn't seem to be trying hard enough. He decides to choose route A with probability p_1, and route B with probability p_2. He also wants to ensure that Charlie's average score will be less than 12, and that Seren's average score will be more than 8. Within these constraints, Andy wants to make his own average score as high as possible.

  b Formulate Andy's problem as a Linear Programming problem.

Remember that total probability = 1, so Andy will choose C with probability $1 - p_1 - p_2$.

15.1 Zero-sum Games

A 'game' in the context of discrete mathematics is defined as being a task or set of tasks where choices exist, and in which the consequences of one person's choice can affect the choice made by one or more others.

In a two-person zero-sum game, the gain of one person is the loss of the other. Consider two players, A and B, playing a game with two choices.

Pay-off for A			
Choice		B	
		1	2
A	1	2	−1
	2	−3	2

Pay-off for B			
Choice		B	
		1	2
A	1	−2	1
	2	3	−2

Since the second matrix is an exact reverse of the first, we only need one of them – convention says we use the former, with the person on the left side being the beneficiary.

Example 1

Alex and Beth each have three playing cards. Alex has a 2, an 8 and a King. Beth has a 5, a Jack and Ace. They each pick one card and the highest card wins. The Ace counts as high against a picture, but low against a number. They each have a pile of counters and pay each other according to the difference in the rank of the cards, as set out in the following pay-off matrix. The matrix shows pay-offs for Alex (i.e. if Alex picks the 8, he gains 3p if Beth picks the 5 but loses 3p if Beth picks the Jack).

		Beth		
		Five	Jack	Ace
Alex	Two	−3	−9	1
	Eight	3	−3	7
	King	8	2	−1

Which card should each of them pick to minimise their potential losses? Is this always the best choice?

Zero-sum does not necessarily mean that the pay-off matrix adds up to zero. If each choice is equally likely and they play enough games, Alex would expect to win overall.

Solution

We calculate for each row, the minimum value (that is, the most that Alex could lose with that card), his *worst case scenario*. For each column we calculate the maximum, since Beth's worst case scenario is when Alex gains the most.

		Beth			Row Minimum
		Five	Jack	Ace	
Alex	Two	−3	−9	1	−9
	Eight	3	−3	7	−3
	King	8	2	−1	−1
	Column maximum	8	2	7	

The strategy of minimising the risk is called a **play-safe** strategy.

So Alex carries the smallest risk, of losing at most 1p, if he chooses the King, whilst Beth carries the smallest risk, of losing at most 2p, if she chooses the Jack.

If a player knows something about the strategy of the other player, their best choice changes. For example, if Beth knows that Alex will play-safe and choose the King, she should choose the Ace and win 1p.

Example 2

Beth decides that the game is unfair and wants to change the cards so they agree a new matrix of scores.

		Beth		
		Five	Jack	King
Alex	Two	−3	−9	−11
	Eight	3	−3	−5
	Queen	7	1	−1

What are their play-safe strategies now? Is this always the best choice?

Solution

We recalculate the row minimums and column maximums

		Beth			Row Minimum
		Five	Jack	King	
Alex	Two	−3	−9	−11	−11
	Eight	3	−3	−5	−5
	Queen	7	1	−1	−1
	Column maximum	7	1	−1	

The play-safe strategy is for Alex to choose the Queen and for Beth to choose the King.

If Alex knows that Beth will choose the King, he will still choose the queen. If Beth knows that Alex will choose the Queen, she will still choose the King. The entry of −1 in the Queen/King position in the matrix is creating play-safe strategies with equal pay-off for both players and is called a **saddle point**. We say that the game has a stable solution, with a value of −1.

Note that there are still potentially better individual results, but only if the other player does not play-safe.

It is possible for a game t have more than one saddle point, in which case there are alternative optimum solutions.

15.1 Zero-sum Games

Exercise

Technique

For each of the pay-off matrices below, state how many saddle points there are. If the game is stable, give the value of the game.

Assume that each of these matrices is of the standard form, giving the pay-offs to player A, whose choices are represented by the rows.

1

0	−3	−3
1	4	−2
2	3	−3

2

5	2	−2
0	1	−4
3	4	−2

3

6	0	−2
−4	1	1
−2	2	−1

4

0	3	−1
1	−1	2
1	−3	2

5

1	−2	−5
−1	3	1
−2	3	−4

6

6	2	2
1	−2	3
−3	0	1

7

3	1	−1
3	−4	2
3	−1	1

8

3	−1	1
−3	−4	−2
−3	−4	1

15.2 Strategy Dominance

Sometimes a particular strategy for a player will have a better pay-off than another strategy, regardless of the choice of the other player. If this is so then the weaker strategy can be eliminated from the game.

Example

Consider again the original game from Section 15.1, and show how the pay-off matrix can be reduced by dominance arguments.

Solution

If we consider the pay-off matrix, we can see that the second row is greater than the first row in every column (that is, the 8 is always a better choice than the 2). We can therefore eliminate the first row.

	Beth		
		Five	Jack	Ace
Alex	Two	−3	−9	1
	Eight	3	−3	7
	King	8	2	−1

If we now consider the columns in the remaining rows, we can see that column one, the 5, always is greater than column 2, the Jack. However, since the matrix is about Alex's winnings, our aim is to minimise column values for Beth, so we eliminate the larger strategy, in column one.

	Beth		
		Five	Jack	Ace
Alex	Eight	3	−3	7
	King	8	2	−1

It is now easier to see that the maximum row minimum for Alex is the − 1 if he chooses the King, whilst the minimum row maximum for Beth is the 2 if she chooses the Jack.

15.2 Strategy Dominance

Exercise

Technique

Reduce each of the following pay-off matrices using dominance arguments.

1

0	2	−3
2	1	4
4	3	1

2

2	−1	4
−4	−2	0
−4	3	1

3

5	−4	−5
1	−1	3
2	−2	−2

4

5	1	4
2	3	6
1	0	0

5

5	−5	2
−4	−5	2
2	3	4

6

−1	0	2
−2	1	−2
−2	−1	3

Sometimes a column dominance will only become apparent after a row has been eliminated or vice versa, in which case we are assuming that both players will aim to play safe.

This is, and always will be, the same play-safe strategy as for the full matrix.

7

6	1	0
−4	3	2
2	−3	−1

8

3	4	−4
−1	2	3
−3	1	−4

15.3 Mixed Strategies

When there is not a stable solution, it is possible to increase the expected winnings by employing a mix of strategies. We assign a probability variable to each strategy and calculate, either by use of a graph or by Linear Programming, the optimum values for these probabilities. In this section we consider games where one of the players has at most two strategies to choose between, and use a graphical approach.

Example 1

For the matrix derived in the previous section:

		Beth	
		Jack	Ace
Alex	Eight	−3	7
	King	2	−1

find:

a the optimum mixed strategy for Alex
b the optimum mixed strategy for Beth
c the value of the game.

Solution

a   Alex's strategy

We assign a probability p to Alex's first choice. Since there are only two strategies available, the second must therefore have probability of $1 - p$.

If Beth chooses the Jack, Alex will win −3 with probability p and 2 with probability $1 - p$. His expected winnings will therefore be $-3p + 2(1 - p) = 2 - 5p$.

Similarly, if Beth chooses the ace, Alex will win $7p - 1(1 - p) = 8p - 1$.

These are drawn on a graph:

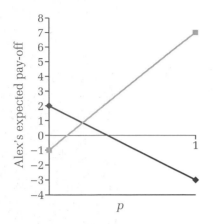

The lower line at any point is the least that Alex can expect. Therefore the optimum strategy occurs at the point where the two lines meet. This point can be calculated by solving the two equations simultaneously to give $p = \frac{3}{13}$.

$$2 - 5p = 8p - 1$$
$$\Rightarrow 13p = 3$$
$$\Rightarrow p = \frac{3}{13}$$

Alex should therefore choose the eight with probability $\frac{3}{13}$ and the King with probability $\frac{10}{13}$.

b Beth's strategy

We now repeat the process for Beth by assigning her first choice the probability q, and her second choice the probability $1 - q$.

Since Alex's loss is Beth's gain, we use the negative of each value in the table to calculate Beth's winnings.

Alex's two choices therefore give Beth winnings of
$3q - 7(1 - q) = 10q - 7$ and
$-2q + (1 - q) = -3q + 1$.
Again we can calculate the optimum probability:
$10q - 7 = -3q + 1$
$q = \frac{8}{13}$

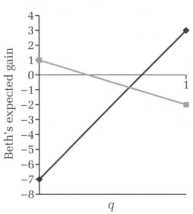

Beth's strategy should therefore be to choose the Jack with probability $\frac{8}{13}$ and the ace with probability $\frac{5}{13}$.

c value

The value of the game is Alex's expected winnings, so we must substitute of value of p into either of the equations giving a value of $8 \times \frac{3}{13} - 1 = \frac{11}{13}$.

This value can also be found by substituting $q = \frac{8}{13}$ into either of Beth's equations and negating the answer.

Example 2

Alex and Beth now try a new game. Beth has first choice of her two cards, and Alex then picks three different ones. The pay-off matrix is as follows:

		Beth	
		Card 1	Card 2
Alex	Card 1	2	−2
	Card 2	−1	5
	Card 3	−2	6

Find the optimum mixed strategy for each of Alex and Beth and state the value of the game.

Solution

We cannot draw a 2-dimensional graph for Alex, because there are three choices. However, since Beth only has two choices we can invert the problem so that it is defined in Beth's favour.

		Alex		
		Card 1	Card 2	Card 3
Beth	Card 1	−2	1	2
	Card 2	2	−5	−6

If Beth chooses card 1 with probability p, and card 2 with probability $1 - p$, then her expected winnings are:

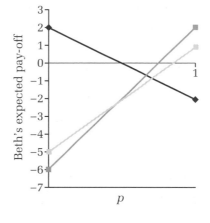

Alex card 1: $-2p + 2(1 - p) = -4p + 2$
Alex card 2: $p - 5(1 - p) = 6p - 5$
Alex card 3: $2p - 6(1 - p) = 8p - 6$

The maximin is at 0.7. This gives the game a value of −0.8 to Beth.

The value to Alex will therefore be 0.8 which comes from the intersection of the lines for him choosing card 1 or 2. We assign the probability p_1 to Alex choosing card 1, p_2 to card 2 and p_3 to card 3.

$2p_1 - p_2 - 2p_3 = 0.8$
$-2p_1 + 5p_2 + 6p_3 = 0.8$
$p_1 + p_2 + p_3 = 1$

Solving these gives $p_1 = 0.6$, $p_2 = 0.4$, $p_3 = 0$

This suggests that Alex should never choose card 3. Assuming that Beth is going to play according to the probabilities calculated above, this is to be expected since although it carries the largest pay-off for him, it also carries a significant loss corresponding to the card which Beth is more likely to choose.

Two choices were represented by p and $1 - p$, one variable.

On the graph, this is shown by the fact that Alex's card 3 gives Beth a larger pay-off at her optimum point than either of the others, which he should aim to avoid.

15.3 Mixed Strategies

Exercise

Technique

Use a graphical approach to find the optimum mixed strategy for each of the following zero-sum games, and state the value of the game.

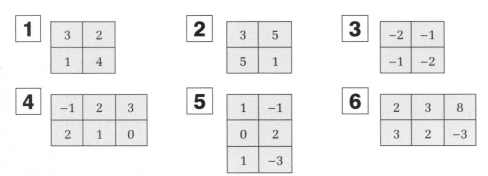

1

3	2
1	4

2

3	5
5	1

3

−2	−1
−1	−2

4

−1	2	3
2	1	0

5

1	−1
0	2
1	−3

6

2	3	8
3	2	−3

15.4 Linear Programming Solutions

We have seen that each strategy can be assigned a probability. For a given probability, there will be a minimum pay-off; our aim is to maximise this. This can be written as a Linear Programme and solved either by the Simplex Algorithm, or by using a computer.

This is known as a maximin problem.

Example

By formulating a Linear Programme, find the value of the game and the optimum strategy for player A, for this pay-off matrix.

3	1	−1
2	−1	3
4	1	−8

Solution

We first have to adjust our matrix to make all values positive – this ensures that our variables remain positive as required by the Simplex algorithm. Since the minimum is −8, we add 8 to each value.

11	9	7
10	7	11
12	9	0

We assign probabilities p_1, p_2 and p_3 to the strategies of player A. If player B chooses their first strategy, the pay-off for player A will be $11p_1 + 10p_2 + 12p_3$.

For strategy two it will be $9p_1 + 7p_2 + 9p_3$ and for strategy three $7p_1 + 11p_2 + 0p_3$.

Our objective is to maximise the value of the game, but this will never be bigger than the smallest of these three expressions, so we can write $v \leqslant$ each of them.

We have an additional constraint which is that the sum of the probabilities cannot exceed 1.

We now have a formulation which reads
maximise v subject to
$$v \leqslant 11p_1 + 10p_2 + 12p_3$$
$$v \leqslant 9p_1 + 7p_2 + 9p_3$$
$$v \leqslant 7p_1 + 11p_2$$
$$p_1 + p_2 + p_3 \leqslant 1$$

The simplex tableau for this is:

P	v	p_1	p_2	p_3	s_1	s_2	s_3	s_4	RHS
1	−1	0	0	0	0	0	0	0	0
0	1	−11	−10	−12	1	0	0	0	0
0	1	−9	−7	−9	0	1	0	0	0
0	1	−7	−11	0	0	0	1	0	0
0	0	1	1	1	0	0	0	1	1

and the solution is $v = 8\frac{1}{3}$
(but we added 8 to every pay-off and therefore to the value of the game) when $p_1 = \frac{2}{3}$, $p_2 = \frac{1}{3}$, $p_3 = 0$.

Player A should therefore play strategies one and two in the ratio 2 : 1, and have an expected pay-off of $\frac{1}{3}$ per game.

$p_1 + p_2 + p_3$ will of course add up to 1. We are using a $\leqslant$ symbol because equalities are harder to deal with in the Simplex algorithm. The first step in our solution to this question was to make all our values positive, so that v, our objective function, is expressed in terms of positive coefficients. Consequently, if at any intermediate stage $p_1 + p_2 + p_3$ is less then 1, it will be possible to increase v by increasing one of the probabilities. The end result is that the Simplex algorithm will always end up with $p_1 + p_2 + p_3 = 1$.

15.4 Linear Programming Solutions

Exercise

Technique

Use the technique in this section to formulate each of the games in Exercise 15.2 as a Linear Programming problem.

Use the Simplex algorithm to solve your Linear Programmes.

Consolidation

Exercise A

1 A stockbroker, B, has three strategies to tempt clients from its main competitor, C, which are referred to as X, Y and Z for simplicity. The competing stockbroker, C, also has three marketing strategies which are referred to as P, Q and R. The table below shows the result, from previous experience, of these strategies from B's point of view (i.e. if B decides upon strategy X and C chooses strategy P then B will lose 1 customer to C). Each stockbroker can only adopt a single marketing strategy in any one month.

	P	Q	R
X	−1	−4	2
Y	4	5	7
Z	6	0	3

  a Show that, regarding this as a zero-sum game, there is no stable solution.
  b Show that it will never be optimal for B to adopt strategy X.
  c By considering mixed strategies, find the optimal mixed marketing strategy for B, giving any probability as an exact fraction. *(AQA)*

2 A two-person zero-sum game is represented by the following pay-off matrix for player A. Find the best strategy for each player and the value of the game.

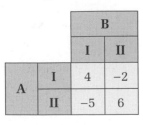

		B	
		I	II
A	I	4	−2
	II	−5	6

(EDEXCEL)

3 Roland and Colleen play a two-person, zero sum game. The table below shows the pay-off matrix for the game. The values in the table are the amounts won by Roland.

		Colleen	
		Stick	Twist
Roland	Stick	−1	4
	Twist	3	−2

a Find Roland's and Colleen's play-safe strategies, and hence show that this game does not have a stable solution.

b i State which strategy Roland should choose if he knows that Colleen will always choose her play-safe strategy.

  ii State which strategy Colleen should choose if she knows that Roland will always choose his play-safe strategy.

Roland and Colleen play the game a large number of times. Colleen uses random numbers to choose the Stick strategy with probability p.

c Show that the expected gain for Roland when he chooses the Stick strategy is given by $4 - 5p$, and find a similar expression for the expected gain for Roland when he chooses the Twist strategy.

d Use a graphical method to find the optimum value of p.

(OCR)

4 Rose is playing a computer game in which she has to defend a planet from aliens. She chooses a defence strategy and the computer chooses an attack strategy.

The number of points scored by Rose with each combination of strategies is shown in the table below.

		Computer		
		Fight	Shoot	Track
Rose	Delay	−2	−5	1
	Hide	3	4	6
	Negotiate	5	−1	2

Rose is trying to maximise the number of points that she scores, and the computer is trying to minimise the number of points that Rose scores.

a Find the play-safe strategies for Rose and the computer, and hence show that this game does not have a stable solution.

b   Explain why Rose will not choose the delay strategy.

c   Which strategy will the computer never choose to play?

Suppose that Rose uses random numbers to choose between her two remaining strategies, choosing the Hide strategy with probability p and the Negotiate strategy with probability $(1-p)$.

d   Find expressions for the expected gain for Rose when the computer chooses each of its remaining strategies.

e   Calculate the value of p for Rose to maximise her guaranteed return.

(OCR)

5   a   Formulate the game from question 4 as a Linear Programme.

b   Parts **b** and **c** of question 4 reduced the table to a 2 × 2 table. Formulate this reduced game as a Linear Programme, and use a graphical method to find Rose's optimum strategy.

Exercise B

1   Richard and Carol play a two-person zero-sum simultaneous play game. The table shows Richard's pay-off matrix for the game.

		Carol		
		Strategy X	**Strategy Y**	**Strategy Z**
	Strategy A	2	3	−2
Richard	**Strategy B**	−4	−1	−1
	Strategy C	−5	0	1

a   Find the play-safe strategy for each player, and hence show that this game does not have a stable solution.

b   Richard's optimal strategy can be found by Linear Programming. Set up a suitable LP formulation, defining the symbols you use, (you are **not** required to solve the LP problem).   *(OCR)*

2   The Rolling Pebbles have been playing as a band for many years. When they tour they sometimes play old songs, they sometimes play new songs and they sometimes play a mixture of old and new songs. Their choice depends upon the age of the audience. The table shows the audience reaction (as a score out of 10) for each of the possible combinations. High scores are good.

		Audience		
		Young	**Mixed**	**Older**
	Old	1	3	8
Songs played	**Mixture**	3	1	2
	New	8	5	3

Explain why, according to this data, the band should never choose to play a mixture of old and new songs.

The band do not know whether their audience will be young, older or of mixed ages. Suppose that they choose to play old songs with probability p and new songs with probability $1 - p$.

a Calculate, in terms of p, the expected reaction from each of the three types of audience.

b Use a graphical method to decide what value p should take to maximise the minimum expected reaction from part **a**. Mark clearly on your graph where the optimal value occurs.

(OCR)

3 Roy and Callum play a two-person, zero-sum game. The table below shows the pay-off matrix for the game. The values in the table are the amounts won by Roy.

		Callum	
		Strategy A	Strategy B
Roy	Strategy P	−1	1
	Strategy Q	4	−3

a Find Roy's and Callum's play-safe strategies, and show that this game does not have a stable solution.

b i State which strategy Roy should choose if he knows that Callum will always choose his play-safe strategy.

ii State which strategy Callum should choose if he knows that Roy will always choose his play-safe strategy.

Suppose that Roy uses random numbers to choose strategy P with probability p.

c Show that the expected gain for Callum when he chooses strategy A is given by $5p - 4$, and find a similar expression for the expected gain for Callum when he chooses strategy B.

d Use a graphical method to find the optimum value of p and the corresponding minimum expected gain for Roy.

(OCR)

4 Robin is playing a computer game in which he has to protect the environment. He chooses an energy source and the computer chooses the weather conditions.

The number of points scored by Robin under each of the combinations of energy type and weather conditions are given in the following table .

		Computer		
		Warm	**Windy**	**Wet**
	Atomic Energy	−6	3	5
Robin	**Bio-gas**	2	4	6
	Coal	5	1	3

Robin is trying to maximise his points total and the computer tries to stop him from doing so.

a Explain why Robin should not choose atomic energy and the computer should not choose windy weather.

b Find the play-safe strategies for the reduced game for Robin and for the computer, and hence show that this game does not have a stable solution.

Suppose that Robin uses random numbers to choose bio-gas with probability p and coal with probability $1 - p$.

c Show that the expected loss for the computer when it chooses warm weather is given by $5 - 3p$ and find a similar expression for the expected loss when it chooses wet weather.

d Use a graphical method to find the optimum value of p and the corresponding expected gain for Robin.

(OCR)

5 **a** Formulate the game from question 4 as a Linear Programme.

b Part **a** of question 4 reduced the table to a 2×2 table. Formulate this reduced game as a Linear Programme, and use a graphical method to find Robin's optimum strategy.

Applications and Extensions

The Prisoner's Dilemma

You and a friend have been arrested on suspicion of burglary, and are being held in separate cells. The police tell you that if you both confess, you will each get a 3 year sentence. If neither of you confesses, they will let you both go. If only one of you confesses, that person will go free, but the other will receive a 10 year sentence. What should you do?

Analysing games

Try analysing a game to see if you can work out an optimum strategy.

Summary

- A **zero-sum game** is one in which the gain of one player constitutes an equivalent loss for their opponent.

- In a **play-safe strategy**, each player chooses in order to minimise their worst-case scenario.

- If a pay-off matrix contains a **saddle point**, this will correspond to both players having a play-safe strategy with the same pay-off and leads to a **stable solution**.

- A strategy is **dominant** if every pay-off for that strategy is better than the corresponding pay-off for another strategy, in which case the weaker strategy can be eliminated from the game.

- In a **mixed strategy** a player varies their choice of strategy, according to a calculated ratio.

16 Decision Trees

What you need to know

● The meaning of an expected value

● How to construct a probability tree diagram

Review

1 Every day Tim plays a game to decide which household chore he does when he gets home. First he rolls a dice. If the score is even, he picks a card from a standard pack. If he gets a club, he does the ironing, which takes half an hour. If he gets any other card, he does the washing up, which takes 10 minutes. If the score on the dice was odd, he rolls a second dice. If he doesn't get a six, he decides to do nothing. If he gets a six, he cooks his brother dinner, which takes 40 minutes. Whichever chores he doesn't do, his brother has to do.

  a Represent this information on a tree diagram.

  b How long can Tim expect to spend doing his chore each evening?

  c How long will his brother expect to have to spend on chores each evening?

  d His brother gets fed up, and decides to load the second dice. What will he have to make the probability of getting a six if Tim is to expect to work for 20 minutes each evening?

16.1 Formulation

When planning a project or course of action, there are often a number of decisions to be made. Whilst at first sight these may appear to offer a complex problem, they can often be reduced to a series of decisions which can be taken one at a time, albeit that later decisions may be dependent on earlier ones.

One method of dealing with such scenarios is to draw a tree diagram – the root node representing the start of the project and each of the end branches representing the possible final outcomes. This is developed in the following example.

Example

Claire and Alan are planning to take part in their local sailing regatta. One of the races involves visiting a number of different points and returning to the start.

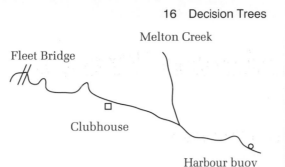

The race starts from the clubhouse at Woodham. They must go upriver to Fleet Bridge, down to the Harbour buoy, and up the other river to Melton Creek.

They consider the tides and wind strength and, based on previous years, estimate the following times for the race. If they go upstream first, the tides will be with them and the return trip will take about 2 hours rather than 3 hours if done at the end. The lower legs will take 4 hours if done first, but if done after going upstream, it could take $4\frac{1}{2}$ hours if the wind keeps up, but $5\frac{1}{2}$ hours if the wind drops off. The chance of the wind dropping is 0.4. Represent these choices, probabilities and timings as a Decision Tree.

Solution

We draw the following tree diagram. Rectangular boxes represent choices that Claire and Alan must make, circles are chance nodes – where they have no control over what will happen, and triangles are the pay-offs, or **expected monetary values** (EMVs) at the end of the branches.

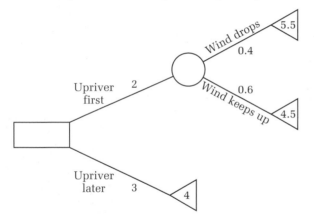

16.1 Formulation

Exercise

Contextual

For each of the situations described below, construct a decision tree, using the appropriate nodes and marking on costs and probabilities. Keep your answers safe, as you will need them in the next exercise.

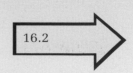

1 A game of tiddlywinks has reached a critical stage, and the player at the table must decide which of two strategies to follow. If she plays safe, she can be sure of ending the game with 4 points (out of a possible 7). If she attempts to pot out, she will get 7 points if she succeeds, but only 1 point if she fails. Based on previous games, the player thinks she has a $\frac{1}{3}$ probability of succeeding at a pot out.

2 Graham is playing a card game called tarot. He must decide whether or not to make a bid. If he bids, he will be allocated a partner at random from among the other players, who may or may not have a good set of cards. The probability that a random partner has a good set of cards is $\frac{1}{3}$. If he does not bid, one of three things may happen. No one else may bid, in which case there is no score for the round and the cards are re-dealt, which Graham thinks has a probability of $\frac{1}{2}$. If someone else bids, there is a 50 : 50 chance that Graham will be picked as that person's partner.

If Graham bids and gets a good partner, he will score 45 points. If he is given a bad partner, he will lose 30 points. If someone else bids and picks Graham, he will score 30 points. If someone else bids and Graham isn't picked, he will lose 20 points.

3 Aisha is going to visit a friend. She has to choose between two routes. The longer route uses motorways; the shorter route uses A-roads. From experience, Aisha knows that there is a 25% chance that the motorways will be busy, in which case her journey will take $2\frac{3}{4}$ hours rather than $2\frac{1}{4}$ hours. If she takes the A-roads, there is $\frac{2}{3}$ chance of a hold up, in which case the journey will take 3 hours rather than 2 hours.

4 John has left his revision to the last minute. The exam paper will ask questions on 2 out of the 4 topics on the syllabus, but he doesn't know which ones. John has time to revise 2 topics thoroughly, or to skim through all 4 topics.

If he does some revision for all 4 topics, he can expect to score 50% on the exam. If he revises only 2, his score depends on how many of those topics come up. If they both appear (probability $\frac{1}{6}$) he will expect to score 80%. If only one appears ($\frac{2}{3}$) he will expect to score 50%. If neither comes up, he will only score 20%.

16.2 Solution

We now need to use our tree to make our decision. This is done by a series of calculations and comparisons – working from the end nodes back towards the root of the tree.

Example

Find the route for Claire and Alan which is likely to give the shortest route.

Solution

We start at the right side. The upper branch on the chance node, which represents the wind dropping off (given that we have gone upstream first), has an expected value of $0.4 \times 5.5 = 2.2$ hours.

The next branch, representing the wind strength being maintained, has an expected value of $0.6 \times 5.5 = 2.7$ hours.

Adding these together gives a total expected value of 4.9 hours, which we place in the circle of our chance node and this becomes the EMV for that branch of the main tree.

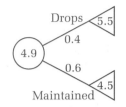

We now have a smaller tree to solve. The upper branch has a total cost of $2 + 4.9 = 6.9$ hours, whilst the lower is $3 + 4 = 7$ hours.

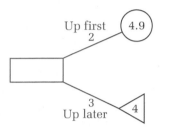

Since we want to minimise the time taken, we reject the lower branch as being a greater time and putting a line across it to show that we will not take that route. The EMV of 6.9 hours is inserted into the initial decision box. Our complete tree is shown below.

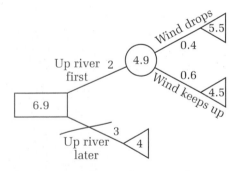

Our recommendation from our decision analysis is that Claire and Alan should go upriver first, taking a chance on the wind strength holding for the remainder of the race (their expected race times are either $6\frac{1}{2}$ or $7\frac{1}{2}$ hours).

16.2 Solution

Exercise

Contextual

Work through the Decision Trees you constructed for Exercise 16.1. In each case, find the best strategy, and state the expected value.

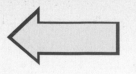

Consolidation

Exercise A

1 Work through the decision tree below to find the best strategy, and the EMV.

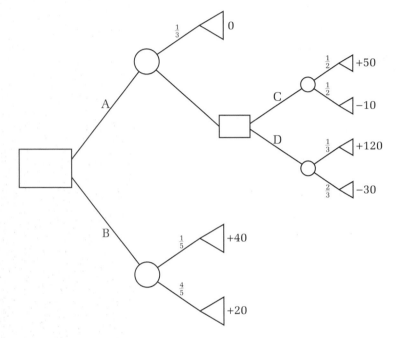

2 Work through the decision tree below to find the best strategy, and the EMV.

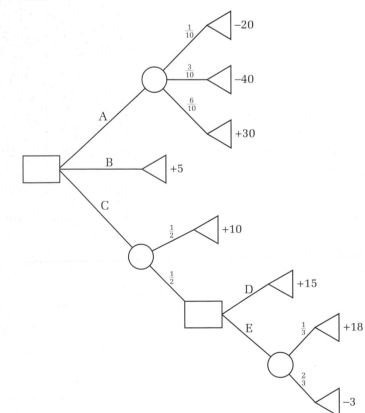

3 Find the value of p which gives an equal EMV for actions A and B.

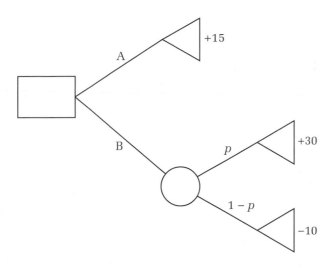

4 A decision has to be made regarding a project. It can be allowed to proceed (A), or it can be cancelled (~ A). Outcomes, pay-offs and probabilities are summarised in the decision tree below.

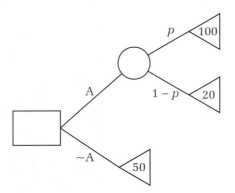

a If the EMV of proceeding is equal to the EMV of cancelling, show that $p = 0.375$.

b Advice can be sought on whether or not to proceed. If advice is sought then there is a probability of 0.2 that the advice will be to proceed, in which case the resultant probabilities will be more favourable. The values are summarised on the decision tree on page 266.

  i   Complete a copy of the tree, showing the EMVs.

  ii   What is the value of the advice?

  iii To what value would the cancellation payoff of 50 have to increase to make it worth not seeking advice?

(AQA)

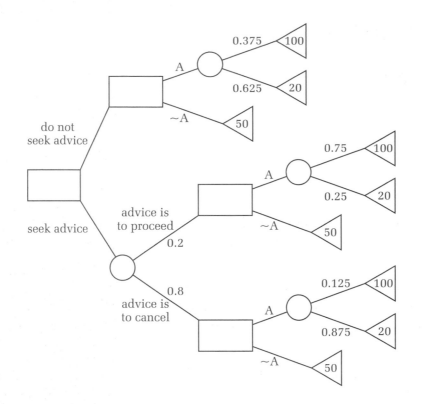

5 A hotel chain wants to build a new hotel on an unspoilt beach site. It has been suggested that the company should consult an environmental protection society for advice on developing environmentally friendly features, and to secure their support for the plans. In the past 60% of development projects submitted to the society have succeeded in securing the society's support.

If the society is not consulted there is a high probability (estimated at 0.60) of disruption from environmental action groups. With the society's support for the project the probability of disruption is much lower at 0.25. However if the society is consulted and withholds its support the probability of disruption is 0.90.

The company has two decisions to make – whether or not to consult the society, and whether or not to go ahead with the project.

In the past disruptive action has added 50% to the costs of construction projects. The company estimates that the cost of the development without interference will be 70 billion pesetas. Should it be decided, at any stage, to cancel the project, it is estimated that it would cost 100 billion pesetas in charges and to develop an alternative site.

a i Complete the decision tree for the company.

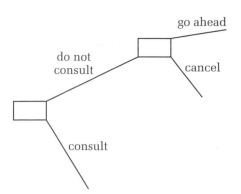

    ii Find the value of consulting to the company i.e. the difference between the expected cost of consulting and the expected cost of not consulting.

b An environmental action group realises that it can increase the worth of consulting the environmental society by increasing the probability p of disruption on projects which are going ahead without consultation.

    i What would be the value of consultation to the company if p were to be increased from 0.6 to 0.8?

    ii Find the maximum level to which the action group can raise the value of consultation, and give the minimum value of p which will achieve this.   *(AQA)*

Exercise B

1 Work through the decision tree below to find the best strategy, and the EMV.

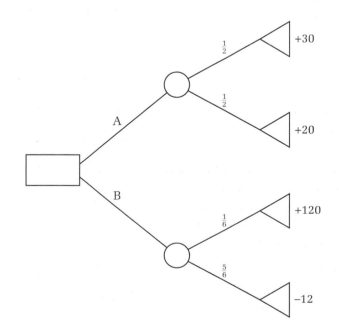

2 Work through the decision tree below to find the best strategy, and the EMV.

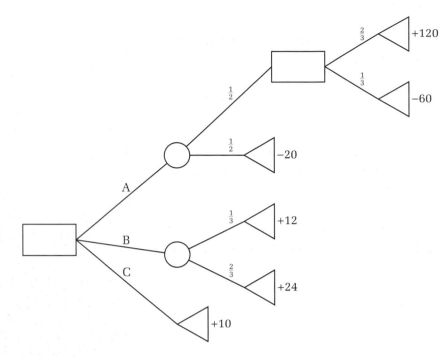

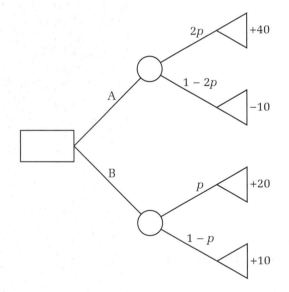

3 Find the value of p which gives an equal EMV for actions A and B.

4 Claudia will be working in London for five years. She has a decision to make about her accommodation.

She could sign a contract now to rent a house for five years at £12 000 per year.

There is a 50% chance that in a year's time she will inherit money which will provide her with a deposit to purchase a house. To allow herself that possibility she could sign a contract to rent for only one year for £13 200.

However, if the money does not become available, then she will have to sign a contract to rent for a further four years, and by that time rents will have increased to £13 500 per year.

If she inherits the money she will borrow the rest of the purchase price of the house. There are two options available.

Option A: a fixed rate loan which will cost £18 000 per year for the four years.

Option B: a variable rate loan which will cost £18 000 per year if interest rates stay steady, £15 000 per year if they fall, and £24 000 per year if they rise.

Claudia estimates that there is a 50% chance that interest rates will stay steady, a 30% chance that they will fall, and a 20% chance that they will rise.

Claudia also estimates that if she buys, she will make a £37,500 profit on re-selling the house at the end of her time in London.

a Complete Claudia's decision tree.

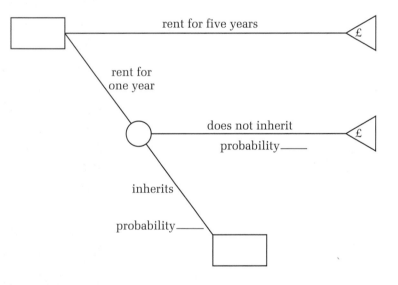

b Find how Claudia can minimise the expected cost of her accommodation. Give the decisions she should take and the expected cost.

c What would be Claudia's best decisions if the probability of inheriting the money is 40% instead of 50%? Justify your answer.

d To what level would the probability of inheriting the money have to fall to make it worthwhile for Claudia to enter into a five year rental contract?

(MEI)

5 A government has to decide how to dispose of nuclear waste material. One possibility is to build a long-term store immediately. This will cost £2500 million.

Alternatively the material can be put into temporary storage for 50 years, after which time the long-term store will be built. The total cost of this alternative depends on the general level of growth in the economy, and is shown in the table.

Growth of economy	total cost
low growth	£6100 million
medium growth	£2400 million
high growth	£1760 million

It is estimated that the probability of low growth is 30%, the probability of medium growth is 50%, and the probability of high growth is 20%.

a Complete the decision tree shown below by marking on outcomes and probabilities, and use it to find which is the best decision for the government to take. Give the cost advantage of that decision compared to the alternative.

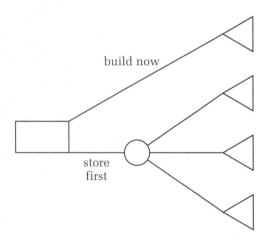

In reviewing the decision the government's economic spokesperson expresses the opinion that low growth will not occur. He estimates that the probabilities of medium growth and high growth are each 50%.

b Find the best decision, and the cost advantage of it, under these assumptions.

In the debate leading to the decision the opposition party calls for an independent enquiry to be set up. The government has to decide whether or not to agree to do so. If an enquiry is set up then a decision will have to be made whether or not to accept its recommendations.

c   Draw a modified decision tree to show all the alternatives:

- whether or not the government sets up an enquiry

- whether such an enquiry recommends building now or storing first

- whether the government decides to build now or store first

- the economic conditions (assuming that high, medium and low growth are all possible).

You are not required to show outcomes or probabilities, but you are required to show the correct structure of the decision tree. Only those nodes representing decisions that are within the control of the government should be shown as decision nodes.

(AQA)

Applications and Extensions

Real Decisions

The techniques introduced in this chapter can be used to analyse any situation involving decisions and outcomes which depend on chance. Investigate real world situations.

Summary

- A tree is drawn, with each path from root node to branch end representing a sequences of choices and chance events.

- The **expected monetary value (EMV)** of a node is the value of the route from that node onwards. The EMVs of end-nodes will be fixed, whilst those at chance and decision nodes will be calculated.

- A chance EMV is the expected value, calculated from all branches leading from it.

- A decision EMV is the largest (or smallest if the aim is to minimise) of the EMVs on each route onward. The route(s) not chosen are crossed through.

- The best decision is found by working from right to left, calculating EMVs and crossing off poor decisions.

17 Simulation

What you need to know

● How to calculate expected values

Review

1 Liz has kept a record of her scores on a computer game on the table below.

Score	1000	2000	3000	4000	5000
Frequency	12	16	10	19	23

If she plays another 10 games, what would she expect her total score to be for those 10 games?

17.1 Single Event Models

Simulation gives us a means of modelling outcomes when we are either unable to actually carry out the event (such as destructive tests) or when it would be impractical to do so (such as those with too great a timescale, or when we are investigating a variety of possible scenarios). Although some simulation is based on predetermined data, we are mostly interested in models which require the use of a random element.

Example 1

The number 42 bus is supposed to run at 20 minute intervals from 8 am to 1 pm. They are never early, and the probability of being late is given in the following table:

On time	1 min late	2 mins late	3 mins late	4 mins late	5 mins late
0.2	0.3	0.2	0.15	0.1	0.05

Using the following table of 2-digit random numbers, simulate the departures times for a morning, and calculate the average lateness.

12   41   74   53   74   48   33   23

51   59   35   80   63   10   32   97

Solution

We assign values to the probabilities as follows:

On time	1 min late	2 mins late	3 mins late	4 mins late	5 mins late
0.2	0.3	0.2	0.15	0.1	0.05
00–19	20–49	50–69	70–84	85–94	95–99

Now we can write out a table for our simulation, filling in first the random numbers, then the corresponding number of minutes late. For example, our first random number is 12. This is in the 00–19 category above so this represents the bus being on time (0 minutes late).

Time due	Random No.	Minutes late	Actual arrival
08:00	12	0	08:00
08:20	41	1	08:21
08:40	74	3	08:43
09:00	53	2	09:02
09:20	74	3	09:23
09:40	48	1	09:41
10:00	33	1	10:01
10:20	23	1	10:21
10:40	51	2	10:42
11:00	59	2	11:02
11:20	35	1	11:21
11:40	80	3	11:43
12:00	63	2	12:02
12:20	10	0	12:20
12:40	32	1	12:41
13:00	97	5	13:05
Total		28	
Average		$\frac{28}{16} = 1.75$	

This average will be considered further in Section 17.3

Example 2

Use a regular die to simulate a random walk in the four main compass directions. Estimate the average number of steps required to return to the starting point.

In a random walk, a sequence of steps is made with the direction of each being determined by chance.

Solution

Let 1 represent North, 2 for East, 3 for South, 4 for West. The scores 5 and 6 will be ignored.

We can place the problem on to co-ordinate axes, with the start point at the origin, and with East being the positive x-axis, North the positive y-axis, etc.

Die score	Direction	x	y
3	South	0	−1
3	South	0	−2
1	North	0	−1
4	West	−1	−1
6		−1	−1
1	North	−1	0
4	West	−2	0
5		−2	0
2	East	−1	0
6		−1	0
1	North	−1	1
4	West	−2	1
1	North	−2	2
5		−2	2
6		−2	2
5		−2	2
5		−2	2
3	South	−2	1
2	East	−1	1
3	South	−1	0
2	East	0	0

So in this first attempt it has taken 14 steps. However, to be more certain of how many steps it was likely to take, we would need to perform the simulation a number of times. This will be considered further in Section 17.3

17.1 Single Event Models

Exercise

Contextual

1 The table below shows the punctuality record of an employee collected over the previous 10 working days.

Minutes late	0	1 to 5	6 to 10	11 to 15	16 to 30
Frequency	2	4	2	1	1

a Explain how you would use random numbers to simulate the employee's likely punctuality over the next 20 days.

b Carry out the simulation.

c Use your simulation to calculate how many minutes, in total, the employee will be late by.

2 A student has collected the following data about weather patterns in December.

Weather	sunny	raining	snowing	foggy
Days	9	16	3	3

a Explain how you would use random numbers to simulate the weather for January, assuming it will follow the same pattern as December.

b Carry out the simulation.

3 Adapt the random walk example above to find the average number of steps needed to be at least 4 steps away from the starting point (measuring the distance away from the origin as a straight line).

4 A student is organising the catering to go with a school play. The table below gives data collected at a previous production showing how many drinks people bought.

Drinks	0	1	2	3	4
Frequency	23	35	22	13	7

a Explain how you would use random numbers to simulate the likely demand for drinks at the next performance.

b Carry out the simulation, assuming that 50 people will attend. (If you don't have access to a spreadsheet, you will find it easier to work with a partner on this question.)

Random numbers may be found from tables, or by using the function available on most scientific calculators. Alternatively a spreadsheet can generate the numbers and can also be programmed to perform the simulation if required.

17.2 Queuing

Many situations can be likened to a queue – an initial (arrival) event with an associated time, followed by a second event (service) and usually another associated time. Queuing simulations are quite common, though the principles can be applied to any multi-stage simulation.

Example

A garage is installing a new multi-function car wash to replace their existing one. Experience from other sites shows that 50% of users are likely to choose the rapid wash (3 minutes), 30% choose the standard (5 minutes), whilst the other 20% are prepared to pay extra for the deluxe (8 minutes).

By analysing their current car wash, the manager has got the following frequencies for the inter-arrival times of cars at the carwash:

Inter-arrival time	2 minutes	4 minutes	6 minutes	8 minutes
Frequency	2	5	6	1

Run the simulation using the random numbers

89, 69, 01, 06, 98, 93, 12, 23, 77, 04, 91, 65, 22, 31, 15, 48, 37

Calculate the average queuing time for cars arriving within the first 30 minutes.

Solution

We set up tables of values for our inter-arrival times and service times according to the proportions given in the question. Since the inter-arrival time frequencies add up to 14 and $100 \div 14 = 7.14$, we use 7 random numbers per customer from the survey, and reject the final two possibilities.

Inter-arrival time	
Range	Value
00–13	2
14–48	4
49–90	6
91–97	8
98–99	reject

Duration of wash	
Range	Value
00–49	3
50–79	5
80–99	8

The first random number is 89, corresponding to an inter-arrival time of 6 minutes. The second random number is 69, corresponding to the standard wash at 5 minutes. This starts immediately and therefore finishes at 11 minutes into the simulation.

The second car arrives 2 minutes later but the wash is not free until the 11th minute, so they queue for 3 minutes.

When the value of 98 is rejected the next value in the sequence is chosen.

The final table is as follows:

Random	Inter-Arrival Time	Random	Service Time	Actual Arrival Time	Start of Service	End of Service	Queuing Time
89	6	69	5	6	6	11	0
1	2	6	3	8	11	14	3
98 93	8	12	3	16	16	19	0
23	4	77	5	20	20	25	0
4	2	91	8	22	25	33	3
65	6	22	3	28	33	36	5
31	4			32	beyond 30 minutes		

The 6 cars in our simulation queue for a total of $3 + 3 + 5 = 11$ minutes, the average queuing time is $\frac{11}{6} = 1.83$ minutes.

The average queue length is found by dividing the total number of queuing minutes by the duration of the queue: $(3 + 3 + 5) \div 32 = 0.34$.

17.2 Queuing

Exercise

Contextual

Each of the following questions gives inter-arrival times, service times and frequencies. In each case:

a Show how you would use random numbers to simulate the queue.
b Run the simulation for an hour, and calculate the average queuing time.

Random numbers may be found from tables, or by using the function available on most scientific calculators. Alternatively a spreadsheet can generate the numbers and can also be programmed to perform the simulation if required.

1

Inter-arrival time	1 minute	2 minutes	3 minutes	4 minutes
Frequency	3	2	3	2

Service time	30 secs	1 minute	90 secs	2 minutes
Frequency	5	3	1	1

2

Inter-arrival time	1 minute	2 minutes	3 minutes	4 minutes
Frequency	4	6	3	2

Service time	30 secs	1 minute	90 secs	2 minutes
Frequency	2	4	3	2

3

Inter-arrival time	0 minute	1 minutes	2 minutes	3 minutes
Frequency	2	5	3	2

Service time	30 secs	1 minute	90 secs	2 minutes
Frequency	6	7	3	2

17.3 Reliability

Simulations do not guarantee to demonstrate what would happen in reality. Indeed, because they are subject to random variation, repeating a simulation will almost certainly give different results. If we perform our simulation a sufficient number of times and take the average of the results, we are likely to get a closer approximation to the expected outcome. But how many times do we need to repeat the simulation to be confident of the results?

Statisticians use a measure called **standard error**, which is calculated as $\sigma/\sqrt{n}$ where σ is the standard deviation of the data, and n is the number of data items. Our aim is for this standard error to be no bigger than our required accuracy. Since 95% of normally distributed data lies within two standard deviations of the mean, 95% confidence is often used, and so the measure $\frac{2\sigma}{\sqrt{n}} \leqslant$ *required accuracy* is required. By required accuracy, we mean the largest amount by which we would expect the mean to differ from our estimated value.

Example

In the example in Section 17.1, we simulated the lateness of buses. Use the measure of standard error to estimate the number of times the simulation needs to be run to have confidence in your estimate of the average delay to within half a minute.

Solution

By running the simulation a number of times, we can calculate the standard deviation in our number of steps. Our first attempt in Section 17.1 gave us an average of 1.75. If we also calculate the standard deviation for this data set, it is 1.29.

Since we want confidence to within half a minute, we require a standard error of less than 0.5.

Therefore we want to choose a value of n so that $\frac{2\sigma}{\sqrt{n}} \leqslant 0.5$. Rearranging gives $n \geqslant \left(\frac{2 \times 1.29}{0.5}\right)^2 = 26.67$ so we must run the simulation at least 27 times.

17.3 Reliability

Exercise

Contextual

In each of the following questions, you are referred back to one of the simulations you carried out earlier in the chapter. In each case, you should use the measure of standard error to estimate the number of times the simulation needs to be run to have confidence in your answer to within the specified amount.

In several cases you will need to run the simulation several times in order to calculate the standard deviation, unless you are able to calculate the standard deviation by applying theory learned in Statistics.

1 Exercise 17.1 question 1.
How often should you run the simulation to have confidence in your estimate of the total lateness to within 10 minutes?

17.1, 17.2

2 Exercise 17.1 question 2.
How often should you run the simulation to have confidence in your estimate of the number of rainy days to within

a 3 days   **b** 1 day?

3 Exercise 17.1 question 3.

How often should you run the simulation to have confidence in your estimate of the number of steps to within 1 step?

4 Exercise 17.2 question 1.

How often should you run the simulation to have confidence in your estimate of the total queuing time to within 2 mins?

5 Exercise 17.2 question 2.

How often should you run the simulation to have confidence in your estimate of the total queuing time to within 2 mins?

6 Exercise 17.2 question 3.

How often should you run the simulation to have confidence in your estimate of the total queuing time to within 2 mins?

Consolidation

Exercise A

Questions **1** – **2** give tables of information about queues, as in Ex. 17.2

1 a Show how you would use random numbers to simulate the queue.
   b Run the simulation for an hour, and calculate the average queuing time.

Inter-arrival time	1 minute	2 minutes	3 minutes	4 minutes
Frequency	4	2	3	1

Service time	30 secs	1 minute	90 secs	2 minutes
Frequency	5	3	1	1

2 a Show how you would use random numbers to simulate the queue.
   b Run the simulation for an hour, and calculate the average queuing time.

Inter-arrival time	1 minute	2 minutes	3 minutes	4 minutes
Frequency	3	5	3	2

Service time	30 secs	1 minute	90 secs	2 minutes
Frequency	2	4	3	2

3 A 'drive-through' fast food restaurant has a single lane for cars, alongside which are three windows. Two are for taking orders and one is for serving food. Once cars have entered the system no overtaking is possible.

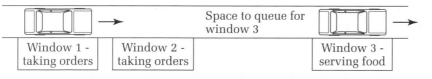

| Window 1 - taking orders | Window 2 - taking orders | | Window 3 - serving food |

A car arrives, queues if necessary, and is then sent either to window 1 or to window 2, where the driver places an order and pays. Having paid, the driver then moves forward to window 3 as soon as possible. At window 3 the food has to be collected, which may involve a wait.

a The time taken to order and pay (either at window 1 or window 2) has the following probability distribution.

Time (minutes)	$\frac{1}{2}$	1	$1\frac{1}{2}$	2	$2\frac{1}{2}$
Probability	$\frac{1}{10}$	$\frac{4}{10}$	$\frac{2}{10}$	$\frac{3}{10}$	$\frac{1}{10}$

(i) Complete the table to give a rule for using two-digit random numbers to simulate times for ordering and paying.

Random numbers	00–				
Time (minutes)	$\frac{1}{2}$	1	$1\frac{1}{2}$	2	$2\frac{1}{2}$

(ii) Use the following two-digit random numbers to simulate order and paying times for three cars.

73 98 14

Car number	1	2	3
Time			

b The time taken from paying until the food is ready for collection at window 3 has the following probability distribution.

Time (minutes)	$\frac{1}{2}$	$\frac{1}{2}$	$1\frac{1}{2}$
Probability	$\frac{1}{3}$	$\frac{1}{2}$	$\frac{1}{6}$

(i) Complete the table to give a rule for using two-digit random numbers to simulate these times. (Your rule should use as many two-digit random numbers as possible).

Random numbers	00–		
Time (minutes)	$\frac{1}{2}$	1	$1\frac{1}{2}$

(ii) Use the following two-digit random numbers to simulate three of these times.

30 24 98 49

Order number	1	2	3
Time			

c Use your times from parts (a) and (b) to simulate the time it takes to process three cars through the system using two different rules. The arrival times of the cars have been simulated for you. Start with all windows free. (The time taken for a car to move between windows should be ignored.)

Rule 1

If both window 1 and window 2 are free the next car is sent to window 2. If window 1 is free but window 2 is occupied the next car is sent to window 1.

Car	Arrival time (hrs:mins)	Window 1 or 2?	Time of arriving at window 1 or 2	Time of completing payment	Time of leaving window 1 or 2	Time of leaving system
1	12.00					
2	$12.01\frac{1}{2}$					
3	12.02					

Rule 2

If both window 1 and window 2 are free the next car is sent to window 2. If window 1 is free and window 2 is occupied it is sent to window 1 if the car at window 2 has been there for 1 minute or less; otherwise the next car is made to wait until window 2 is free

Car	Arrival time (hrs:mins)	Window 1 or 2?	Time of arriving at window 1 or 2	Time of completing payment	Time of leaving window 1 or 2	Time of leaving system
1	12.00					
2	$12.01\frac{1}{2}$					
3	12.02					

d Comment on your results from part **c**.

4 The time intervals between cars travelling along a one-way road are distributed as follows.

gap (seconds)	Less than 4 seconds (mean = 2 seconds)	Between 4 seconds and 10 seconds (mean = 7 seconds)	Between 10 seconds and 60 seconds (mean = 35 seconds)
Probability	$\frac{1}{2}$	$\frac{1}{6}$	$\frac{1}{3}$

a A student uses a table of random numbers to simulate the time intervals beween cars, using the rule:

$$00, 01, 02 \rightarrow 2 \text{ seconds}$$
$$03 \qquad\quad \rightarrow 7 \text{ seconds}$$
$$04, 05 \quad\; \rightarrow 35 \text{ seconds}$$
$$06\text{–}99 \quad\; \rightarrow \text{ignore}$$

Explain why this is an inefficient use of the random number table.

b Give a rule for using 2-digit random numbers. Use the mean time intervals to simulate time intervals between cars.

You should give an efficient rule.

c Use your rule, together with the list of 2-digit random numbers given below to simulate the fifteen intervals between sixteen cars. Read the random numbers from left to right.

Interval	1	2	3	4	5	6	7	8	9	10	11	12	13	14	15
Length (seconds)															
Cumulative time (for use in part (iv)															

Random numbers: 98 01 11 49 58 52 83 43 14 82 65
21 21 89 23 74 37

Other cars arrive from a side road at a junction with the main one-way road. They have to turn left to join the flow of traffic along the main road. They can turn out of the side road and on to the main road only when there is a gap of at least 10 seconds before the next car tavelling along the main road arrives at the junction.

When a car leaves the side road it takes 4 seconds for any car queuing immediately behind to move up to the junction

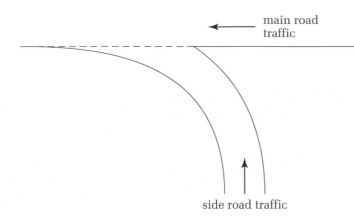

d The side road serves an industrial estate. Assume that in the late afternoon cars leave the estate at a steady rate of 6 per minute (one every 10 seconds exactly).

Using as many of your simulated time intervals between cars on the main road as are needed, simulate the arrival and departure times of six cars arriving at the junction along the side road. Start your simulation as the first car arrives at the junction from the side road, and assume that at that instant a car passes the junction along the main road.

Car Number	1	2	3	4	5	6
Time of arrival at junction (s)						
Time of departure from junction (s)						

e During the first 60 seconds of your simulation, what is the maximum length of the queue of cars from the side road at the junction?

Give the time interval during which the queue is at its maximum length.

Max length of queue: .... cars

Time: from .... to ....

f Suggest two ways in which the simulation might be improved.

Exercise B

Questions **1** – **2** give tables of information about queues, as in Ex. 17.2

1 a Show how you would use random numbers to simulate the queue.
b Run the simulation for an hour, and calculate the average queuing time.

Inter-arrival time	1 minute	2 minutes	3 minutes	4 minutes
Frequency	2	3	2	3

Service time	30 secs	1 minute	90 secs	2 minutes
Frequency	5	3	1	1

2 a Show how you would use random numbers to simulate the queue.
b Run the simulation for an hour, and calculate the average queuing time.

Inter-arrival time	1 minute	2 minutes	3 minutes	4 minutes
Frequency	1	7	5	1

Service time	30 secs	1 minute	90 secs	2 minutes
Frequency	2	4	3	2

3 The weather bureau in a particular country defines each day to be either wet or dry.

Records show that if the weather today is dry then the probability that it will be dry tomorrow is $\frac{4}{5}$, and the probability that it will be wet tomorrow is $\frac{1}{5}$. If the weather today is wet then the probability that it will be wet tomorrow is $\frac{2}{7}$, and the probability that it will be dry tomorrow is $\frac{5}{7}$.

Future weather is to be simulated. Each day a two-digit random number is to be used, together with a simulation rule based on that day's weather, to simulate the weather for the next day.

When the weather is dry the rule to be used is as follows:

$00 - 79 \longrightarrow$ weather tomorrow is dry
$80 - 99 \longrightarrow$ weather tomorrow is wet.

a Give a simulation rule to simulate the weather for a day following a wet day.

b The weather today is *dry*. Use the rules, together with the random numbers below, to simulate the weather for the next 14 days. Read the two-digit numbers from left to right.

Random numbers:

39 16 44 89 01 56 90 99 11 37 47 84 29 52 21
06 39 43 06 42 82 52 16 39 89 58 61 74 93 82

c Use the 14 results from your simulation to calculate an estimate of the overall proportion of wet days.

d Use the 14 results from your simulation to calculate an estimate of the probability of the weather tomorrow being the same as the weather today.

e Give two ways in which the simulation of the weather could be improved.

[MEI]

4 a A small post office has one server. Customer inter-arrival times follow the following distribution:

Inter-arrival times (minutes)	2	3	4
Probability	$\frac{1}{4}$	$\frac{1}{2}$	$\frac{1}{4}$

Using the following two-digit random numbers, simulate *five* inter-arrival times.

40 22 03 80 19 37 62 93

Describe the rule that you used to generate your inter-arrival times.

b Service times have the following distribution:

Length of service	1	2	4
Probability	$\frac{1}{3}$	$\frac{1}{2}$	$\frac{1}{6}$

Using the following two-digit random numbers, simulate service times for *six* customers.

35 92 78 98 16 06 31 34

Describe the rule that you used to generate your service times.

c Assuming that the service of the first customer has just begun, simulate the service of six customers. Number the customers from 1 to 6, and record your results in a copy of the table.

Customer number	Arrival time	Start of service	End of service
1	0	0	
2			
3			
4			
5			
6			

d Compute the mean queuing time (i.e. the mean of the times for which each customer queues), the mean length of the queue (i.e. the total time spent queueing divided by the total elapsed time) and the server utilisation (i.e. the percentage of elapsed time for which the server is busy).

e Say how the reliability of the results from your simulation could be improved.

Applications and Extensions

Queuing
Try using simulation techniques to model a queue in real life. You will need to collect data about actual inter-arrival and service times.

Spreadsheets
Try running some simulations on a spreadsheet. MS Excel has the following functions which you may find useful: rand, lookup, if, max, min. Other spreadsheets will usually have equivalents.

Game of Life
In the game of life, a cell lives and may breed if it has sufficient other cells nearby, but dies if it is isolated, or if it is smothered. Create a set of rules and investigate different starting patterns.

Summary

- A **simulation** is a means of modelling real life.

- Many simulations use a **random event**. This can be generated manually (e.g. with a die), from random number tables, or with a calculator or computer.

- In a simulation, each possible outcome will have an associated

18.1 Exploring Sequences

Exercise

Contextual

Give the next four terms of each of the following sequences.

1   a $u_n = 2u_{n-1} + 3$ $u_0 = 3$ **2** $u_n = 3u_{n-1} + 2$ $u_0 = 3$

3   a $u_n = 5u_{n-1} + 1$ $u_0 = 2$ **4** $u_n = 7u_{n-1}$ $u_0 = 2$

5   a $u_n = -u_{n-1} + 2$ $u_0 = 3$ **6** $u_n = u_{n-1} + 2$ $u_0 = 3$

18.2 Linear First Order

A first order recurrence relation is one in which each value is expressed in terms of only the previous ones. If the expression is linear, then it only involves a multiple of the previous one, and possibly a constant. The solutions are given as follows:

Type	Form	Solution
1st order homogeneous	$u_n = au_{n-1}$	$u_n = a^n u_0$
1st order non-homogeneous	$u_n = au_{n-1} + b$	$u_n = \lambda a^n + \mu \quad a \neq 1$ $u_n = u_0 + nb \quad a = 1$

These solutions are derived from the summation of series in Pure Mathematics.

Example 1

On his fifth birthday Matthew starts receiving 50p pocket money per week. He is promised a 20% increase every year on his birthday. How much will he get on his tenth birthday?

Solution

A 20% increase means multiplying by 1.2. The recurrence relation is therefore $u_n = 1.2u_{n-1}$

Matthew's tenth birthday is in 5 years time, so we want $n = 5$; $u_0 = 50$p
From the table of solutions on the previous page, $u_n = 1.2^n u_0$
$u_5 = 1.2^5 \times 50 = 124.4 = £1.24$

Example 2

A gardener has dandelions in her lawn and tries to remove them. Each year she manages to remove 80% of the plants, but unfortunately gains 12 new ones from seeds blowing in from her neighbour's garden.

a Write a recurrence relation to describe the number of dandelions in her lawn, and solve it to find a formula for the number of dandelions in n years time, u_n, in terms of the number now, u_0.

b If she currently has 150 plants, how many will she have in 3 years time? Will she ever get rid of them?

Solution

a Removing 80% means leaving 20% so each year is 20% of the previous, plus 12 new ones.

$u_n = 0.2u_{n-1} + 12$

From the table of solutions we know that it will be of the form
$u_n = \lambda 0.2^n + \mu$

putting $n = 0$ gives $u_0 = \lambda + \mu$
putting $n = 1$ gives $u_1 = 0.2\lambda + \mu$, but we know that $u_1 = 0.2u_0 + 12$

$$u_0 = \lambda + \mu$$
$$0.2u_0 + 12 = 0.2\lambda + \mu$$

subtracting gives $0.8u_0 - 12 = 0.8\lambda$
so $\lambda = (0.8u_0 - 12) \div 0.8 = u_0 - 15$
$\mu = u_0 - \lambda = 15$

$u_n = (u_0 - 15) \times 0.2^n + 15$

b $u_0 = 150$
$u_3 = (150 - 15) \times 0.2^3 + 15 = 135 \times 0.008 + 15 = 16.08$

As n gets large, 0.2^n will become very small and so the term $(u_0 - 15) \times 0.2^n$ will approach zero. However, the +15 means that the number of dandelions will never reach 0, but will stabilise at 15.

18.2 Linear First Order

Exercise

Technique

Solve each of the recurrence relations given in Exercise 18.1.
Check that you have got the right answer by using your solution to calculate u_4 in each case.

18.3 Second Order Homogeneous

A second order recurrence relation is one in which each value is expressed in terms of the previous two values. If it is also homogeneous, then there is no other constant involved, and it can therefore be written in the form $u_n + au_{n-1} + bu_{n-2} = 0$.

The solution is found by considering the quadratic equation $m^2 + am + b = 0$, where a and b are the coefficients from the recurrence relation.

If this quadratic has real distinct roots p and q, then the solution to the recurrence relation is given by $u_n = Ap^n + Bq^n$ where A and B are constants to be found.

If the quadratic has a repeated root p, then the solution is given by $u_n = (A + Bn)p^n$.

The case where the quadratic has complex roots is similar, but beyond the scope of this book.

> If you have studied 2nd order differential equations, you may recognise the form of these solutions.

Example

Strawberry plants are propagated from runners – new plants growing on the end of a stalk from the main plant. One year old plants produce an average of 2 runners each, whilst two year-old plants produce an average of 3. The runners from older plants are removed and not used.

a Formulate and find the general solution for a recurrence relation to model the number of new plants each year.

b If a nursery starts with 1 new plant in year 0, how many new plants will there be in the 6th year?

Solution

a Number of new plants $u_n = 2u_{n-1} + 3u_{n-2}$
Re-arranging to required format gives $u_n - 2u_{n-1} - 3u_{n-2} = 0$

Auxiliary equation (quadratic) $m^2 - 2m - 3 = 0$
$$(m + 1)(m - 3) = 0$$
$$m = -1 \text{ or } 3$$
General solution is $u_n = A(-1)^n + B3^n$

b $u_0 = 1$

Since one year old plants produce 2 runners, $u_1 = 2$

Using the general solution:

$1 = A + B$ {$n = 0$ so the powers disappear}
$2 = -A + 3B$ {$n = 1$}

adding gives $3 = 4B$ so $B = 0.75$, $A = 0.25$

Solution: $u_n = 0.25(-1)^n + 0.75 \times 3^n$
In the 6th year, $u_6 = 0.25(-1)^6 + 0.75 \times 3^6$
$$= 0.25 + 0.75 \times 729$$
$$= 547 \text{ new plants}$$

If we had defined the start as year 1 rather than year 0, we would have different values of A and B, but the resulting sequence would be unchanged.

18.3 Second Order Homogeneous

Exercise

Technique

For each of the following recurrence relations:

a find the general solution
b find the particular solution for the given values of u_0 and u_1
c check that your answer is correct by finding u_3 both from your solution and by finding the next two terms using the original formula.

1 | $u_n = 2u_{n-1} + 3u_{n-2}$ $u_0 = 1$ $u_1 = 2$

2 | $u_n = 3u_{n-1} - 2u_{n-2}$ $u_0 = 3$ $u_1 = 1$

3 | $u_n = -u_{n-1} + 2u_{n-2}$ $u_0 = 4$ $u_1 = 4$

4 | $u_n = 6u_{n-1} - 9u_{n-2}$ $u_0 = 2$ $u_1 = 3$

5 | $u_n = 2u_{n-1} - 0.75u_{n-2}$ $u_0 = 2$ $u_1 = 1$

18.4 Second Order Non-homogeneous

A non-homogeneous equation has an additional term to those considered in Section 18.3. This term can be a constant, or a function of the value of n (i.e. relating it to the position in the sequence).

To solve these recurrence relations requires a specific solution which satisfies the full relationship, and adding this to the general solution of the associated homogeneous equation.

The general rule for finding a specific solution is to choose a multiple of a general function of the same order. For example, if the function is $3n^2$, choose a general quadratic $an^2 + bn + c$.

Example

The strawberry grower discovers that from the second year onwards, $2n$ new plants will be rejected as being substandard.

Formulate and solve the recurrence relation as before.

Solution

Number of new plants $u_n = 2u_{n-1} + 3u_{n-2} - 2n$

The associated homogenous equation is $u_n - 2u_{n-1} - 3u_{n-2} = 0$ as before and has general solution $u_n = A(-1)^n + B3^n$.

We now seek a specific solution to satisfy the additional function:

Let $u_n = pn + q$
Then $u_{n-1} = p(n-1) + q$ and $u_{n-2} = p(n-2) + q$
Substituting into the initial recurrence relation gives

$pn + q = 2(p(n-1) + q) + 3(p(n-2) + q) - 2n$
$pn + q = 2pn - 2p + 2q + 3pn - 6p + 3q - 2n$
$\quad\quad = 5pn - 8p + 5q - 2n$

Equating coefficients of n gives $p = 5p - 2$ so $p = 0.5$.
Equating constants gives $q = -8p + 5q$ so $q = 1$.

General solution is therefore $u_n = A(-1)^n + B3^n + \frac{1}{2}n + 1$.

Again using $u_0 = 1$ and $u_1 = 2$ and substituting into the general solution:

$1 = A + B + 1$ {$n = 0$ so the powers disappear}
$2 = -A + 3B + \frac{1}{2} + 1$ {$n = 1$}
adding gives $3 = 4B + 2\frac{1}{2}$ so $B = \frac{1}{8}$ and $A = -\frac{1}{8}$

Note that we must use a general linear equation here, even though our function did not have a constant term in it.

Specific solution: $u_n = -\frac{1}{8}(-1)^n + \frac{1}{8} \times 3^n + \frac{1}{2}n + 1$

In the 6th year, $u_6 = -\frac{1}{8}(-1)^6 + \frac{1}{8} \times 3^6 + \frac{1}{2} \times 6 + 1$
$$= -\frac{1}{8} + \frac{729}{8} + 3 + 1$$
$$= 95$$

18.4 Second Order Non-homogeneous

Exercise

Technique

Solve each of the recurrence relations given below.

1 $u_n = 2u_{n-1} + 3u_{n-2} + 2n$ $u_0 = 1$ $u_1 = 2$

2 $u_n = 6u_{n-1} - 9u_{n-2} + 0.5n$ $u_0 = 2$ $u_1 = 3$

3 $u_n = 2u_{n-1} - 0.75u_{n-2} - 2n^2 + 3$ $u_0 = 2$ $u_1 = 1$

Consolidation

Exercise A

1 A shrub with six new twigs is purchased from a garden centre. The shrub is of a type in which every year a new twig develops at the base of each old twig. New twigs do not develop at the base of twigs which are in their first year, but they do in subsequent years.

Let u_n be the number of twigs n years after purchase, so that $u_0 = 6$, $u_1 = 6$ and $u_2 = 12$.

a Find u_3, the number of twigs on the shrub three years after it was purchased.

b Explain why $u_{n+1} = u_n + u_{n-1}$ $(n \geqslant 1)$

c   i   Solve the recurrence relation to find an expression for u_n in terms of n.

    ii   Show that your expression gives the correct value for u_2.

At the end of year 5 the gardener prunes a number of old twigs (without losing any of the newest growth) so as to keep the shrub healthy and under control.

d How many twigs are there at the end of year 5 (i.e. u_5), and how many of these are old twigs (i.e. u_4)? How many old twigs should the gardener prune at the end of year 5 so that there are exactly 60 twigs at the end of year 6 (i.e. so that $u_6 = 60$)?

e Given that pruning as in part **d** above has taken place, so that there are 60 twigs at the end of year 6, how many of the 60 twigs are old and how many are new? Prove that the gardener will not be able to achieve $u_7 = 60$ by pruning old twigs at the end of year 6.   *(AQA)*

2 A charity worker writes to a number, w, of her friends asking each for a £1 donation towards the charity. Suppose that a number x of those friends each donate £1 and in turn write to w of their friends repeating the request, etc. Call the worker's letters 'level 1' letters, and the letters from the worker's immediate friends 'level 2' letters etc.

Suppose that whenever w letters are written x result in both a £1 donation and in w further letters being written, and the remainder are ignored.

a Express the number of letters written at level 2 in terms of w and x.

Give an expression for the total amount of money donated as a result of level 1 and level 2 letters.

b Let u_n be the number of letters written at level n. Explain why the recurrence relation for u_{n+1} in terms of u_n is $u_{n+1} = xu_n$.
Assuming $x > 1$, solve the recurrence relation to give u_n in terms of w and x.

c Let v_n be the total amount of money donated as a result of letters at levels 1 through to n inclusive. Show that $v_{n+1} = v_n + x^{n+1}$.
Solve the above recurrence relation to give an expression for v_n in terms of w and x.

d Given that $w = 6$ and $x = 3$ find u_{10} and v_{10}.
Should the charity worker expect to her scheme to raise this much money? If not, why not?   *(AQA)*

3 **a** Solve the recurrence relation $u_{n+1} = au_n + b$ (where a and b are constants and a $\neq$ 1), given that $u_0 = c$.

b Sketch a graph of u_n against n in the case where a = 0.5, b = 10, and c = 0.   *(AQA)*

4 In a model for the growth of a population, p_n is the number of individuals at the end of n years. Initially the population consists of 1000 individuals.

In each calendar year the population increases by 20% and on December 31st 100 individuals leave the population. Thus $p_1 = 1200 - 100 = 1100$.

a   Calculate the value of p_2.

b   Write down a first-order recurrence relation between p_{n+1} and p_n, and solve it to find p_n as a function of n.

c   Calculate the smallest value of n for which $p_n > 10\,000$.   *(OCR)*

5   A 100 litre tank of water has been polluted with liquid waste. Initially the pollution is at a concentration of 10%; this means that the tank contains 90 litres of pure water and 10 litres of liquid waste well mixed together.

The pollution is reduced by taking 10 litres of fluid out of the tank and replacing it with 10 litres of pure water. You may assume that the fluid that remains in the tank mixes completely with the pure water that is added.

Let c_n% be the concentration of the pollution after this dilution procedure has been carried out n times. The value of c_0 is 10.

a   Work out the values of c_1 and c_2.

b   Write down a first-order recurrence relation between c_{n+1} and c_n. Determine how many times the dilution process must be carried out to reach a concentration of pollution that is less than 1%.   *(OCR)*

Exercise B

1   Grundy the gardener cuts a lawn to a length of 1 cm. He notes that, on average, the growth during the $(n+1)$th day after a cut is 0.8 times the growth during the nth day after a cut. His report on this to Lord Whimsey states that $G_{n+1} = 0.8G_n$.

Lord Whimsey, keen to use his mathematical ability to organise the estate's activities efficiently, decides to model L_n, the length of grass n complete days after a cut.

a   Explain why the recurrence relation for L_{n+1} in terms of L_n and G_n is $L_{n+1} = L_n + G_{n+1}$.

b   Given that $G_{n+1} = 0.8 \times G_n$ and that $G_n = L_n - L_{n-1}$, produce a second order recurrence relation giving L_{n+1} in terms of L_n and L_{n-1}.

c   You are given that $G_1 = 1$, so that $L_1 = 2$ (because $L_0 = 1$). Solve your recurrence relation to find an expression for L_n in terms of n.

Grundy has no time for new-fangled ideas such as second order recurrence relations. He argues that if

$$G_{n+1} = 0.8G_n \text{ and } G_1 = 1, \text{ then } G_n = (0.8)^{n-1} \text{ and } \sum_{i=1}^{n} G_i = 5 - 5(0.8)^n$$

d   Grundy aims to cut the lawn when it reaches a length of about 4 cm. How often should he cut the lawn (to the nearest whole number of days)?

e   If the lawn grows for 200 days per year, approximately what will be the total length of grass that he cuts in a year?

f   What will be the approximate total length cut in the year if he cuts it only when it has reached a length of 4.7 cm?   *(AQA)*

2   An engine's cooling system has a capacity of 10 litres. It leaks at the rate of 1 litre per week. Initially, at time 0, the system is full, and contains water only. Every week (i.e. at times 1, 2, 3 ...) it is topped up with a litre of antifreeze mixture of concentration 25% (a mixture of 750 ml of water and 250 ml of antifreeze).

a   What is the concentration of antifreeze in the cooling system after it has been topped up at time 1?

b   How much antifreeze will leak from the system during the following week?

c   How much antifreeze is there in the system after it has been topped up at time 2? What is its concentration?

Let u_n be the number of millilitres of antifreeze in the system immediately after the top-up at time n. Let c_n be the concentration.

d   Express u_{n+1} in terms of u_n.

e   Express c_{n+1} in terms of c_n.

f   Give the long-run concentration, i.e. the value to which c_n tends as n becomes large.   *(AQA)*

3   Robbie keeps stick insects. At the beginning of week n Robbie has u_n stick insects, and $u_1 = 600$.
The population is modelled as follows.
In the middle of the week the population is multiplied by the factor 1.5, and at the end of the week 200 stick insects die.

a   Calculate the values of u_2 and u_3.

b   Write down a recurrence relation between u_{n+1} and u_n.

c   Solve the recurrence relation in part **b**, and hence find u_n in terms of n.

(OCR)

4   Katie takes out a loan for £1000. At the end of each month she is charged interest on her debt at 2% on the outstanding loan, and she then pays off £X of her debt.

a   Write down a first-order linear recurrence relation between u_n and u_{n+1} where £u_n is the amount owing at the start of month n, and $u_1 = 1000$.

b   Solve the recurrence relation in part **a** to express u_n in terms of n and X.

c   The loan is to be paid off in 18 months. Use your answer to part **b** to find the value of X.   *(OCR)*

5 Consider the second-order recurrence relation

$u_{n+2} = 2u_{n+1} + 3u_n$, $n \geqslant 0$ with $u_0 = 1$, $u_1 = 2$.

a Find the values of u_2 and u_3.
b Obtain u_n as a function of n. *(OCR)*

Applications and Extensions

Spreadsheets

Model some recurrence relations on a spreadsheet. Set the initial values and produce a formula, which can be replicated down the column. Beware that row numbers only match 'n' value if you start at $n = 1$ (some relations start at 0) and you put no column headings in.

Logarithms and Exponential Equations

Find out about logarithms and their use in solving exponential equations such as $a^n = b$. If you have found a formula for u_n in terms of n, and want to know when u_n will first exceed a given value, you can solve an exponential equation. This is covered in Chapter 7 of the Pure Mathematics book in this series.

Summary

- A **recurrence relation** is one in which each value is defined in terms of previous values and constants.

- A **first order equation** only involves the previous term of the sequence, a second order the previous two etc.

- Solutions can be found as follows:

Type	Form of equation	Solution
1st order homogeneous	$u_n = au_{n-1}$	$u_n = a^n u_0$
1st order non-homogenous	$u_n = au_{n-1} + b$	$u_n = \lambda a^n + \mu$ $a \neq 1$ $u_n = u_0 + nb$ $a = 1$
2nd order homogeneous	$u_n + au_{n-1} + bu_{n-2} = 0$	solve $m^2 + am + b = 0$ $u_n = Am_1^{\ n} + Bm_2^{\ n}$
2nd order non-homogeneous	$u_n + au_{n-1} + bu_{n-2} = f(n)$	$u_n = Am_1^{\ n} + Bm_2^{\ n} + g(n)$

19 Logic and Boolean Algebra

19.1 Propositional Logic

In this section we will look at how statements can be represented using symbols. We will be using the following symbols, which are explained in more detail in the example below.

∧ and   ⇒ if ... then
∨ or   ⇔ if and only if
~ not

When these symbols are combined with letters representing individual propositions, the results are often referred to as **Boolean expressions**.

Example

Use the symbols of propositional logic to write down a Boolean expression to represent the statements:

a Black cats are unlucky and elephants are memorable.
b Black cats are unlucky or elephants are memorable.
c Black cats are lucky.
d If I bribe my teacher then I will pass my exams.
e If I score more than 40% I will pass my exams, and if I pass my score will be more than 40%.

Solution

First we must identify individual elements of these statements, and represent them with letters. Let:

p = black cats are unlucky
q = elephants are memorable
r = I bribe my teacher
s = I pass my exams
t = my score is more than 40%

We then proceed to write down the statements using the letters we have chosen and the symbols defined above.

a $p \wedge q$
   Note that ∧ has the identical meaning to 'and' in English.

Another name for this topic is *Formal Logic*. Thi is because the subject is concerned with the form of statements, not with the meanings of the individual propositions, or even whether the statements make sense in the real world.

b $p \lor q$

Note that in English 'or' is ambiguous. The question: 'Would you like tea or coffee?' could be answered with 'tea' or 'coffee' but not 'both'. However, the question 'Are you studying Maths or Physics?' could well get the answer 'both'. In logic, we use or in the second, **inclusive**, sense.

c Lucky is the opposite of unlucky. We can rewrite this statement as 'Black cats are not unlucky' so the answer is $\sim p$.

d $r \Rightarrow s$

This example is relatively straightforward. In English, there are different ways of saying if ... then. For example, we could also say that I won't pass my exams unless I bribe my teacher.

e This is a much stronger implication than in **d**. In **d**, if I pass my exam you don't know that I bribed my teacher – I might have done enough revision to pass honestly. However, the consequence of combining the two statements made in this question is that as well as knowing that a score of 40% means I passed, you also know that if I passed my exams, then I scored more than 40%. This is an example of **if**, **and only if**, so the answer is $t \Leftrightarrow s$. (This is equivalent to saying $(t \Rightarrow s) \land (s \Rightarrow t)$.)

> In formal logic, we say that r implies s. Implication is a difficult concept, and its exact meaning depends on which set of logical rules you are using.

19.1 Propositional Logic

Exercise

Technique

Let p = 'It is raining'
Let q = 'I am carrying an umbrella'
Let r = 'I am on holiday'

1 Express the following in English:

  a $q \Rightarrow p$

  b $p \land r$

  c $\sim q$

  d $p \land \sim r$

  e $(p \land \sim q) \Rightarrow r$

  f $\sim p \Rightarrow \sim r$

  g $r \Rightarrow p$

2 Express the following using p, q, r and logical symbols:

  a If it is raining then I am not carrying an umbrella.

  b I am on holiday or it is raining.

c   I am carrying an umbrella or it is raining.

d   If it is raining then I am holiday and not carrying an umbrella.

e   It is raining unless I am carrying an umbrella.

f   It is raining unless I am not on holiday.

19.2 Switching Circuits

Example 1

The diagram below shows an electrical circuit. It contains a battery, three switches and a bulb. In order for the bulb to light, the switch labelled a must be closed, and so must at least one of the switches labelled b and c.

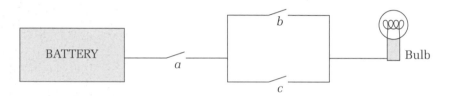

Write down a Boolean expression equivalent to the switching circuit.

Solution

For the bulb to light, a must be true AND so must b OR c. We can write this as $a \wedge (b \vee c)$.

Example 2

Draw a switching circuit equivalent to the propositional statement:
$a \vee (b \wedge c)$.

Solution

The $\vee$ indicates that there are going to be two possible routes; $\wedge$ means that there will be two switches in a row.

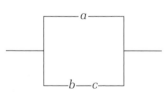

Example 3

Simplify the switching circuit drawn below.

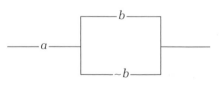

If you are familiar with electrical circuits you ma[y] find it helpful to think of $\wedge$ as the same as 'in series' and $\vee$ as the same as 'in parallel'.

Note that the battery and the bulb are not drawn in and the position of the switches is indicated by the letters without drawing the physical switch.

Solution

For the bulb to light, switch a must be on. Once we have got past a, there are two possible routes. If b is on, we can take the upper route. If b is off, we can go via the bottom route. (It may help to think of a switch labelled $\sim b$ to be like a traffic light – cars travelling in one direction may only be able to go if the light in the opposite direction is not green.)

This means that whether b is on or off doesn't matter – the only bit of the circuit that makes a difference is a, and we could do without the other two switches, leaving the circuit below.

———a———

We say that these two circuits are **equivalent** because they always produce the same output given the same inputs.

19.2 Switching Circuits

Exercise

Technique

1 Write down a Boolean expression equivalent to each of the switching circuits below:

a
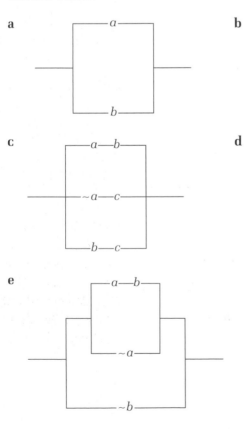

b
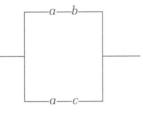

c

d

e
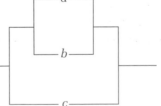

2 Draw a switching circuit equivalent to each of the following Boolean expressions.

    a $(\sim b \wedge c) \vee (b \wedge \sim c)$

    b $(a \wedge b \wedge c) \vee (\sim a \wedge \sim b \wedge c) \vee (a \wedge b \wedge c)$

19.3 Truth Tables

Most statements are sometimes true and sometimes false, but some are always true or always false. These are equivalent to circuits which are designed so that the light is always on (or always off). A statement which is always true is a **tautology**. A statement which is never true is a **contradiction**. Sometimes two statements are **equivalent** to each other.

This section will look at ways of establishing whether two propositions are equivalent, and whether a proposition is always true, sometimes true or never true. To do this, we need to define the concept of a truth table.

A **truth table** is a way of showing whether a complex statement ends up being true or false for each of the possible combinations of truth and falsity of its components.

Example 1

Construct the truth table for the statement $a \wedge b$.

Solution

We draw up a table with a column for each of the components a and b, and another column for the overall statement. We then have one row for each possible combination of true and false for a and b, and decide what the truth of the overall statement is for each combination.

a	b	$a \wedge b$
F	F	F
F	T	F
T	F	F
T	T	T

The statement is true only if both the inputs are true, so it will only be true in the last row.

Notice that we have used T and F instead of true and false. This is the traditional approach, but it is nowadays more common to use 1 to represent true and 0 to represent false. This reflects the crucial links between logic of this type and the principles of computing. This results in the table below.

a	b	$a \wedge b$
0	0	0
0	1	0
1	0	0
1	1	1

Notice the order in which the combinations of 1 and 0 were listed. Counting in binary, from 00 to 11, ensures that no combination is left out, and also enables us to have standard truth tables.

Example 2

Construct truth tables for the statements

a $\sim a$
b $a \vee b$
c $a \Rightarrow b$
d $a \Leftrightarrow b$

Solution

a

a	$\sim a$
0	1
1	0

b

a	b	$a \vee b$
0	0	0
0	1	1
1	0	1
1	1	1

Remember we define $\vee$ to be inclusive – see page 301.

c

a	b	$a \Rightarrow b$
0	0	1
0	1	1
1	0	0
1	1	1

This always seems strange at first sight. This truth table arises because we consider a statement to be true unless we can prove it to be false (innocent until proved guilty). The only way to prove an if ... then statement false is for the first part to happen, and then for the second part to fail to happen. For example, if a teacher said to you: if you buy this book you will pass your exam, you might:

● *not buy the book* – in which case you could never prove that they were lying. This is represented in the first two lines of the truth table.
● *buy the book and fail* – in which case you decide they were lying (or perhaps they meant you had to read it as well!) – the third line.
● *buy the book and pass* – in which case they appear to be telling the truth – the fourth line.

This is similar to the assumption in law that a suspect is innocent until proven guilty.

d

a	b	$a \Leftrightarrow b$
0	0	1
0	1	0
1	0	0
1	1	1

This table was constructed by remembering that $a \Leftrightarrow b$ means the same as $(a \Rightarrow b) \wedge (b \Rightarrow a)$. Constructing the table for this compound statement, we get:

Note the use of brackets to ensure that the statement is unambiguous

a	b	$a \Rightarrow b$	$(a \Rightarrow b) \wedge (b \Rightarrow a)$	$b \Rightarrow a$
0	0	1	1	1
0	1	1	0	0
1	0	0	0	1
1	1	1	1	1

Note that it is often helpful to highlight the column representing the overall statement. This is always the last column to be filled in.

Example 3

Use truth tables to decide whether the following statements are **tautologies**, **contradictions** or neither.

a $a \wedge \sim a$
b $a \vee \sim a$
c $a \vee b$

Solution

a

a	$\sim a$	$a \wedge \sim a$
0	1	0
1	0	0

This statement is never true, so it is a contradiction.

b

a	$\sim a$	$a \vee \sim a$
0	1	1
1	0	1

This statement is always true, so it is a tautology.

c

a	b	$a \vee b$
0	0	0
0	1	1
1	0	1
1	1	1

This statement is sometimes true, sometimes false, so it is neither a tautology nor a contradiction.

Example 4

Use truth tables to show that the statements $\sim a \vee \sim b$ and $\sim(a \wedge b)$ are equivalent.

This is one of de Morgan's rules. This result appears again on page 311.

Solution – Truth Tables

We construct the truth tables for each statement separately, and note that the final result is the same in each case.

a	b	$\sim a$	$\sim b$	$\sim a \vee \sim b$
0	0	1	1	**1**
0	1	1	0	**1**
1	0	0	1	**1**
1	1	0	0	**0**

a	b	$a \wedge b$	$\sim(a \wedge b)$
0	0	0	**1**
0	1	0	**1**
1	0	0	**1**
1	1	1	**0**

This shows that the overall value of each statement is the same, given the same combination of inputs, so the two statements are equivalent.

It is important to realise that if two statements are equivalent, then if one is true the other must be true, and if one is false the other must be false, i.e. one is true if and only if the other is true.

This leads to a different way of setting out our solution. Rather than constructing two separate truth tables, we construct a single table for the compound statement $\sim a \vee \sim b \Leftrightarrow \sim(a \wedge b)$. This has the advantage of not needing duplicate columns for a and b (which is perhaps of limited benefit in this case, but could be very helpful when dealing with more variables).

These two approaches are equally valid, and it is up to you which you prefer to use. However, the concept that equivalent statements imply each other is an important one.

a	b	$\sim a$	$\sim b$	$\sim a \vee \sim b$	$\sim a \vee \sim b \Leftrightarrow \sim(a \wedge b)$	$a \wedge b$	$\sim(a \wedge b)$
0	0	1	1	**1**	1	0	**1**
0	1	1	0	**1**	1	0	**1**
1	0	0	1	**1**	1	0	**1**
1	1	0	0	**0**	1	1	**0**

Here we have used bold to indicate the main connective in each of the separate statements, and then shaded the column giving the value of $\Leftrightarrow$. Since this final column is all 1s, we conclude that $\sim a \vee \sim b \Leftrightarrow \sim(a \wedge b)$ is a tautology and so the two statements are equivalent.

19.3 Truth Tables

Exercise

Technique

1 By drawing up truth tables for the following statements identify two pairs of equivalent statements.

a $p \wedge \sim q$ **b** $\sim p \wedge \sim q$ **c** $\sim(p \vee q)$
d $\sim q \Rightarrow \sim p$ **e** $\sim p \Rightarrow \sim q$ **f** $p \Rightarrow q$

2 Draw up truth tables for the following statements:

a $(\sim b \wedge c) \vee (b \wedge \sim c)$
b $(a \wedge b \wedge c) \vee (\sim a \wedge \sim b \wedge c) \vee (a \wedge b \wedge \sim c)$

3 Use truth tables to decide whether the following statements are tautologies, contradictions or neither.

a $(p \wedge (p \Rightarrow q)) \Rightarrow q$
b $[(p \wedge q) \wedge (p \Rightarrow r)] \Rightarrow r$
c $[(p \vee q) \wedge (p \Rightarrow r)] \Rightarrow r$
d $[(p \Rightarrow q) \wedge \sim q] \Rightarrow \sim p$
e $[(p \vee r) \wedge (r \Rightarrow q) \wedge (p \Rightarrow q)] \Rightarrow q$
f $\sim(p \vee \sim q) \Rightarrow \sim p$
g $[((p \wedge q) \vee r) \wedge ((p \vee r) \Rightarrow s)] \Rightarrow s$

19.4 Combinatorial Circuits

In this section we look at a very common practical application of the concepts discussed so far.

Computers are based on silicon chips containing millions of **logic gates**. These logic gates take binary input, and ultimately produce what you see on the screen. The gates, and the standard symbols for them, are given below.

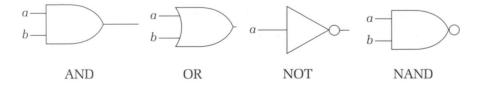

AND   OR   NOT   NAND

A NAND gate has output of 0 if both its inputs are 1, otherwise the output will be 1.

These gates have the same truth tables as the equivalent propositional expressions. For example a AND $b \equiv a \wedge b$.

Example 1

Show that a NAND gate is equivalent to an AND gate followed by a NOT gate.

Solution

We can do this using a truth table.

a	b	$a \wedge b$	$\sim(a \wedge b)$
0	0	0	1
0	1	0	1
1	0	0	1
1	1	1	0

The column for $\sim(a \wedge b)$ matches the definition given above, so the two are equivalent.

> NAND gates are important because any circuit can be replaced with an equivalent circuit constructing only using NAND gates.

Example 2

Construct a combinatorial circuit which is equivalent to $(a \vee b) \wedge (\sim c \wedge a)$.

Solution

The main connective is AND, with its two inputs being an OR gate and another AND. One of the inputs to this second AND gate is NOT.

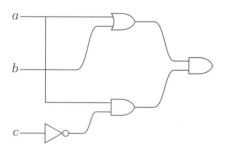

Notice that although a is used as an input to two gates, it is only listed once on the left hand side, with two branches coming off it.

Example 3

Express the following combinatorial circuit using a Boolean expression.

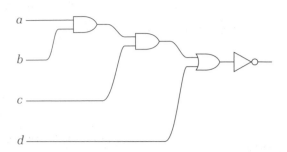

Solution

Working from right to left, the last gate is NOT, coming after an OR, so the whole circuit must be ~(? ∨ ?).

One of the inputs is d, the other is an AND gate, so the circuit is ~[(? ∧ ?) ∨ d].

This AND gate has two inputs. One is just c, the other is another AND gate, with inputs a and b, so the final expression is ~[((a ∧ b) ∧ c) ∨ d].

19.4 Combinatorial Circuits

Exercise

Technique

1 Write down a Boolean expression equivalent to each of the following combinatorial circuits:

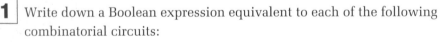

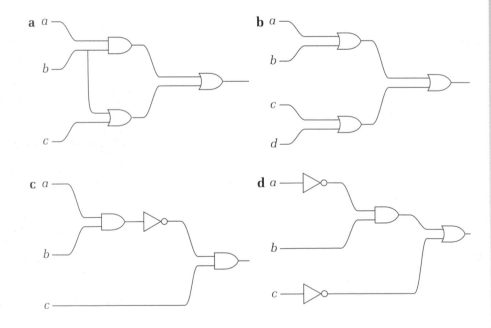

2 Draw a combinatorial circuit equivalent to each of the following Boolean expressions:

   a $(\sim b \wedge c) \vee (b \vee \sim c)$
   b $(a \wedge b \wedge c) \vee (\sim a \wedge \sim b \wedge c) \vee (a \wedge b \wedge c)$

19.5 Boolean Algebra

You will have noticed a lot of similarities between the examples and exercises in the previous sections. On the surface statements involving words, switching circuits and combinatorial circuits may seem to have little in common, but we have seen that they can all be represented using Boolean expressions. This section looks at the theory which underpins the concepts of modern logic.

Boolean Algebra is the term used to describe the rules which can be used to manipulate statements of the form that we have been using. It is based upon the idea of equivalent expressions. Some of these equivalences will be proved in the example below; others are left for you to derive for yourselves.

You may recognise some of these rules from work you have done using Venn Diagrams, since Boolean algebra also applies to set theory.

Distributive rules

$a \wedge (b \vee c) \equiv (a \wedge b) \vee (a \wedge c)$
$a \vee (b \wedge c) \equiv (a \vee b) \wedge (a \vee c)$

Associative rules

$a \wedge (b \wedge c) \equiv (a \wedge b) \wedge c$
$a \vee (b \vee c) \equiv (a \vee b) \vee c$

Commutative rules

$a \vee b \equiv b \vee a$
$a \wedge b \equiv b \wedge a$

Double negation

$\sim(\sim a) \equiv a$

Absorption rules

$a \wedge (a \vee b) \equiv a$
$a \vee (a \wedge b) \equiv a$

De Morgan's rules

$\sim(a \vee b) \equiv \sim a \wedge \sim b$
$\sim(a \wedge b) \equiv \sim a \vee \sim b$

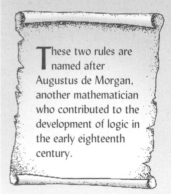

The notation used in this section was devised by George Boole in 1847, and the rules for using these symbols is named after him.

There are also distributive, associative and commutative rules in the algebra of numbers, which are similar but not identical to the rules in Boolean Algebra.

These two rules are named after Augustus de Morgan, another mathematician who contributed to the development of logic in the early eighteenth century.

Identity and complement rules

Where 0 and 1 stand for expressions which are tautologies or contradictions.

$a \wedge a \equiv a$ $a \wedge \sim a \equiv 0$

$a \vee a \equiv a$ $a \vee \sim a \equiv 1$

$a \wedge 0 = 0$ $a \wedge 1 \equiv a$

$a \vee 0 = a$ $a \vee 1 \equiv 1$

Example 1

Use the rules of Boolean Algebra to simplify $[(b \wedge a) \vee (b \wedge c)] \wedge (\sim a \wedge b)$

Solution

$[(b \wedge a) \vee (b \wedge c)] \wedge (\sim a \wedge b)$

$= [b \wedge (a \vee c)] \wedge (\sim a \wedge b)$ **distributive rule**

$= b \wedge (a \vee c) \wedge \sim a \wedge b$ **removing unnecessary brackets**

$= b \wedge b \wedge (a \vee c) \wedge \sim a$ **commutative rule**

$= b \wedge (a \vee c) \wedge \sim a$ **identity**

$= b \wedge [(\sim a \wedge a) \vee (\sim a \wedge c)]$ **distributive rule**

$= b \wedge [0 \vee (\sim a \wedge c)]$ **complement**

$= b \wedge \sim a \wedge c$ **identity**

Example 2

Use Venn diagrams to show that $\sim a \wedge \sim b$ and $\sim (a \vee b)$ are equivalent statements.

Solution

To use Venn diagrams, we need to replace $\vee$ with $\cup$ and $\wedge$ with $\cap$.

$\sim (a \vee b)$ is everything which is not in a or in b.

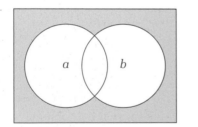 $\sim a \wedge \sim b$

$\sim a \wedge \sim b$ is the intersection (overlap) of $\sim a$ and $\sim b$

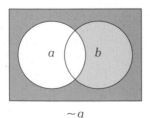   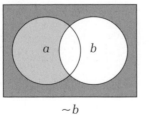

$\sim a$ $\sim b$

Since these two diagrams shade the same area, they have the same meaning, so the two expressions are equivalent.

Activity

Check the result in Example 1 using Venn diagrams.

19.5 Boolean Algebra

Exercise

Technique

Prove the following statements, using the laws of Boolean Algebra

1 $(a \wedge b) \vee (a \wedge c) \equiv a \wedge (b \vee c)$

2 $(a \vee b) \wedge (a \wedge b) \equiv (a \wedge b)$

3 $(a \wedge b) \vee (a \wedge \sim b) \equiv a$

4 $a \wedge [(b \wedge c) \vee (b \wedge \sim c)] \equiv a \wedge b$

5 $\sim a \wedge (\sim b \vee a) \equiv \sim (a \vee b)$

Consolidation

Exercise A

1 Use a truth table to prove that the following two statements are equivalent:

If the north wind blows then we shall have snow.
If we have no snow then the north wind does not blow.

(AEB)

2 **a** Write down a Boolean expression for the following circuit.

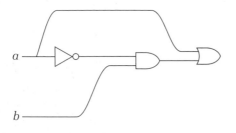

b Show, algebraically or otherwise, that your expression reduces to
a ∨ b

(AEB)

3 A two-way switch is a device which has two connected switches
arranged so that when one part is open, the other is closed, and vice
versa. It is convenient to label the two connected parts as (say) A and ~A.
When a two-way switch is operated (flicked) then A closed and ~A open
is changed to A open and ~A closed, or vice versa.

a There are two two-way switches, switch A and switch B, controlling
the light in a room. The circuit below controls the flow of current.
Describe what happens when a switch is flicked.

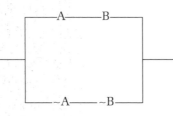

b The light in a room is to be controlled in such a way that flicking any
one of three separate switches will turn a light on if it is off, and off it
is on. Design a circuit which will achieve this.

(AEB)

4 **a** The logical connective NAND ↑ is defined by

$a \uparrow b = \sim(a \wedge b)$

Give the truth table of NAND
b Give a combinatorial circuit equivalent
to this which uses **only** a NAND gate.
c Give a combinatorial circuit equivalent
to this which uses **only** NAND gates.

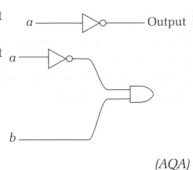

(AQA)

Exercise B

1 Consider the following switching circuit:

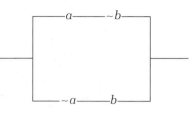

a Write down a Boolean expression for the circuit.

b Use the distributive rules to prove that the Boolean expression for the circuit is equivalent to $(a \lor b) \land (\sim a \lor \sim b)$.

c Use part **b** to draw an alternative, equivalent switching circuit to that given in part **a**.

(AQA)

2 a The following is a combinatorial circuit for a half adder:

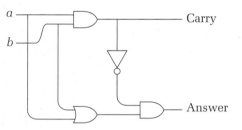

Draw a table of inputs and associated outputs.

b The following circuit uses two half adders:

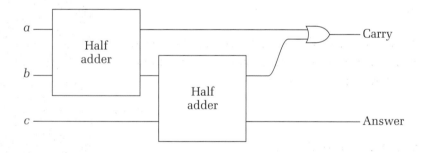

Draw a table of associated inputs and outputs, and explain briefly the purpose of the circuit.

(AQA)

3 Each member of a committee has a button to press in order to register a 'Yes' vote on a proposal. Design two different circuits for the buttons of a committee with three members, which will allow current to pass only when two or more members press their buttons.

(AEB)

4 'Use a truth table to show that (a and b) AND (a if...then b) is a valid argument.'

AND should be replaced with an upside down ∨; if...then with a double-arrow pointing to the right

Below is the question repeated, hopefully with the symbols correct (depends on your e-mail program)

'Use a truth table to show that $(a \wedge b) \wedge (a \Rightarrow b) \Rightarrow b$ is a valid argument.'

Applications and Extensions

Valid arguments

Another important application of logic is in evaluating arguments. Consider the following:

If the moon is made of green cheese it will taste good. The moon is made of green cheese. Therefore the moon will taste good.

Is this a valid argument?

If a = the moon is made of green cheese
    b = the moon tastes good
then the argument can be rewritten as

$$[(a \Rightarrow b) \wedge a] \Rightarrow b$$

You should be able to use truth tables to show that this is valid. This means that

$$(a \Rightarrow b) \wedge a \equiv b$$

This is an important rule, which can be used to simplify arguments without using truth tables. Try using this rule to decide which of the statements in Exercise 19.3 question 3 are valid arguments.

Lighting circuits

Try designing a lighting circuit that is to be controlled by several switches, and use the techniques of Boolean Algebra to simplify the resulting circuit.

Note that validity refers to the structure of the argument, not the truth of the conclusion. If a valid argument has a false conclusion, then one of the premises of the argument must be false.

Summary

- **Boolean Expressions** consist of statements, represented by letters, and symbols representing the connections between the statements.

- **Boolean Algebra** contains a set of rules for manipulating Boolean Expressions.

- **Switching circuits**, **Combinatorial circuits** and **Venn diagrams** are alternative ways of representing Boolean Expressions.

- **Truth tables** show whether a Boolean Expression is true or false for each possible combination of input values.

- **Symbols to learn**

and	∧	
or	∨	
not	~	
not NAND	↑	
if ... then	⟹	

20 Coding

What you need to know

● How to add in modulus arithmetic

When adding in modulus arithmetic we ignore any carried over digits. In this chapter we will be using Mod(2).

When adding in Mod(2), the answer is the remainder when the total is divided by 2.

$0 + 0 = 0$
$1 + 1 = 0$
$0 + 1 = 1$
$1 + 1 + 1 = 1$

A simpler way of looking at this is that if there is an odd number of 1s, the answer is 1; if there is an even number of 1s the answer is 0.

● How to multiply matrices

Multiplying matrices involves multiplying an element in a row of the first matrix by the corresponding element in a column of the second matrix and adding the results of those calculations.

In this chapter you will only need to be able to pre-multiply a column vector (a 1 dimensional matrix) by a matrix. This means your answer will also be a column vector, with the same number of rows as the first matrix.

$$\begin{pmatrix} 1 & 2 & 3 \\ 4 & 5 & 6 \end{pmatrix} \times \begin{pmatrix} 7 \\ 8 \\ 9 \end{pmatrix} = \begin{pmatrix} 1 \times 7 + 2 \times 8 + 3 \times 9 \\ 4 \times 7 + 5 \times 8 + 6 \times 9 \end{pmatrix} = \begin{pmatrix} 50 \\ 122 \end{pmatrix}$$

In this chapter we will be multiplying matrices using Mod(2) addition, as shown below.

$$\begin{pmatrix} 1 & 0 & 1 \\ 0 & 1 & 1 \end{pmatrix} \times \begin{pmatrix} 1 \\ 0 \\ 1 \end{pmatrix} = \begin{pmatrix} 1 \times 1 + 0 \times 0 + 1 \times 1 \\ 0 \times 1 + 1 \times 0 + 1 \times 1 \end{pmatrix} = \begin{pmatrix} 1 + 0 + 1 \\ 0 + 0 + 1 \end{pmatrix} = \begin{pmatrix} 0 \\ 1 \end{pmatrix}$$

You may have come across this topic under the name of *clock arithmetic*.

This is similar to what happens when working in base 2 (binary), but with the important difference that we are not carrying digits across. In binary, $1 + 1 = 10$.

Matrices have important applications throughout mathematics, and are a field of study in their own right.

Review

1 Calculate the following:

a $\begin{pmatrix} 2 & 1 & 3 \\ 1 & 4 & 2 \end{pmatrix} \times \begin{pmatrix} 5 \\ 3 \\ 1 \end{pmatrix}$ **b** $\begin{pmatrix} 3 & 5 & 2 \\ 6 & 0 & 4 \end{pmatrix} \times \begin{pmatrix} 2 \\ 1 \\ 3 \end{pmatrix}$ **c** $\begin{pmatrix} 1 & 2 & 2 & 3 \\ 3 & 1 & 5 & 2 \end{pmatrix} \times \begin{pmatrix} 4 \\ 7 \\ 6 \\ 8 \end{pmatrix}$

2 Calculate the following, working in Mod(2).

a $\begin{pmatrix} 1 & 1 & 0 \\ 0 & 1 & 1 \end{pmatrix} \times \begin{pmatrix} 1 \\ 0 \\ 1 \end{pmatrix}$

b $\begin{pmatrix} 1 & 1 & 0 & 1 & 1 \\ 0 & 1 & 1 & 0 & 1 \\ 0 & 1 & 1 & 1 & 0 \end{pmatrix} \times \begin{pmatrix} 1 \\ 1 \\ 0 \\ 1 \\ 0 \end{pmatrix}$

c $\begin{pmatrix} 1 & 0 & 1 & 1 & 0 & 1 & 0 \\ 1 & 1 & 1 & 0 & 0 & 0 & 1 \\ 0 & 1 & 1 & 0 & 1 & 1 & 0 \end{pmatrix} \times \begin{pmatrix} 1 \\ 1 \\ 0 \\ 1 \\ 1 \\ 0 \\ 0 \end{pmatrix}$

20.1 Check Digits

When most people think of codes, they think of secrecy – the use of codes to disguise information and prevent other people reading your messages. This chapter looks at a very different use of codes – ways of making it easier for other people to read your messages. In particular, it looks at ways of letting the person reading your message know that a mistake has been made, and that what they are looking at is not what you wrote. Barcodes appear in lots of places, from shopping to library books to bank

cards. The lines in the code represent numbers – which are often also written below the barcode. However, what happens in cases like the picture above, where the barcode has been creased/crumpled? It would be inconvenient to have to type in a number manually every time the barcode is slightly damaged. This chapter will look at ways of adding extra information to messages so that the recipient can check whether they have received the correct message, and even correct mistakes without having to ask the sender for confirmation.

Example

Paul has written down his phone number for Ben, and wants to check that Ben can read his handwriting, but is fed up with repeating his number. What could he do to enable Ben to check that he has read the number correctly.

Solution 1 – Totals

Paul's number is 507400. The digits should add up to
$5 + 0 + 7 + 4 + 0 + 0 = 16$. He tells Ben this total, by writing down his number as 50740016.

When Ben adds up the digits of what he thinks is Paul's phone number, he gets the total 25. He knows he has misread the number, but he doesn't know where the mistake is. It could be that he has mistakenly read a 9 instead of one of the 0s, but he doesn't know which one.

Solution 2 – Repetition

Since his handwriting is so bad, Paul decides that when he gives his phone number to Ben, he will write it down twice. He writes 507400507400, but he doesn't get a call from Ben. Next time they meet, he asks what went wrong.

'I read your number as 507400507409' said Ben. 'I knew it must be the last number that was wrong, but I didn't know which was right – 0 or 9'.

Solution 3 – ISBN numbers

Paul has been reading about ISBN numbers. They contain 9 numbers which identify the book, and an extra check digit at the end. The check digit is calculated by multiplying each of the first nine digits by a different number, from 10 down to 2, and adding up the total. The check digit is the smallest number that needs to be added to make the grand total an exact multiple of 11.

For example, for the book with ISBN 0 3491 0649 5, This gives the result in the table below.

Digit	0	3	4	9	1	0	6	4	9	
Multiplier	10	9	8	7	6	5	4	3	2	
Result	0	27	32	63	6	0	24	12	18	Total = 182

The next multiple of 11 is 187, so the check digit is 5.
Paul decides to modify this system. Because there are only 6 digits in his phone number, he multiplies the first digit by 7, and will be looking for the next multiple of 8 to find the check digit, as shown below.

Digit	5	0	7	4	0	0	
Multiplier	7	6	5	4	3	2	
Result	35	0	35	16	0	0	Total = 86

Paul could of course just write his number out lots of times, but that takes a lot of time.

The next multiple of 8 is 88, so the check digit is 2. What Paul writes down is 5074002.

Ben understands this system. When he looks at what Paul has written down, he sees 5074092. He uses the method above, and gets the following result:

Digit	5	0	7	4	0	9	
Multiplier	7	6	5	4	3	2	
Result	35	0	35	16	0	18	Total = 104

Adding the check digit gives a total of 106.

Ben knows that 106 is not a multiple of 8. The nearest multiples of 8 are 104 and 112. Assuming he has only read one digit incorrectly, he needs to change one digit to reduce the total by 2 or increase it by 6. This gives him two possibilities: 517409 and 507400.

Activity

The following is a valid ISBN number. What does the X stand for, and why is it needed?

0 3251 1322 X

We are assuming that.
- the check digit is correct
- that only one digit is correct
- that the incorrect digit is only out by 1.

The assumption that the minimum possible correction should be made continues through out the chapter.

20.1 Check Digits

Exercise

Contextual

1 Calculate the check digits for the following phone numbers using **i** the totals method of Example 1, and **ii** the method used in Example 2.

   a 653409
   b 212308

2 A phone number has been written down, using repetition, as 402345412345402345. What is the most likely correct number?

3 Calculate the ISBN check digit for the following numbers.

   a 0 1245 3109
   b 0 0032 2370

4 The following is an invalid ISBN number. Assuming that the check digit is correct, and that only one digit is incorrect, what is the most likely correct number?

1006152473

20.2 Binary Codes

The examples in the previous section used arabic numbers. However, computers work in binary, and since many of the applications of coding apply to messages transmitted from one computer to another, for the rest of this chapter we will focus on binary codes.

A binary code is made up of **codewords** each of which consists of 1s and 0s. If a **word** has an even number of 1s, we say that it has even **weight**. A 100% **efficient** code is one that uses the minimum number of bits. As we shall see, this can have disadvantages, so we will also need to measure the efficiency of codes which make use of extra bits.

In all codes, individual **codewords** are often simply referred to as **words**. This does not mean that they are necessarily words in any language.

Example 1

A satellite regularly transmits a brief message to Earth to indicate its current status. There are 8 possible states it could be in.

a What is the minimum number of bits needed to transmit all possible states?

b How can an extra digit be added to each word to check whether it has been received correctly?

c How efficient is this code?

When dealing with binary codes, a digit is usually referred to as a **bit**.

Solution

a In a binary system, each additional digit doubles the number of possible words. $8 = 2 \times 2 \times 2$, so the satellite will need to use a 3 bit code. The set of words is 000, 001, 010, 011, 100, 101, 110, 111.

b One way of adding an extra digit would be to make sure that the final word has an even **weight**. This results in the final set of codewords 0000, 0011, 0101, 0110, 1001, 1010, 1100, 1111.
If the ground station receive the word 1000, they will know that a mistake has been made. However, they will not know whether the correct word was 0000, 1001, 1100 or 1010.

c The final code is a 4-digit code. The maximum number of 4-digit words is 2^4. However, only 8 of these possible words are used. Since $8 = 2^3$, the efficiency of this code is $\frac{3}{4}$.
Without the parity check digit, the code would use 2^3 out of 2^3 possible words, giving an efficiency of $\frac{3}{3} = 1$.

Example 2

It is simpler to programme the satellite to send a longer code word than to send a message asking it to repeat an incorrect word. How can repetition be combined with a parity check digit to make it less likely that the ground station will have to tell the satellite to repeat a word?

Solution

Simply repeating a word would give a 6-digit word. However, if the received word was 000001, the ground station would not know whether the correct word was 000000 or 001001. Adding a check digit to make a 7-digit word would give a code set of

0000000
0011001
0101010
0110011
1001100
1010101
1100110
1111111

If the received word was 0000001, the ground station would expect that the correct word was 0000000.

The check digit of the original 3 bit code appears in the middle column, and is not repeated. This is only one of several possible arrangements. For example, each bit could be sent twice in a row, followed by a check digit at the end. This would make the 7th word 1111000.

20.2 Binary Codes

Exercise

Technique

1 Add a check digit to each of the following 4-digit codewords.

   a 1011   **b** 1100   **c** 0010

2 Which of the following codewords, which include a parity check digit at the end of the word, are incorrect?

   a 01011   **b** 01101   **c** 10011

3 How efficient is the 7-digit code word in Example 2?

4 The following codewords come from a system using a 4-digit codeword, a check digit, and repetition. In each case, decide if the word is correct and, if it is not correct, give the most likely intended word.

   a 100101001   **b** 110101001   **c** 001010000

20.3 Hamming Distance

In the example in Section 20.1, Ben had a problem because Paul's 0s looked a lot like 9s. It is unlikely that Ben would have mistaken a 0 for a 4, however badly it had been written. In general, mistakes are more likely to be made if the different words in a code are similar to each other.

In a binary code, we are only dealing with 1s and 0s, which are not very similar. However, interference during the transmission (e.g. a bad telephone connection), can cause some of the 0s to turn into 1s, and vice-versa. Consequently, code designers will try to ensure that the words in their code are as different as possible. The measure of how different the words in a code set are is called the **Hamming Distance**, abbreviated as δ ('*delta*').

> The Hamming distance is named after RW Hamming, who introduced the concept in 1950.

Example 1

A code is to consist of 2 different 4-digit words.

a How different can they be?
b How many errors in such a code can be corrected?
c How many errors in such a code can be detected?

Solution

a If the two words are 0000 and 1111, then these words differ in each digit, so the code set has a Hamming distance of 4.

Parts **a** and **b** of this question are clearly related. We shall tackle them by considering what would happen in the case of 1, 2, or 3 errors occurring with a transmitted codeword.

b If there is one error, then if the received word is read as 0010, the intended word must have been 0000. So if there is only one error, the receiver can work out the correct codeword.

c However, if there were two errors, then the received word 0011 could have been intended to be 1111 or 0000. In this case, the receiver will have detected the presence of errors, because the word is incorrect, but will not know what the correct word was.
If there are three errors, then a word sent as 0000 might arrive as 1110. In this case, the receiver would assume that only one error had been made, and would think that the correct word was 1111. In this case the receiver would have detected the presence of errors, but was not able to correct them.
Overall, we conclude that this code will correct one error, and detect 2 or 3.

Activity

Why do we not need to consider 4 or more errors?

Example 2

a What is the Hamming distance of the code set below?
b How many errors can be detected and corrected?

Word 1	1	1	1	1
Word 2	1	1	0	1
Word 3	0	0	0	1
Word 4	0	0	1	0

Solution

a Words 1 and 2 differ in 1 place (3rd).
   Words 1 and 3 differ in 3 places (1st, 2nd and 3rd).
   Words 1 and 4 differ in 3 places (1st, 2nd and 4th).
   Words 2 and 3 differ in 2 places (1st and 2nd).
   Words 2 and 4 differ in all 4 places.
   Words 3 and 4 differ in 2 places (3rd and 4th).
   The Hamming distance is the distance between the two most similar words, which is 1.
b This means that in the worst case scenario, a word transmitted as 1101 might arrive as 1111, and the receiver would have no way of knowing that an error had occurred. Consequently, for this code we say that no errors can be detected (or corrected), even though in some cases errors would be picked up.

Example 3

What is the connection between Hamming distance and error detection and correction?

Solution

If δ is even, then $\frac{\delta}{2}$ errors can be detected, and $\frac{\delta-2}{2}$ errors can be corrected.

If δ is odd, then $\frac{\delta-1}{2}$ errors can be detected, and $\frac{\delta-1}{2}$ errors can be corrected.

Activity

Test out this theorem with your own set of codewords, and see if you can understand why it works.

20.3 Hamming Distance

Exercise

Technique

1 List all the sets of 2 codewords of 3 digits with a Hamming distance of 3.

Each of the codes below is a repetition code with a central check digit. For each of the codes:

(a) Work out the Hamming distance.
(b) State how many errors can be (i) detected and (ii) corrected.
(c) State the efficiency of the code.

2 1 0 1 1 0	**3** 1 1 1 1 1 1 1	**4** 1 1 1 0 1 1 1 1 0
1 1 0 1 1	1 0 1 0 1 0 1	0 1 0 1 0 0 1 0 1
0 1 1 0 1	1 1 0 0 1 1 0	0 0 1 1 0 0 0 1 1
0 0 0 0 0	0 1 1 0 0 1 1	1 0 0 1 0 1 0 0 1

20.4 Linear Codes and Parity Check Matrices

A **linear code** is one in which any word in the code can be made by adding two other words in the code.

If a code is **linear**, then it is possible to construct a parity check matrix which can be used to see if a codeword has been transmitted correctly.

A **parity check matrix** (usually abbreviated as H) is constructed so that H × any valid codeword = 0; H × any invalid codeword ≠ 0.

Example 1

Is the code set 00, 01, 10, 11 linear?

Solution

When we add codewords, we add each digit separately, and do not carry over.

00 = 01 + 01
01 = 10 + 11
10 = 11 + 01
11 = 01 + 10

Any codeword added to itself gives 0.

Each word can be found by adding two other words together, so this is a linear code.

Example 2

What is the biggest linear code set that can be generated using 001, 010, and 100 as the starting point?

Solution

By using all possible pairs we can generate

000 = 100 + 100
001 given
010 given
011 = 010 + 001
100 given
101 = 001 + 100
110 = 100 + 010

Counting in binary, we have made all the numbers from 000 to 111. A linear code will not always have all these possibilities, and codewords are not binary numbers, but using binary provides a systematic way of searching.

We can also get 111 by adding 100 (given) to 011.

Example 3

Construct a parity check matrix for the code

00000   10110   01101   11011

Solution

We notice that this code is based on a 2-digit code, repeated and with a check digit in the middle. This means that the 1st and 4th digits will be the same; the 2nd and 5th digits will be the same; and the first three digits must have an even number of ones. This produces the parity check matrix:

$$\begin{pmatrix} 1 & 0 & 0 & 1 & 0 \\ 0 & 1 & 0 & 0 & 1 \\ 1 & 1 & 1 & 0 & 0 \end{pmatrix}$$

Notice that all the columns in the matrix are different; if they weren't, we would be able to detect errors but might not be able to correct them.

Example 4

a Use the parity check matrix

$$H = \begin{pmatrix} 1 & 0 & 1 & 0 & 0 \\ 0 & 1 & 0 & 1 & 0 \\ 1 & 1 & 0 & 0 & 1 \end{pmatrix}$$

to check the received message 1010111011.

b If any word in the message is incorrect, use the parity check matrix to correct it.

c Use the resulting correct words to generate the rest of the code set.

Solution

The parity check matrix has five columns. This means that there will be four bits in each codeword, so we can split the received message into the two words 10101 and 11011.

a $\begin{pmatrix} 1 & 0 & 1 & 0 & 0 \\ 0 & 1 & 0 & 1 & 0 \\ 1 & 1 & 0 & 0 & 1 \end{pmatrix} \times \begin{pmatrix} 1 \\ 0 \\ 1 \\ 0 \\ 1 \end{pmatrix} = \begin{pmatrix} 0 \\ 0 \\ 0 \end{pmatrix}$ so 10101 is a valid word.

$\begin{pmatrix} 1 & 0 & 1 & 0 & 0 \\ 0 & 1 & 0 & 1 & 0 \\ 1 & 1 & 0 & 0 & 1 \end{pmatrix} \times \begin{pmatrix} 1 \\ 1 \\ 0 \\ 1 \\ 1 \end{pmatrix}$ so 11011 is not a valid word.

b If there has only been one error, then the result of our multiplication will be the same as one of the columns in the check matrix. The error will be in the corresponding bit in the message received. In this case the first column in the matrix is the same as the result, so the error was in the first bit. We can check this by changing the first bit of the received word, and checking again using the matrix.

$\begin{pmatrix} 1 & 0 & 1 & 0 & 0 \\ 0 & 1 & 0 & 1 & 0 \\ 1 & 1 & 0 & 0 & 1 \end{pmatrix} \times \begin{pmatrix} 0 \\ 1 \\ 0 \\ 1 \\ 1 \end{pmatrix}$ so 01011 is a valid word, and is probably what

was intended.

If there had been more than one error, this method would not have worked. The result of the multiplication would not have been all 0s (unless several errors had combined to produce another valid word), but it would not have been a column in the check matrix.

c Our two valid words are 10101 and 01011. From these we can generate:

    00000 = 10101 + 10101
    01011 given
    10101 given
    11110 = 01011 + 10101

The two valid words each have two 1s, with no overlap. Consequently the result of any addition will have an even number of 1s.

Activity

Why will the resultant vector always be the sum of 1 or more of the columns of the check matrix?

20.4 Linear Codes and Parity Check Matrices

Exercise

Technique

1 Use the set <0110, 1100, 1001> to create a linear code.

2 Use the parity check matrix

$$\begin{pmatrix} 0 & 1 & 1 & 0 & 1 & 1 & 0 \\ 0 & 1 & 0 & 0 & 1 & 0 & 1 \\ 0 & 1 & 0 & 1 & 0 & 1 & 0 \\ 1 & 0 & 0 & 0 & 1 & 0 & 0 \end{pmatrix}$$

to test the words:

a 1001111
b 0111001
c 0101100

3 Construct a parity check matrix with four columns and two rows for the code set:

0000
0011
1100
1111

4 Construct a parity check matrix with five columns and three rows for the code set:

00000
00111
11001
11110

Consolidation

Exercise A

1 A binary code has the following parity check matrix.

$$\begin{pmatrix} 1 & 1 & 0 & 0 & 0 & 0 & 0 \\ 0 & 1 & 1 & 1 & 0 & 0 & 0 \\ 0 & 0 & 0 & 1 & 1 & 1 & 0 \\ 0 & 0 & 0 & 0 & 0 & 1 & 1 \end{pmatrix}$$

  a Use the matrix to correct the following message.
    110110000110010000100

  b If the digits of any codeword are numbered x_1 to x_7, then the first line of the parity check matrix could be written as $x_1 + x_2 = 0$ Mod(2). Write down three more equations based on the parity check matrix.

  c Using your answer to part **b**, or by any other method, find the other five valid codewords in this code.

(AEB)

2 Products sold in the EU are marked with an 8-digit EAN bar code. This number incorporates a check digit (the eighth digit) so that the following result is divisible by 10:

$3 \times$ (the sum of digits in places 1, 3, 5 and 7) + (the sum of digits in places 2, 4, 6 and 8).

  a Show that the number 00337793 is valid.
  b Given that $5021421a$ is valid, find a.
  c The number 50268024 is not valid. Find two valid numbers which differ from 50268024 by a single digit.
  d Find how many valid numbers differ from 50268024 by a single digit.
  e Say how many 8-digit numbers are valid, and how many are invalid.

(AEB)

3 A linear code consists of the following codewords.

00000   01101   10110   11 011

It is proposed that the following matrix be used to identify and correct single errors.

$$\begin{pmatrix} 0 & 1 & 1 & 1 & 0 \\ 1 & 1 & 1 & 0 & 0 \end{pmatrix}$$

a Prove that this matrix confirms correct messages.
b Show that it does not detect all single errors.
c Show that if it detects a single error it may not correct it.
d Add a row to the matrix to overcome the problems identified in parts **b** and **c**.
e Describe what will happen when the amended matrix is applied to a codeword which contains two errors.

(AEB)

4 **a** A binary code is to be used to transmit one of the following eight directions:

i Explain why 3 bits will be needed.
ii Construct a suitable 3 bit code.

b The transmission device occasionally makes errors – seldom more than one per codeword. To counter this it is proposed to add a parity check bit to each codeword.

i Add a parity check bit to each codeword of your code.
ii Give the Hamming distance of your new code and describe its error detection and correction capabilities.

c The detection and correction capabilities given by the parity check bit are not considered to be adequate. Instead, the original 3 bit codeword will be transmitted twice, giving a 6 bit code. Give the Hamming distance of this 6 bit code, and comment on its error detection and correction capabilities.

Again, the error detection and correction capabilities are not thought to be adequate. Thus, the following code is constructed incorporating both the repetition and a check bit:

N	0	0	0	0	0	0	0
NE	0	0	1	1	0	0	1
E	0	1	0	1	0	1	0
SE	0	1	1	0	0	1	1
S	1	0	0	1	1	0	0
SW	1	0	1	0	1	0	1
W	1	1	0	0	1	1	0
NW	1	1	1	1	1	1	1

d Describe how to check that this code is linear.

e Give the Hamming distance of the code and describe its error detection and correction capabilities.

f Construct a parity check matrix for the code.

g Use your matrix to check and correct the following message consisting of three directions.

010101010101001100110

(AEB)

5 A Braille symbol has six positions, each of which may or may not be occupied by a raised dot. For example

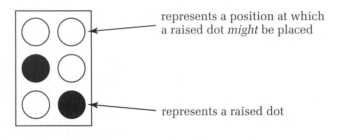

represents a position at which a raised dot *might* be placed

represents a raised dot

a How many different symbols are possible?

b How many positions would be needed to allow for 200 different symbols?

(AEB)

Exercise B

1 The eight words of a linear code are as follows.

0000000
0000111
0011001
0011110
1100001
1100110
1111000
1111111

a Calculate the efficiency of this code.

b What is the Hamming distance of this code?

c How many errors per received codeword can this code detect?

d How many errors per received codeword can this code correct?

e Construct a parity check matrix for this code.

f Show how to use your matrix to correct the following received word which has an error in one digit: 1000110

(AEB)

2 In Morse code, a character is represented by at least one, and up to four, 'dots' or 'dashes', in which the order is important. How many different characters are **possible** in the code?

(AEB)

3 The parity check matrix for a 6 bit linear code is

$$\begin{pmatrix} 1 & 1 & 0 & 0 & 0 & 0 \\ 0 & 1 & 1 & 0 & 1 & 0 \\ 0 & 0 & 1 & 0 & 0 & 1 \end{pmatrix}$$

a The words 111001 and 101011 are received. Use the matrix to decide whether or not the words are likely to have been correctly transmitted and to suggest the correct word if one error has occurred.

b List all the valid codewords.

(AEB)

4 A Huffman code is to be designed for four letters, E, H, L and P. In a Huffman code, each letter is coded by a series of 0s and 1s which indicate a route through a tree, starting at **S** and finishing at the end of the branch where the letter will be found.

So one possible tree for the code is:

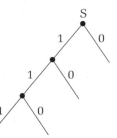

(The letters have not been marked on, but it can be seen that there are four ends of the branches for the letters.)

a Draw each of the other four possible trees for this code.

b One of the trees is selected and the code is constructed. The message 'HELP' is coded 001011010. Show which tree was used.

c Using the dame code, encode the message 'PEEL'.

(AEB)

5 The following code is constructed incorporating both repetition and a check bit:

M	0000000
A	0011001
T	0101010
H	0110011
E	1001100
I	1010101
C	1100110
S	1111111

a Construct a parity check matrix for the code.

b Use your matrix to check and correct the following message:

111111101011100011001010100001100

Applications and Extensions

Huffman Codes

Question 4 in Consolidation Exercise B introduced a Huffman code. Investigate different ways of constructing Huffman codes in order to reduce the average length of messages. Do Huffman codes detect and correct errors?

Bar codes

Bar codes consist of a pattern of wide and thin bars that represent numbers. By looking at examples, can you work out the patterns?

Summary

- Codes are a means of transmitting information.

- A binary code consists of 1s and 0s.

- Ways of detecting and correcting errors in codes include:
  ○ repetition
  ○ check digits
  ○ parity check matrices.

- The **Hamming distance** of a code is the minimum number of different digits seen when comparing the two most similar words in a code.

  The relationship between Hamming distance and the error detection and correction capabilities of a code are given in the table below.

	Detect	Correct
δ **even**	$\frac{\delta}{2}$	$\frac{(\delta - 2)}{2}$
δ **odd**	$\frac{(\delta - 1)}{2}$	$\frac{(\delta - 1)}{2}$

- In a **linear code**, each word is the result of adding two other words in the code.

- When a valid codeword is multiplied by the appropriate parity check matrix, the result is a column vector containing only 0s.

- When an invalid codeword is multiplied by the appropriate parity check matrix, the result is a column vector with at least one 1. If there has only been one error, the vector will be the same as one of the columns of the check matrix, and the error will be in the corresponding digit of the codeword.

Answers

1 Algorithms

1.1 Contextual (p. 3)

2 Structured code
a **STEP 1** Set total = 0, and counter = 0.
STEP 2 Add next mark to total.
STEP 3 Add 1 to counter.
STEP 4 If counter = 200 then stop, else go to 3.

b Alter step 4
4 If counter = 200 then go to 5, else go to 3.
5 Divide total by 200.

Flow chart
a   b Replace end with

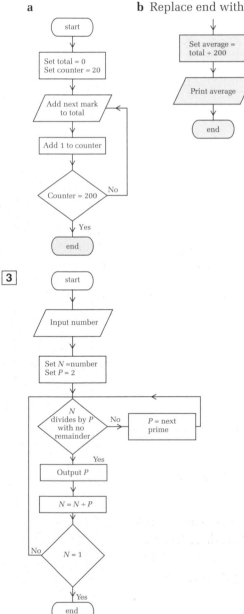

3

1.2 Contextual (p. 5)

1 The stopping condition is when $N = 1$.
It would fail if the initial number was negative, or not an integer.

2 a 40 mins   b 5 mins

3 a 160 mins   b $2\frac{1}{2}$ mins

4 a 2.59×10^{53} mins   b 1.5×10^{-5} mins

5 a $O(n)$
b People can make instantaneous comparisons of lots of lengths; computers have to make comparisons 2 at a time.
c If the lengths are very similar; or spread over too big a range to be represented by standard spaghetti; too many pieces to handle easily.
This question illustrates the difference between people and computers. For small problems, people will get solutions quickly and without using step-by-step methods. For large problems, computers have to be used.

2 Sorting, Searching and Packing

Review (p. 7)

1 a $O(n^2)$ b $O(n)$ c $O(n^3)$

2 a 45 mins   b 135 mins

2.1 Contextual (p. 8)

1 Start in the History section.
Find the English History section
Find the Civil War

2 Take the bus to the end of the street.
Walk down the street, checking each shop in turn.

2.2 Contextual (p. 10)

1 Start with M or N.
If told earlier, guess F; if later U.
i.e.: keep halving the remaining letters.

2 a i Does it have 4 sides?
Are all sides equal?
Are all the angles right-angles?
ii Does it have 4 sides?
Are all sides curved?
Does it only have 1 side?

b

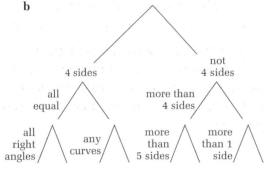

3 a Edward III, Black Prince, Richard II, John, Henry IV, Thomas of Exeter.

b Edward III, Black Prince, John, Thomas of Gloucester, Richard II, Henry IV, Thomas of Exeter.

c No. If you don't know what order items are placed in the tree, all you can do is check them all until you find what you want.

2.3 Technique (p. 15)

1 a 11   b 36   c 15

2 a 11   b 15 if starting from 1st each time.

3 a 21   b 7

2.3 Contextual (p. 15)

1
```
3 6 2 7 4 1 5
1 6 2 7 4 3 5
1 2 6 7 4 3 5
1 2 3 7 4 6 5
1 2 3 4 7 6 5
1 2 3 4 5 6 7
```

2 Darker numbers indicate a swap. Dotted lines indicate the end of a pass

```
3 6 2 7 4 1 5
2 6 3 7 4 1 5
1 6 3 7 4 2 5
1 3 6 7 4 2 5
1 2 6 7 4 3 5
1 2 4 7 6 3 5
1 2 3 7 6 4 5
1 2 3 6 7 4 5
1 2 3 4 7 6 5
1 2 3 4 6 7 5
1 2 3 4 5 7 6
1 2 3 4 5 6 7
```

3 a 15   b 6

2.4 Technique (p. 18)

1 Darker numbers indicate a swap.

```
7 8 3 6 5 1 2 9 4
6 8 3 7 5 1 2 9 4
6 5 3 7 8 1 2 9 4
6 5 1 7 8 3 2 9 4
6 5 1 2 8 3 7 9 4    end of phase 1
2 5 1 6 8 3 7 9 4
2 1 5 6 8 3 7 9 4
2 1 5 6 3 8 7 9 4
2 1 5 6 3 7 8 9 4
2 1 5 6 3 7 8 4 9
1 2 5 6 3 7 8 4 9
1 2 5 3 6 7 8 4 9
1 2 5 3 6 7 4 8 9
1 2 3 5 6 7 4 8 9
1 2 3 5 6 4 7 8 9
1 2 3 5 4 6 7 8 9
1 2 3 4 5 6 7 8 9
```

2
```
12 14  8 10 16  4 18  2  6
10 14  8 12 16  4 18  2  6
10 14  4 12 16  8 18  2  6
10 14  4 12  2  8 18 16  6
10 14  4 12  2  6 18 16  8    end of phase 1
10  2  4 12 14  6 18 16  8
 2 10  4 12 14  6 18 16  8
 2  4 10 12 14  6 18 16  8
 2  4 10 12  6 14 18 16  8
 2  4 10 12  6 14 16 18  8
 2  4 10 12  6 14 16  8 18
 2  4 10  6 12 14 16  8 18
 2  4 10  6 12 14  8 16 18
 2  4  6 10 12 14  8 16 18
 2  4  6 10 12  8 14 16 18
 2  4  6 10  8 12 14 16 18
 2  4  6  8 10 12 14 16 18
```

3
```
49 56  7 21 61 35 14 28 42
21 56  7 49 61 35 14 28 42
21 56  7 49 61 35 14 28 42
21 56  7 14 28 35 49 61 42
14 56  7 21 28 35 49 61 42
14 28  7 21 56 35 49 61 42    end of phase 1
14  7 28 21 56 35 49 61 42
14  7 21 28 56 35 49 61 42
14  7 21 28 35 56 49 61 42
14  7 21 28 35 49 56 61 42
14  7 21 28 35 49 56 42 61
 7 14 21 28 35 49 56 42 61
 7 14 21 28 35 49 42 56 61
 7 14 21 28 35 42 49 56 61
```

2.5 Technique (p. 20)

1 Circles indicate pivot at each stage.

```
3 6 5 1 2 4 (7) 8 9
1 2 (3) 6 5 4 7 (8) 9
(1) 2 3 5 4 (6) 7 8 9
1 2 3 4 (5) 6 7 8 9
```

2
```
8 10 4 2 6 (12) 14 16 18
4 2 6 (8) 10 12 (14) 16 18
2 (4) 6 8 10 12 14 (16) 18
```

3
```
7 21 35 14 28 42 (49) 56 63
(7) 21 35 14 28 42 49 (56) 63
7 14 (21) 35 28 42 49 56 63
7 14 21 28 (35) 42 49 56 63
```

2.6 Contextual (p. 22)

1 Using First-fit decreasing:
7 + 6 + 6 + 1 = 20
5 + 4 + 4 + 3 + 2 + 2 = 20

2 a 3

b First tape: 100 + 75 = 175
Second tape: 90 + 90 = 180
Third tape: 30 + 30 + 30 + 25 + 25 + 25 = 165
Fourth tape: 20

c Possible solution is
First tape: 100 + 30 + 30 + 20 = 180
Second tape: 90 + 90 = 180
Third tape: 75 + 30 + 25 + 25 + 25 = 180

Consolidation A (p. 22)

1   **a** 4, 7, 13, 8, 15, 6, 26, 56
       4, 7, 8, 13, 6, 15, 26, 56
       4, 7, 8, 6, 13, 15, 26, 56
       4, 7, 6, 8, 13, 15, 26, 56
       4, 6, 7, 8, 13, 15, 26, 56
  b 28

2 5, 7, 2, 8, 6, **9**, 11, 17
    2, **5**, 7, 8, 6, 9, **11**, 17
    2, 5, 6, **7**, 8, 9, 11, 17

3 FULLER, LEECH, GRANT, GREGORY

4 **a** 6 tapes: ABCD, EFG, HI, J, K, L
  b 5 tapes: KD, LE, JF, HI, JABC

Consolidation B (p. 23)

1 3 5 12 11 14 2 10 19
    3 5 11 12 2 10 14 19
    3 5 11 2 10 12 14 19
    3 5 2 10 11 12 14 19
    3 2 5 10 11 12 14 19
    2 3 5 10 11 12 14 19

2 3 2 **5** 12 19 11 14 10
    2 **3** 5 11 10 **12** 19 14
    2 3 5 10 **11** 12 14 **19**

3 1st pick FULLER, then COUTTS or DENYER, then DENYER

4 **a** Tape 1: $\frac{1}{2}, \frac{1}{4}, \frac{1}{2}, \frac{3}{4}, 1 = 3$ hrs
    Tape 2: $1\frac{1}{4}, \frac{1}{4}, \frac{1}{4}, 1 = 2\frac{3}{4}$
    Tape 3: $1\frac{1}{4}, 1\frac{1}{2} = 2\frac{3}{4}$
    Tape 4: $\frac{1}{2}$
  b Tape 1: $1\frac{1}{2}, 1\frac{1}{4}, \frac{1}{4}$
    Tape 2: $1\frac{1}{4}, 1, \frac{3}{4}$
    Tape 3: $1, \frac{1}{2}, \frac{1}{2}, \frac{1}{2}, \frac{1}{4}, \frac{1}{4}$

3 Graph Theory

3.1 Contextual (p. 28)

1 a and d
  e and b
  f and c
  g and h

2 **a**

	A	B	C	D
A		1	1	1
B	1		1	1
C	1	1		1
D	1	1	1	

  b

	A	B	C
A		1	1
B	1		2
C	1	2	

c

	A	B	C	D
A	2	1	1	1
B	1		1	1
C	1	1		1
D	1			

3 These are possible solutions – there will be many isomorphic alternatives.

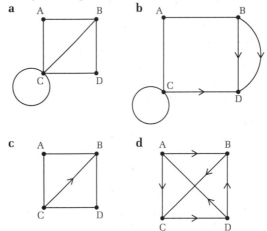

3.2 Contextual (p. 31)

1

	A	B	C	D	E
A		3	2	5	
B	3		4		5
C	2	4		2	7
D	5		2		3
E		5	7	3	

2

	A	B	C	D	E	F
A		5	2			
B	5			2	4	1
C	2	2		3	4	
D		4	3		2	6
E		1	4	2		8
F				6	8	

3

	A	B	C	D	E	F	G	H
A		7	4	8				
B	7		5		9			
C	4	5		3		6		
D	8		3				4	
E		9				2		5
F			6		2		3	12
G				4		3		4
H				5	12	4		

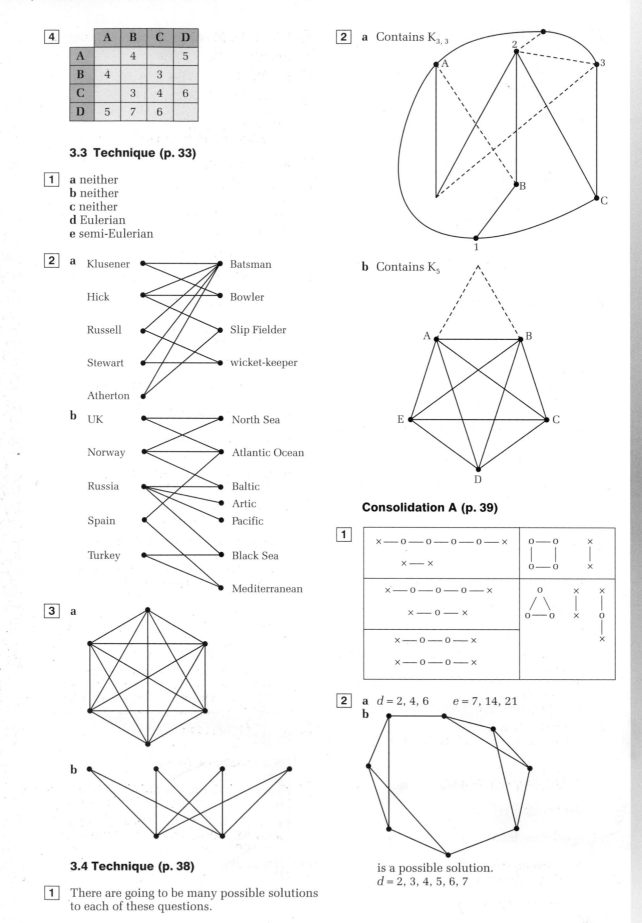

4

	A	B	C	D
A		4		5
B	4		3	
C		3	4	6
D	5	7	6	

3.3 Technique (p. 33)

1 **a** neither
b neither
c neither
d Eulerian
e semi-Eulerian

2 **a**

Klusener — Batsman
Hick — Bowler
Russell — Slip Fielder
Stewart — wicket-keeper
Atherton

b

UK — North Sea
Norway — Atlantic Ocean
Russia — Baltic
— Artic
Spain — Pacific
Turkey — Black Sea
— Mediterranean

3 **a**

b

3.4 Technique (p. 38)

1 There are going to be many possible solutions to each of these questions.

2 **a** Contains K$_{3,3}$

b Contains K$_5$

Consolidation A (p. 39)

1

2 **a** $d = 2, 4, 6$ $e = 7, 14, 21$
b

is a possible solution.
$d = 2, 3, 4, 5, 6, 7$

3 **a** 1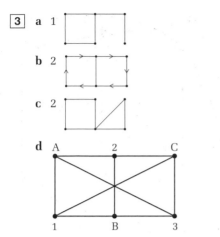

b 2

c 2

d

This contains $K_{3,3}$, with A → C and 1 → 3 on the sets of vertices.

4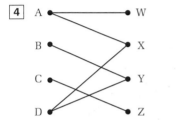

5 **a** Semi-Eulerian **b** Many possible answers.

Consolidation B (p. 41)

1 **a** Contains $K_{3,3}$ (A, C, E; B, D, F) or by failure of planarity algorithm.
  b **i** Many solutions. One is (3, 5, 8; 2, 4, 9).
    ii it is non-planar.

2 Fig. 1 is planar.
Fig. 2 is not.

3 **a** AB, ACB, ADB, ACDB, ADCB
  b 16
  c Part **b**, because all vertices of even order.

4 **a** A = 5 B = 4 C = 4
    D = 5 E = 4
    Semi-Eulerian because all vertices except 2 are of even order.
  b C must be entered twice and left twice.
  c Many solutions.
  d Adding F as described creates K_5.

5 **a** Semi-Eulerian.
  b One solution uses (A, C, E; B, D, F).

4 Spanning Trees

Review (p. 46)

1 **a** and **e** are trees.

4.1 Technique (p. 50)
Edges listed in order:

1 FG, DG, BG, AB, BC, ED = 21

2 FC, AD, BC (FD and BE in either order) = 59

3 AB, BD, CE, BC, EF = 103

4 DE, BD, CE, AE = 358

5 CG, AF, EF, BC, DE, AC = 69

4.2 Technique (p. 54)
Edges listed in order:

1 AB, BG, FG, DG, BC, DE = 21

2 BC, CF, FD, AD, BE = 59
or
BC, CF, BE, FD, AD = 59

3 CE, BC, AB, BD, EF = 103

4 DE, BD, CE, AC = 358

5 EF, AF, DE, AC, CG, BC = 69

4.3 Technique (p. 57)

1 **a** AB, AF, DF, CD, DE = 16
  b AC, AD, AB, BE, CF = 16
  c DF, CF, BF, AB, CE = 25
  d EF, FC, FD, FA, AB = 125
  e Several possible orders, total = 26.

Consolidation A (p. 58)

1 (i) **a** DE, BF, CF, CE, AB = 15
  (ii) **a** AB, BF, CF, CE, ED = 15

  (i) **b** CF, EF, AE, CD, BD = 18
  (ii) **b** AE, EF, CF, CD, BD = 18

2 **a** Cost = 165 pence.
  b New cost = 115 pence.

3 **a** Diag (i) does not represent a proof. It shows D being proved from A, which according to the table is not possible. Diag (ii) shows a proof of 55 lines.
  b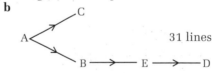
    31 lines
  c The new value makes no difference to the algorithms solution. However, there is a better solution, of 30 lines, shown below.
    A → B → E → D → C

4 AD, AE, EF, BF, CF = £69

Consolidation B (p. 60)

1 (i) **a** FG, CG and AD, EH, CD, DH, BF = 126
  (ii) **a** AD, CD, CG, FG, DH, EH, BF = 126

  (i) **b** AB, BH, BC, BG, GE, GF, ED = 430
  (ii) **b** BH and EG, FG and AB, DE and BC, BG = 430

2 1250 metres

3   **a**   Office → A, AE, CE, Office → D, BE

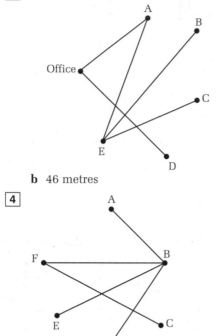

b   46 metres

4

Cost: 530

5 Shortest Paths

Activity

1   4

2   ABCD = 7

5.1 Technique (p. 68)

1   A–C–D–E = 7

2   A–C–D–F = 11

3   A–C–D–G–H = 15

4   A–B–D–E–G = 16

5   A–D–F–G = 21
    or A–C–D–F–G = 21
    or A–B–E–F–G = 21

5.2 Technique (p. 71)

1

	A	B	C	D
A	–	4	5	3
B	4	–	1	2
C	6	5	–	3
D	3	2	3	–

2

	A	B	C	D	E
A	–	3	4	5	6
B	3	–	3	2	3
C	4	3	–	1	2
D	5	2	1	–	1
E	6	3	2	1	–

5.3 Technique (p. 74)

1   **a**

	A	B	C	D
A	–	2	6	3
B	2	–	4	1
C	6	4	–	3
D	3	1	3	–

b

	A	B	C	D
A	–	4	3	2
B	4	–	2	6
C	3	2	–	5
D	2	6	5	–

c

	A	B	C	D
A	–	3	8	5
B	3	–	5	2
C	8	5	–	7
D	5	2	7	–

Consolidation A (p. 74)

1

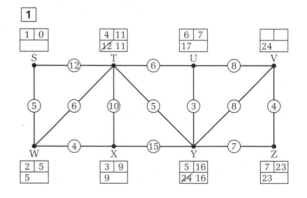

S–W–T–Y–Z = 23

2   **a**   A–B–E–F–G–H–I–J = 292
     b   A–B–D–E–F–G–H–I–J = 282
       DE = 82

3   B–D–E–G–F = 90

4

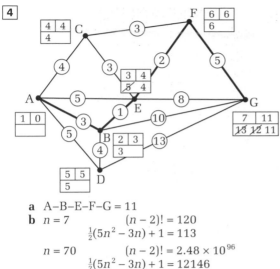

a A–B–E–F–G = 11
b $n = 7$ $(n-2)! = 120$
  $\frac{1}{2}(5n^2 - 3n) + 1 = 113$

  $n = 70$ $(n-2)! = 2.48 \times 10^{96}$
  $\frac{1}{2}(5n^2 - 3n) + 1 = 12146$
  For large value of n, Dijkstra is more efficient than trial and improvement.

5 **a**

	A	B	C	D
A	–	4	3	4
B	4	–	2	3
C	3	2	–	1
D	4	3	1	–

	A	B	C	D
A	A	B	C	C
B	A	B	C	C
C	A	B	C	D
D	A	B	C	D

b

	A	B	C	D
A	–	3	2	2
B	3	–	5	1
C	2	5	–	4
D	2	1	4	–

	A	B	C	D
A	A	D	C	D
B	D	B	D	D
C	A	D	C	D
D	A	B	C	D

Consolidation B (p. 76)

1 **a** A–F–H–J = 43
  b J–G–C–A = 52

2 **a**

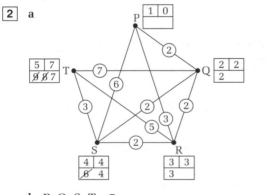

b P–Q–S–T = 7

3 **a** A–B–D–G = 47

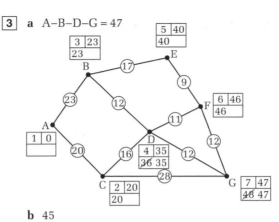

b 45

4 A–B–C–D–E = 57

5

	A	B	C	D	E
A	–	2	4	7	3
B	2	–	2	5	4
C	4	2	–	3	6
D	7	5	3	–	4
E	3	4	6	4	–

	A	B	C	D	E
A	–	B	B	B	E
B	A	–	C	C	E
C	B	B	–	D	E
D	C	C	C	–	E
E	A	B	C	D	–

6 Route Inspection

Review (p. 80)

1 **a** S–A–B–T = 9   **b** S–B–C–D–T = 6
2 **a** neither   **b** semi-Eulerian
  c neither

6.1 Contextual (p. 82)

1 **a** 5   **b** 55   **c** 17
  d 14   **e** 15

2 In each question there will be a number of possible answers for part ii.
  a i 3   **b i** 6

Consolidation A (p. 83)

1 **a** 56

2 **a** The network is not Eulerian; vertices B, C, D and E are odd.
  b length = 95.5

3 **a** 2800. Vertices A, C, D, G are odd. Inspection gives A B E C and D F G on minimum extra length.
  b 4600 Each road now appears twice on the network, making all vertices even. Consequently there is an Eulerian cycle.
  c No. He will still only go along each road twice, as in **a** and will be able to choose his direction each time.

4 **a** Length of route = 61

5 **a** 12

Consolidation B (p. 86)

1 **a** 8

2 **a** **A** is neither.
B is semi-Eulerian.
C is Eulerian.
b **A** is neither – no route.
B is semi-Eulerian – route starts at one odd vertex, finishes at the other.
C is Eulerian – numerous routes; can start and finish anywhere.

3 **a** B, D, F, G
b because not all vertices are of even order
c length = 2200

4 **a** Vertices B, C, D, G are odd.
b Length = 3325

5 **a** 17

7 Travelling Salesperson Problems

Review (p. 89)

1

A connected, but not complete graph would:
- not have every possible edge
- have a route (not necessarily direct) between any pair of vertices.

2 Use edges AD, BE, DE, CE, total 13.

3 A–E–C = 9

7.1 (p. 92)

1 **a** CEDACBC = 21 (other answers are possible)
b A–F–B–E–D–C–B–A = 41
c A–B–H–C–D–E–G–F–A = 34

2

	A	B	C	D	E
A	–	7	3	5	5
B	7	–	4	9	6
C	3	4	–	5	2
D	5	9	5	–	3
E	5	6	2	3	–

3

	A	B	C	D	E	F
A	–	5	15	16	7	4
B	5	–	10	11	2	3
C	15	10	–	8	12	13
D	16	11	8	–	9	14
E	7	2	12	9	–	5
F	4	3	13	14	5	–

4

	A	B	C	D	E	F	G	H
A	–	4	11	13	13	5	6	7
B	4	–	7	9	13	9	10	3
C	11	7	–	2	7	16	14	4
D	13	9	2	–	5	16	12	6
E	13	13	7	5	–	11	7	11
F	5	9	16	16	11	–	4	12
G	6	10	14	12	7	4	–	17
H	7	3	4	6	11	12	13	–

7.2 Technique (p. 95)

1 C–E–F–A–D–B–C = 108

2 D–A–B–C–E–D = 72

3 D–C–H–G–B–A–F–E–D = 146

4 P–R–Q–T–S–P = 59
Q–R–P–S–T–Q = 59
R–P–S–T–Q–R = 59
S–P–R–Q–T–S = 59
T–S–P–R–Q–T = 59

5 A–D–B–E–C–F–H = 216
B–D–C–E–F–A–B = 204
C–E–F–D–B–A–C = 198
D–B–E–C–F–A–D = 216
E–C–D–B–F–A–E = 232
F–E–C–D–B–A–F = 204

7.3 Contextual (p. 99)

1 **a** MST uses all regular services. Length = 13; UB = 26.
b e.g.: A–I–A–T–A–H–A–M–S–A = 25

2 **a** 150
b e.g.: A–B–C–D–E–F–A = 100

3 **a** 94
b e.g.: A–B–C–D–E–A = 77

4 **a** 202
b e.g.: A–B–G–C–D–E–H–F–A = 133

5 **a** 84
b e.g: P–R–Q–J–S–P = 59

6 **a** 286
b e.g.: A–D–C–E–F–B–A = 205

7.4 Technique (p. 101)

1 89

2 63

3 118

4 55

5 177

7.5 Contextual (p. 103)

1 a i 440 mins
ii Any feasible solution represents an Upper Bound.
iii A–D–C–E–B–F–A = 330 mins
b 300

Consolidation A (p. 103)

1 a

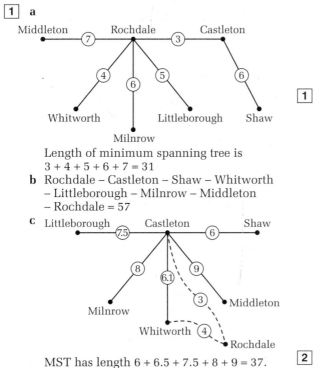

Length of minimum spanning tree is
3 + 4 + 5 + 6 + 7 = 31

b Rochdale – Castleton – Shaw – Whitworth – Littleborough – Milnrow – Middleton – Rochdale = 57

c

MST has length 6 + 6.5 + 7.5 + 8 + 9 = 37. Two shortest from Rochdale are 3 and 4 so total length of lower bound is
37 + 3 + 4 = 44.

2 a <13 is ⩽12, of which at least 2 minutes is return to P after last delivery, so maximum 10. Add on 10 for cooking $4 × 2\frac{1}{2}$ stop/deliver = 30 minutes.
b D A B C; 30 minutes

3 a A D B C E A; 97
b 78
c No, because **b** says it will be at least 78; 72 is less precise.
d A E D C B A; 92

4 a

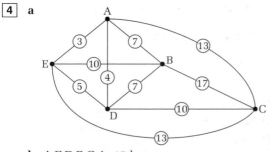

b A E D B C A; 45 km
c BC not in the original network, actual route A E D B D C A.

5 a

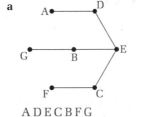

A D E C B F G
b 2 × MST = 596
c Shortcut from F to G and from B to A reduces upper bound to 420.
d 352

Consolidation B (p. 106)

1 a

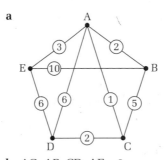

b AC, AB, CD, AE = 8
c A–B–C–D–E–A = 18
A–B–E–D–C–A = 21
A–C–B–E–D–A = 28
A–D–C–B–E–A = 26
d Because this network is not in classical form (not all shortest routes are indicated between pairs of vertices).

2 a AC, AD, DF, CE, BE = 251

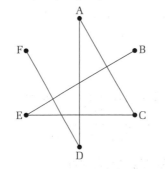

b i 502
ii F–D–A–C–E–B–F = 351
c 351
d 351 is optimum.
e

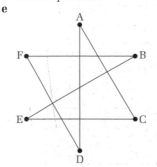

3 **a** A–H–G–F–C–B–D–E–J–I–G–H–A = 229
b e.g.: Replacing CBD with CBBD reduces
total to 216.

4 **a** JK, KL, KM, KN = 16
b

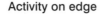

c 32
d JL, LM, MN + JK, KL = 23
e JKLMNJ = 26

5 **a** Nearest Neighbour
b A–C–B–D–A = 6.7 km.

8 Critical Path Analysis

8.1 Technique (p. 115)

Activity on edge

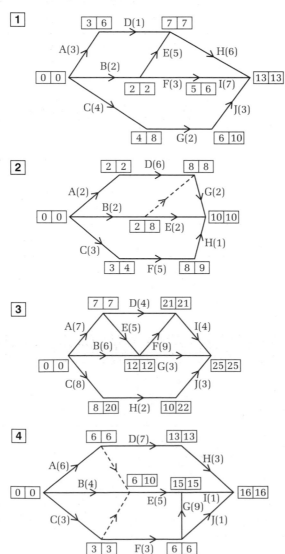

Activity on node

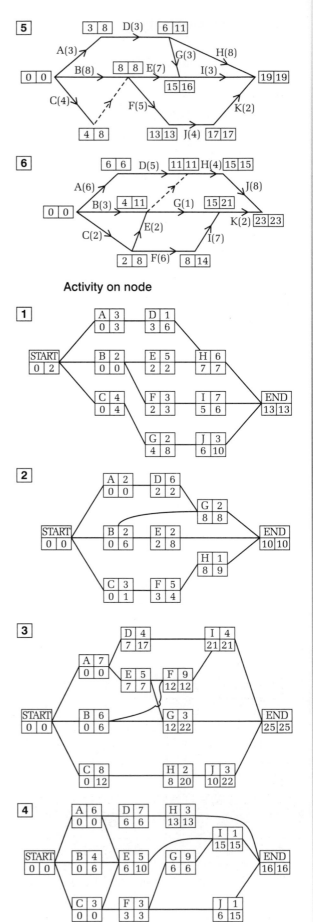

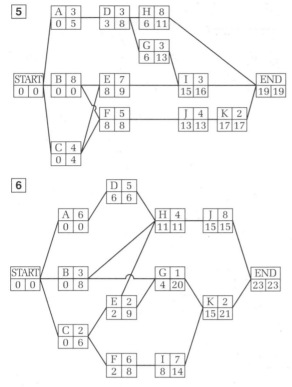

3

Activity	Earliest start	Latest start	Total float	Independent float	Interfering float
A	0	0	0	0	0
B	0	6	6	6	0
C	0	12	12	0	12
D	7	17	10	10	0
E	7	7	0	0	0
F	12	12	0	0	0
G	12	22	10	10	0
H	8	20	12	0	12
I	21	21	0	0	0
J	10	22	12	0	12

4

Activity	Earliest start	Latest start	Total float	Independent float	Interfering float
A	0	0	0	0	0
B	0	6	6	2	4
C	0	0	0	0	0
D	6	6	0	0	0
E	6	10	4	0	4
F	3	3	0	0	0
G	6	6	3	0	0
H	13	13	0	0	0
I	15	15	0	0	0
J	6	15	9	9	0

5

Activity	Earliest start	Latest start	Total float	Independent float	Interfering float
A	0	5	5	0	5
B	0	0	0	0	0
C	0	4	4	0	4
D	3	8	5	0	5
E	8	9	1	0	1
F	8	8	0	0	0
G	6	13	7	1	6
H	6	11	5	0	5
I	15	16	1	0	1
J	13	13	0	0	0
K	17	17	0	0	0

6

Activity	Earliest start	Latest start	Total float	Independent float	Interfering float
A	0	0	0	0	0
B	0	8	8	1	7
C	0	6	6	0	6
D	6	6	0	0	0
E	2	9	7	0	7
F	2	8	6	0	6
G	4	20	16	3	13
H	11	11	0	0	0
I	8	14	6	0	6
J	15	15	0	0	0
K	15	21	6	0	6

8.2 Technique (p. 121)

1 B, F, I = 12   **2** A, D, G = 9, so is C, F, H

3 A, E, F, I = 25

4 A, D, H = 16 and C, F, G, I = 16

5 B, F, J, K = 19   **6** A, D, H, J = 23

8.3 Technique (p. 123)

1

Activity	Earliest start	Latest start	Total float	Independent float	Interfering float
A	0	3	3	0	3
B	0	0	0	0	0
C	0	4	4	0	4
D	3	6	3	0	3
E	2	2	0	0	0
F	2	3	1	0	1
G	4	8	4	0	4
H	7	7	0	0	0
I	5	6	1	0	1
J	6	10	4	0	4

2

Activity	Earliest start	Latest start	Total float	Independent float	Interfering float
A	0	0	0	0	0
B	0	6	6	0	6
C	0	1	1	0	1
D	2	2	0	0	0
E	2	8	6	0	6
F	3	4	1	0	1
G	8	8	0	0	0
H	8	9	1	0	1

8.4 Technique (p. 125)

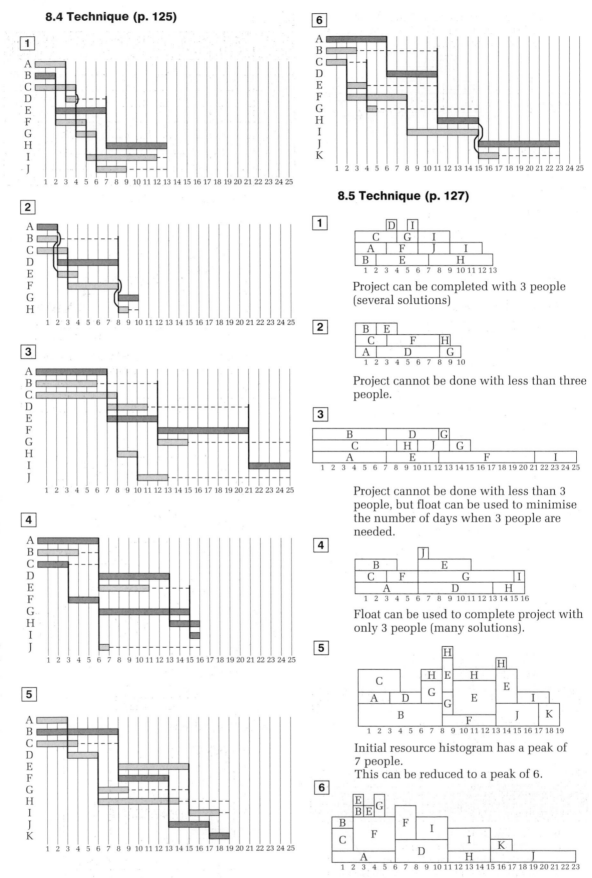

8.5 Technique (p. 127)

1

Project can be completed with 3 people (several solutions)

2

Project cannot be done with less than three people.

3

Project cannot be done with less than 3 people, but float can be used to minimise the number of days when 3 people are needed.

4

Float can be used to complete project with only 3 people (many solutions).

5

Initial resource histogram has a peak of 7 people.
This can be reduced to a peak of 6.

6

Initial resource histogram has a peak of 6 people.

This can be reduced to 5 people by splitting activity F. The histogram below shows one possibility.

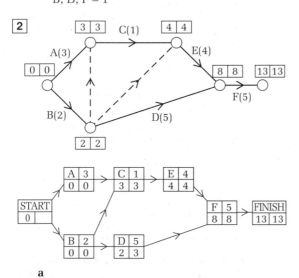

8.6 Technique (p. 129)

1 C, G, J = 10

2 A, D, G = 9

3 A, E, F, I = 19 and B, F, I = 19

4 C, F, G, I = 16 (A, D, H no longer critical)

5 C, F, J, K = 15

6 C, F, I, K = 17 and B, F, J, K = 15

Consolidation A (p. 130)

1 a

Activity	Earliest start	Latest start	Total float
A	0	0	0
B	0	1	1
C	4	4	0
D	3	4	1
E	6	6	0
F	8	9	1

b ACE = 11

c A, C, E = 0
B, D, F = 1

2

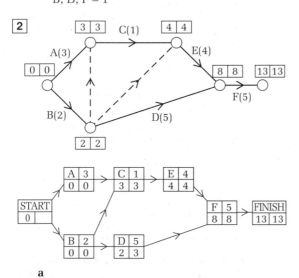

a

Activity	A	B	C	D	E	F
Earliest starting time	**0**	**0**	**3**	**2**	**4**	**8**
Latest starting time	0	0	3	3	4	8

b A, B, C, E, F 13 days.

c 5 – from peak on histogram.

d 1 by deferring D until C is complete (3 is the minimum number of people because C needs 3 people).

3 a, b

Activity	Earliest start	Latest start	Total float	Independent float	Interfering float
A	0	0	0	0	0
B	0	1	1	1	0
C	0	6	6	0	6
D	2	2	0	0	0
E	7	7	0	0	0
F	5	11	6	0	6
G	13	13	0	0	0
H	5	14	9	3	6

Critical path: A, D, E, G = 17

c

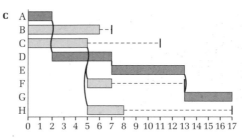

d Project can be completed with 2 people: a possible schedule is shown below.

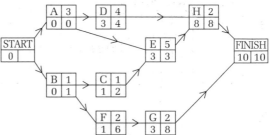

4 a

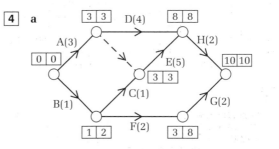

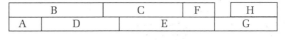

b A, E, H, 10 days

c

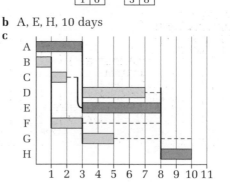

d D–5, F–3, G–8.

5 a

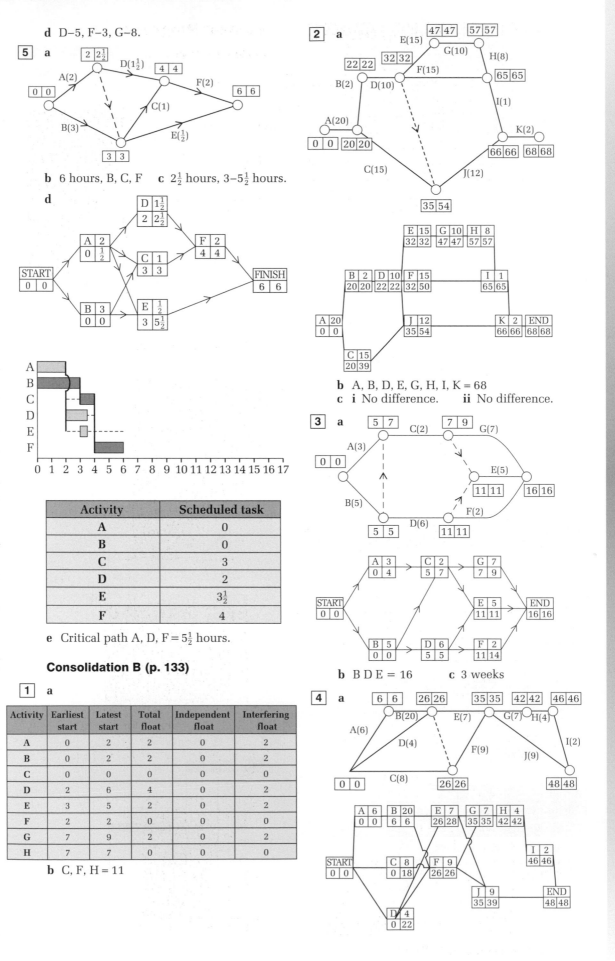

b 6 hours, B, C, F   **c** $2\frac{1}{2}$ hours, $3-5\frac{1}{2}$ hours.

d

Activity	Scheduled task
A	0
B	0
C	3
D	2
E	$3\frac{1}{2}$
F	4

e Critical path A, D, F = $5\frac{1}{2}$ hours.

Consolidation B (p. 133)

1 a

Activity	Earliest start	Latest start	Total float	Independent float	Interfering float
A	0	2	2	0	2
B	0	2	2	0	2
C	0	0	0	0	0
D	2	6	4	0	2
E	3	5	2	0	2
F	2	2	0	0	0
G	7	9	2	0	2
H	7	7	0	0	0

b C, F, H = 11

2 a

b A, B, D, E, G, H, I, K = 68

c i No difference.   **ii** No difference.

3 a

b B D E = 16   **c** 3 weeks

4 a

b

Task	Early start	Late start
A	0	0
B	6	6
C	0	18
D	0	22
E	26	28
F	26	26
G	35	35
H	42	42
I	46	46
J	35	39

Critical path is A, B, F, G, H, I = 48 weeks.

c 44 weeks

F(−3 weeks), G(−1 week), E(−1 week)

Extra cost: £120,000

5 a

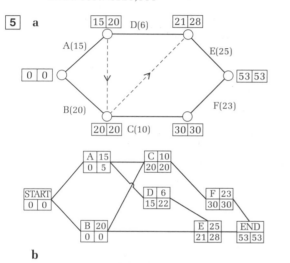

b

Activity	Earliest start	Latest start	Total float	Independent float	Interfering float
A	0	5	5	0	5
B	0	0	0	0	0
C	20	20	0	0	0
D	15	22	7	0	7
E	21	28	7	0	7
F	30	30	0	0	0

Critical path: B, C, F = 53

c

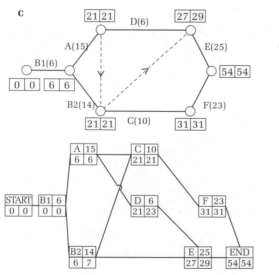

Critical path: B, A, C, F = 54

9 Linear Programming

Review (p. 139)

1 $3x + y = 4$

2 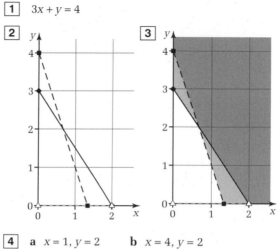 **3**

4 **a** $x = 1, y = 2$ **b** $x = 4, y = 2$

9.1 Technique (p. 142)

1

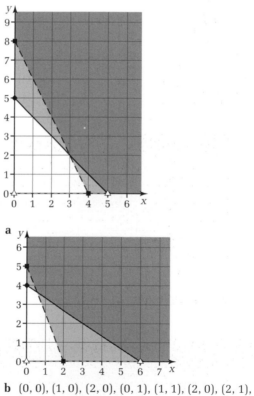

2 a

b (0, 0), (1, 0), (2, 0), (0, 1), (1, 1), (2, 0), (2, 1), (3, 0), (4, 0)

3 a

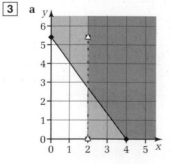

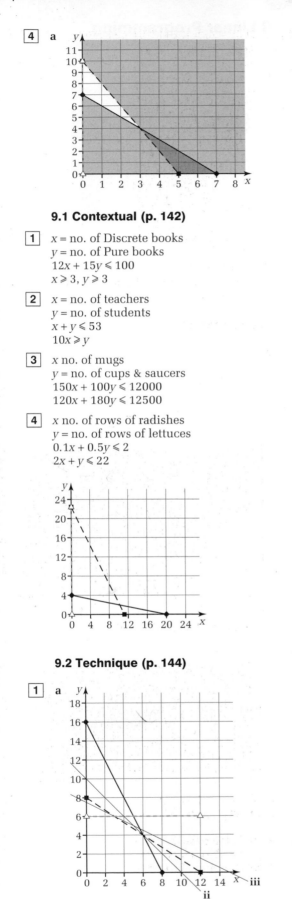

4 a

9.1 Contextual (p. 142)

1 x = no. of Discrete books
y = no. of Pure books
$12x + 15y \leqslant 100$
$x \geqslant 3, y \geqslant 3$

2 x = no. of teachers
y = no. of students
$x + y \leqslant 53$
$10x \geqslant y$

3 x no. of mugs
y = no. of cups & saucers
$150x + 100y \leqslant 12000$
$120x + 180y \leqslant 12500$

4 x no. of rows of radishes
y = no. of rows of lettuces
$0.1x + 0.5y \leqslant 2$
$2x + y \leqslant 22$

9.2 Technique (p. 144)

1 a

b Optimum at $(6, 4)$, value 10.
c Optimum at $(3, 6)$, value 15.

2 a Optimum at $(\frac{6}{11}, 3\frac{7}{11})$, value $4\frac{8}{11}$
b Optimum at $(2, 0)$, value 6.

3 a $(0, 5\frac{1}{3})$; $5\frac{1}{3}$.
b $(2, 2\frac{2}{3})$; $6\frac{2}{3}$

4 a $(0, 10)$, Profit = 10 **b** $(0, 10)$, Profit = 20

9.3 Technique (p. 146)

1 a $(0, 4)$, Profit = 16 **b** $(0, 4)$, Profit = 32

2 $(4, 2)$; 32

3 $(5, 0)$; 10

9.3 Contextual (p. 146)

1 a $P = x + y$ **b** 4 Discrete and 3 Pure books.

2 a $P = y$ **b** 48 students (with 5 staff)

3 a $P = 5x + 7.5y$
b 59 mugs, 30 cup and saucer sets, Profit £520

4 a $50x + 75y$
b 10 rows of radishes, 2 rows of lettuces, £6.50.

9.4 Technique (p. 148)

1 Any point on $4x + 3y = 24$ between $(6, 0)$ and $(2\frac{8}{11}, 4\frac{4}{11})$; profit = 48

2 $(0, 8)$ or $(1, 7)$; profit = 8

9.5 Contextual (p. 149)

1 $3x + 2y + s_1 = 18$
$2x + y + s_2 = 10$
$(0, 0, 18, 10)$
$(5, 0, 3, 0)$
$(2, 6, 0, 0)$
$(9, 0, 0, 1)$

2 $150x + 100y + s_1 = 12000$
$120x + 180y + s_2 = 12500$
$(0, 0, 12000, 12500)$
$(80, 0, 0, 2900)$
$(60\frac{2}{3}, 29, 0, 0)$
$(0, 69\frac{4}{9}, 5055\frac{5}{9}, 0)$

3 $0.1x + 0.5y + s_1 = 2$
$2x + y + s_2 = 22$
$(11, 0, 0.9, 0)$
$(10, 2, 0, 0)$
$(0, 4, 0, 18)$

4 a

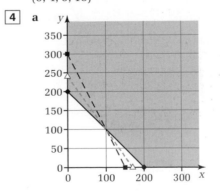

b $5x + 5y + s_1 = 1000$
$10x + 5y + s_2 = 1500$
$14x + 10y + s_3 = 2400$
c (x, y, s_1, s_2, s_3):
$(0, 200, 0, 500, 400)$
$(100, 100, 0, 0, 0)$
$(150, 0, 250, 0, 300)$

9.6 Technique (p. 151)

1 $(10, 0)$, cost $= 10$

2 **a** $(6\frac{2}{3}, 2)$, Cost $8\frac{2}{3}$ **b** $(6, 3)$, Cost 9 or $(7, 2)$

3 Let x be no. of days of first mine and y the no. of days of the second mine.

a $x = 5\frac{1}{7}$ days, $y = \frac{5}{7}$ days, Cost £92857
b $x = 5$ days, $y = 1$ day, Cost £97000

Consolidation A (p. 151)

1 **a** Minimise $265A + 205B$
subject to $13A + 10B \geqslant 500$
$A + B \geqslant 45$
b $A = 16\frac{2}{3}$, $28\frac{1}{3}$, cost £10225
c $A = 10$, $B = 37$
d Integer solution has 47 people, otherwise both meet the constraints.

2 **a** Maximise $80C + 350T$
subject to $20C + 100T \leqslant 10000$
$4C + 15T \leqslant 1950$
b 450 chairs, 10 tables, £39,500
c Unused resources; both zero.
d 45 chairs for each table.

3 **a** Maximise/minimise $20x + 25y$
subject to $8x + 8y \leqslant 7200$
$2x + 3y \leqslant 2200$
$x \geqslant 300$
$y \geqslant 300$
$x + y \geqslant 800$
b

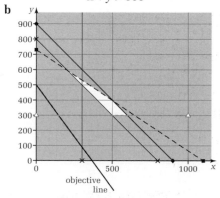

c Maximum $=$ £20000 at 9500, 400)
Minimum $=$ £17500 at $(500, 300)$

4 **a** $10a + 25b + 80c \leqslant 785$
$90a + 60b \leqslant 540$
b They are integer.
c $P = 70a + 120b + 180c$

5 **a** $200x + 200y \leqslant 2800$ divide by 200
$125x + 50y \leqslant 1000$ divide by 25
b $50x + 30y \leqslant 480$
c

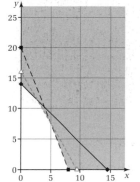

d $P = 3.5x + 1.5y$
e $x = 6$, $y = 5$ (nearest integer to $(4.8, 8)$)
f $P = $ £28.50

Consolidation B (p. 154)

1 **a** $a + b + c \geqslant 4$
$c \geqslant 2$
b $b \geqslant \frac{1}{2}(a + c)$

2 $x = 3$, $y = 4$, $P = 29$

3

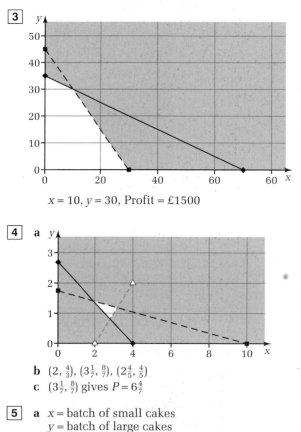

$x = 10$, $y = 30$, Profit $=$ £1500

4 **a**

b $(2, \frac{4}{3})$, $(3\frac{1}{7}, \frac{8}{7})$, $(2\frac{4}{5}, \frac{4}{5})$
c $(3\frac{1}{7}, \frac{8}{7})$ gives $P = 6\frac{4}{7}$

5 **a** $x = $ batch of small cakes
$y = $ batch of large cakes
b $x + 2y \leqslant 8$ $2x + y \leqslant 7$

c $P = 20x + 12y$

d

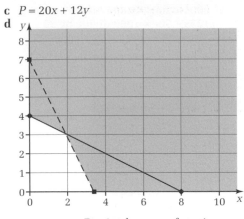

$x = 2, y = 3, P = £76$ by tour of vertices.

10 The Simplex Method

Review (p. 157)

1. **a** Maximise $3x + 5y$
   subject to
   $2x + 3y \leqslant 1000$
   $2x + 5y \leqslant 1600$
   b $0.2x + 0.3y + s_1 = 100$
   $12x + 30y + s_2 = 9600$
   c

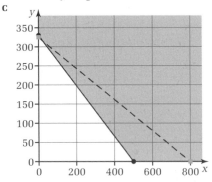

   d $(0, 0, 100, 9600)$ 100 kg stuffing and 9600 minutes spare
   $(500, 0, 0, 3600)$ no stuffing, 3600 minutes spare
   $(50, 300, 0, 0)$ no spare stuffing or time
   $(0, 320, 4, 0)$ 4 kg stuffing spare, no spare time

10.1 Technique (p. 163)

1. $x = 4, y = 2$, Profit = 32
2. $x = 3.5, y = 2.25$, Profit = 5.75
3. $x = 0, y = 8\frac{1}{3}, z = 6\frac{2}{3}$, Profit = $23\frac{1}{3}$
4. $x = 6, y = 0$, Profit = 48
   or $x = \frac{30}{11}, y = \frac{48}{11}$, Profit = 48
   and same profit at all points in between, on the constraint
5. $x = 0, y = 8.5$, Profit = 8.5
6. $x = 1, y = 0, z = 4$, Profit = -15

10.2 Technique (p. 166)

1. $x = 8, y = 0$, Profit = 8
2. $x = 6, y = 1$, Profit = 7
3. $x = 1.2, y = 4.2$, Profit = 14.4

10.3 Technique (p. 169)

Answers as given in 10.2 Technique above.

Consolidation A (p. 169)

1. **a** $x = 4, y = 5\frac{1}{3}$, Profit = $22\frac{2}{3}$
   b $x = 3.6, y = 5.6$, Profit = 22

2. $x = 3.6, y = 5.6$, Profit = 22

3. **a** Maximise $14x + 12y + 13z$
   subject to
   $4x + 5y + 3z < 16$
   $5x + 4y + 6z < 24$
   b r, s are slack variables.
   c

P	x	y	z	r	s	
1	0	5.5	−2.5	3.5	0	56
0	1	1.25	0.75	0.25	0	4
0	0	−2.25	2.25	−1.25	1	4

   d make 4 lions only, giving profit of £56

4. **a** maximise $3x + 2y + 5z$
   subject to
   $2x + 5y + 4z \leqslant 60$
   $2y + z \leqslant 10$
   $2x + 4y + 2z \leqslant 70$
   $4x + 3y + 2z \leqslant 180$
   b $x = 30$, Profit = 90
   c $y \geqslant 5$ becomes $y - s_5 + a = 5$
   d Minimise a becomes maximise $-a$:
   objective is $Q - y + s_5 = 5$ or Maximise
   $3x + (2 - M)y + 5z - Ms_5 - 5M$

5. **a**

P	x	y	s_1	s_2	s_3	RHS
1	−2	−1	0	0	0	0
0	1	1	1	0	0	7
0	1	2	0	1	0	10
0	2	3	0	0	1	16

   b

P	x	y	s_1	s_2	s_3	RHS
1	0	1	2	0	0	14
0	1	1	1	0	0	7
0	0	1	−1	1	0	3
0	0	1	−2	0	1	2

   c $x = 7, y = 0, P = 14$
   d Optimum: no negative values in 1st row so cannot increase.

Consolidation B (p. 171)

1. **a** $x = 4.846$, $y = 1.538$, Profit $= 6.384$
   b $x = 5$, $y = 2$, Profit $= 16$

2. $x = 5$, $y = 2$, Profit $= 31$

3. **a** no negative to increase in first row
   b $P = -\frac{3}{2}x - \frac{3}{4}r$: increasing x would decrease profit.
   c **i** £840   **ii** A(0), B(56), C(75)

4. **a**

P	x	y	s_1	s_2	RHS
1	−1	−3	0	0	0
0	2	3	1	0	8
0	1	6	0	1	10

   b increase x

P	x	y	s_1	s_2	LHS
1	0	−1.5	0.5	0	4
0	1	1.5	0.5	0	4
0	0	4.5	−0.5	1	6

   increase y

P	x	y	s_1	s_2	LHS
1	0	0	$\frac{1}{3}$	$\frac{1}{3}$	6
0	1	0	$\frac{2}{3}$	$-\frac{1}{3}$	2
0	0	1	$-\frac{1}{9}$	$\frac{2}{9}$	$\frac{4}{3}$

   c $x = 4$, $y = 0$, $P = 4$
   then $x = 2$, $y = \frac{4}{3}$, $P = 6$

5. **a**

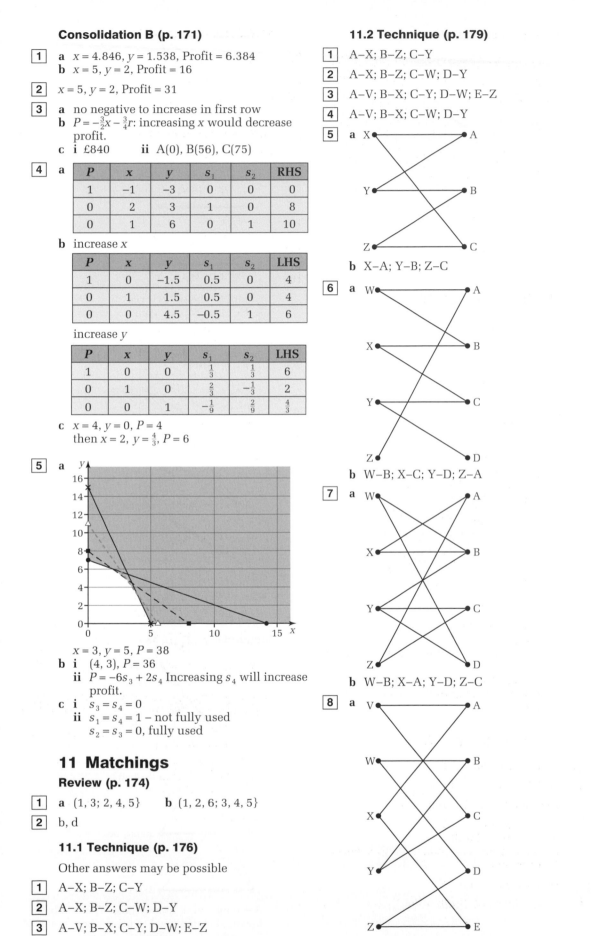

   $x = 3$, $y = 5$, $P = 38$
   b **i** (4, 3), $P = 36$
   ii $P = -6s_3 + 2s_4$ Increasing s_4 will increase profit.
   c **i** $s_3 = s_4 = 0$
   ii $s_1 = s_4 = 1$ – not fully used
   $s_2 = s_3 = 0$, fully used

11 Matchings

Review (p. 174)

1. **a** {1, 3; 2, 4, 5}   **b** {1, 2, 6; 3, 4, 5}

2. b, d

11.1 Technique (p. 176)

Other answers may be possible

1. A–X; B–Z; C–Y

2. A–X; B–Z; C–W; D–Y

3. A–V; B–X; C–Y; D–W; E–Z

4. A–V; B–X; C–W; D–Y

11.2 Technique (p. 179)

1. A–X; B–Z; C–Y

2. A–X; B–Z; C–W; D–Y

3. A–V; B–X; C–Y; D–W; E–Z

4. A–V; B–X; C–W; D–Y

5. **a**
   b X–A; Y–B; Z–C

6. **a**
   b W–B; X–C; Y–D; Z–A

7. **a**
   b W–B; X–A; Y–D; Z–C

8. **a**
   b V–A; W–B; X–E; Y–C; Z–D

Consolidation A (p. 181)

1 a
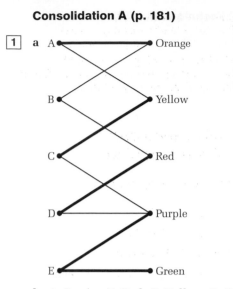

b A Orange; B–Red; C–Yellow; D–Purple;
E–Green

2 a
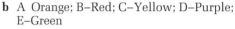
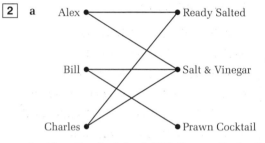
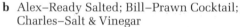

b Alex–Ready Salted; Bill–Prawn Cocktail;
Charles–Salt & Vinegar

3 a
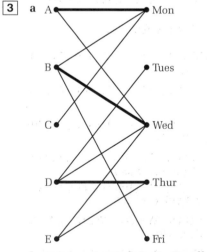

b C–Mon–A–Wed–B–Fr; D still Thur
c Tues–D–Thur–E
Complete matching: A–Wed; B–Fri;
C–Mon; D–Tue; E–Thur

4 a
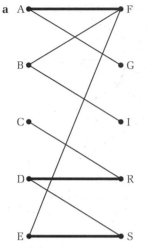

b C + R – D + S – E + F – A + G; B + I
Complete matching: A–G; B–I; C–R; D–S;
E–F

5 a,b
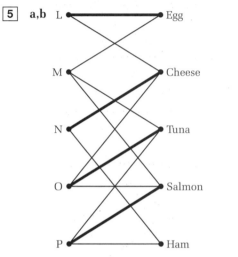

c M + E – L + C – N + H
Complete matching: L–C; M–E; N–H; O–T;
P–S

Consolidation B (p. 183)

1 a
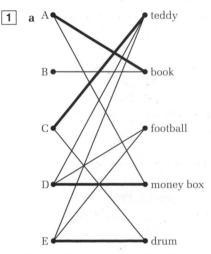

b B + book – A + money-box – D + football
Maximal matching: A + money-box; B + book;
C + teddy; D + football; E + drum

2 a

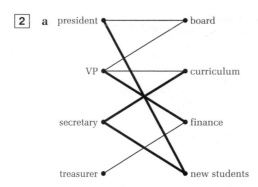

president — board
VP — curriculum
secretary — finance
treasurer — new students

b treasurer + finance – VP + board
Complete matching: President–new
students; VP–board; secretary –curriculum;
treasurer–finance

3 a

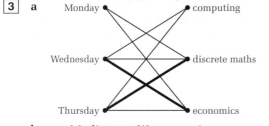

Monday — computing
Wednesday — discrete maths
Thursday — economics

b e.g.: M–discrete; W–computing;
Thurs–econ (other solutions possible)

4 a, b

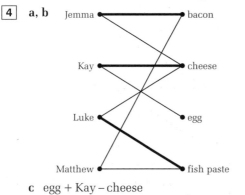

Jemma — bacon
Kay — cheese
Luke — egg
Matthew — fish paste

c egg + Kay – cheese
–Jemma ··· bacon–Matthew
Complete matching: Jemma–cheese;
Kay–egg; Luke–fishpaste; Matthew–bacon

5 a, b

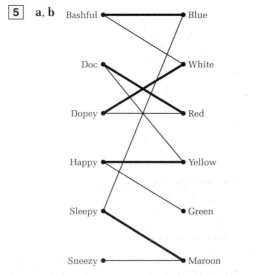

Bashful — Blue
Doc — White
Dopey — Red
Happy — Yellow
Sleepy — Green
Sneezy — Maroon

c Sneezy + Maroon – Sleepy + Blue –
Bashful + White – Dopey + Red –
Doc + Yellow – Happy + Green

Maximal matching: Bashful–White;
Doc–Yellow; Dopey–Red; Happy–Green;
Sleepy–Blue; Sneezy–Maroon

12 Allocation and Transportation

12.1 Technique (p. 190)

1 A–V, B–Y, C–W, D–X; 12

2 A–V, B–W, C–Y, D–X; 12

3 A–Y, B–X, C–W, D–V; 19

4 A–X, B–Y, C–W, D–V; Z unallocated; 7

5 A–Y, B–X, C–V, D–Z; W unallocated; 19

12.2 Technique (p. 195)

1 A–Z, B–Y, C–X, D–V, E–W; 17

2 A–Z, B–V, C–W, D–X, E–Y; 22

3 A–V, B–Y, C–X, D–Z, E–W; 38

4 A–W, B–Y, D–X, E–V (C unallocated); 23

5 A–V, B–Z, D–X, E–Y, F–W (C unallocated); 41

6 A–X, B–V, C–Y, D–W; Profit = 48

7 A–W, B–Y, C–X, D–V; Profit = 56

8 A–Z, B–X, C–Y, D–W, E–V; Profit = 83

12.3 Contextual (p. 199)

1 VA(30), VB(20), WB(40), WC(10), XC(40),
XD(40); cost 640

2 VA(50), VB(20), WC(30), XC(10), XD(60);
COST 370

3 VA(50), VB(30), WB(20), WC(10), XC(40),
XD(50); COST 740

4 VA(40), WA(10), WB(20), XB(10), SC(10),
YC(30), YD(30); cost 550

5 VA(20), VB(20), WB(10), WC(30), XC(10),
XD(30), YD(20); cost 480

6 VC(20), VD(20), WB(30), WC(10), XA(30),
XD(10); Cost 630

7 VA(10), VD(40), WA(10), WB(50), XA(40),
XC(30); Cost 2510

8 VC(40), WA(30), XB(20), YA(20), YB(10),
YD(30); Cost 610

12.4 Technique (p. 204)

1. Not optimum
2. Not optimum
3. Not optimum
4. Not optimum
5. Not optimum
6. Optimum
7. Not optimum
8. Not optimum

12.5 Technique (p. 206)

1. AX = 30, BV = 10, BX = 50, CW = 50, DV = 40;
Cost = 340

2. AW = 30, AX = 20, BV = 20, CX = 40, DV = 50,
DX = 10; Cost = 340

3. VB = 50, VC = 30, WA = 30, XA = 20, XC = 20,
XD = 50; Cost = 570

4. AV = 40, AW = 10, BY = 30, CX = 10, CY = 30,
DW = 20, DX = 10; Cost = 410

5. VC = 30, VD = 10, WD = 40, XA = 20, YA = 20,
YB = 30, YC = 10; Cost = 410

6. Optimum

7. AV = 50, AW = 10, BW = 50, CX = 30,
DX = 40; Cost = 2190

8. AV = 20, AW = 30, BY = 30, CV = 20, CX = 20,
DY = 30; Cost = 570

Consolidation A (p. 206)

1. Debby–R, Carl–Q, Bert–P, Elaine–S: cost 334.

2. a i

	A	B	C	D
I	2	0	0	0
II	0	3	1	1
III	0	0	3	0
IV	0	4	3	0

   ii A–II, C–I, B–III, D–IV
   b 69 minutes.

3. a Annie–Under stairs, Benny–Trunk Room,
Connie–Veranda, Danny–Wardrobe
   b 16 minutes
   c All values in the table would be made
negative. The smallest in each row/column
is then subtracted as before – this will turn
the non-zero values positive again and the
algorithm continues.

4. a Art Gallery–Thursday, Castle–Wednesday,
Beach–Saturday, Exhibition–Friday
   b 4.50 + 4.50 + 1.50 + 6.00 = £16.50

5. a

	Farm A	Farm B	Farm C	Farm D
Shop A	6 (40)	7	5	9
Shop B	8 (10)	3 (20)	16	4
Shop C	13	15 (10)	12 (10)	3
Shop D	11	14	2 (30)	12 (30)

   Cost = 1070

   b

	Farm A	Farm B	Farm C	Farm D
Shop A	6 (40)	7	5	9
Shop B	8	3 (30)	16	4
Shop C	13	15	12	3(20)
Shop D	11 (10)	14	2 (40)	12

   Cost:
   $40 \times 6 + 30 \times 3 + 20 \times 3 + 10 \times 11$
   $+ 40 \times 2 + 10 \times 12 = 700$

Consolidation B (p. 209)

1. a $F_1 W_1(2), F_1 W_2(2), F_2 W_2(3), F_3 W_2(4),$
$F_3 W_3(4)$; cost 72
   b

	W_1	W_2	W_3	R_i
F_1	7	8	6[1]	7
F_2	9[8]	2	4[5]	1
F_3	5[0]	6	3	5
K_i	0	1	−2	

   c nothing negative to improve

2. a Jenny–Drainage, Kenny–Building,
Lenny–Carpentry, Penny–Electrics.
   b £14000

3. A–1, B–2, C–3, D–4 = 179 seconds

4. a All values negated.
   b Add a 'dummy' grandchild.
   c Arnie–Maps, Beth–Views, Cyril–Puppies,
Des–Seaside, Erin–Railway.

5. The following table gives information about
the supply, demand and transportation costs
of sacks of organic potatoes between farms
and shops.
   a FA–SA–40, FA–SD–10, FB–SB–30,
FC–SD–40, FD–SC–20, FD–SD–10
   b Optimal, 900.

13 Network Flow

Review (p. 212)

1 **a**

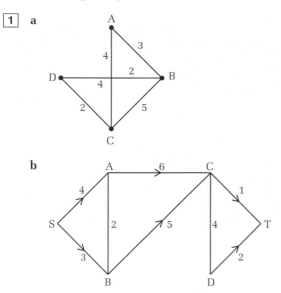

b

13.1 Technique (p. 214)

1

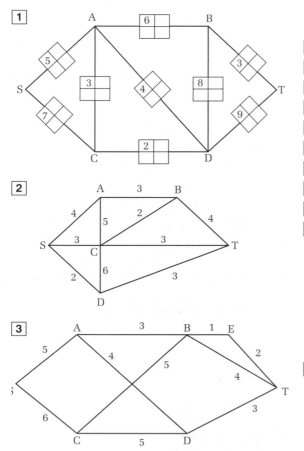

2

3

4

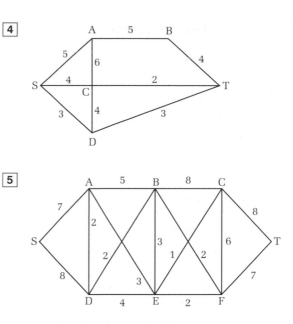

5

13.2 Technique (p. 216)

There are many possible answers to each of these questions.

13.3 Technique (p. 219)

The answers below give the maximum flow, and the edges used for the minimum cut.

1 10 SA, AC, CD

2 9 SA, SC, SD

3 8 BE, BT, DT

4 9 BT, CT, DT

5 13 BC, EC, BF, EF

6 9 BT, CT, DT

7 11 BT, BC, DC

8 14 SE, CE, CD, BD, BT

9 21 BT, ET

10 25 SA, DA, DB, DE

13.4 Technique (p. 222)

Many different answers are possible for these questions. However, any answer will use the full capacity of all the edges included in the minimum cut.

Consolidation A (p. 222)

1 **a** 11
b

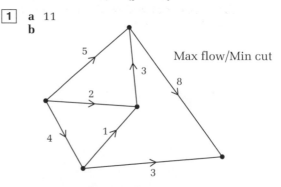

Max flow/Min cut

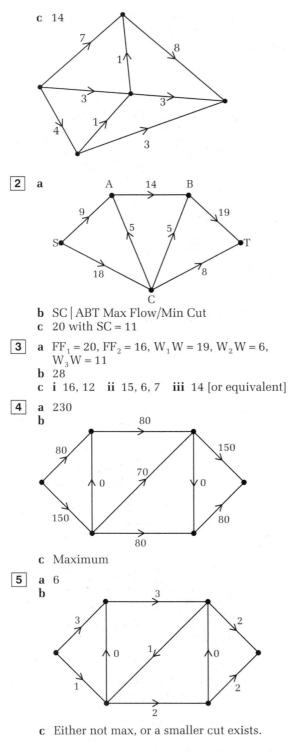

c 14

2 a

b SC | ABT Max Flow/Min Cut

c 20 with SC = 11

3 a $FF_1 = 20$, $FF_2 = 16$, $W_1W = 19$, $W_2W = 6$, $W_3W = 11$

b 28

c i 16, 12 **ii** 15, 6, 7 **iii** 14 [or equivalent]

4 a 230

b

c Maximum

5 a 6

b

c Either not max, or a smaller cut exists.

Consolidation B (p. 225)

1 a several answers **b** max flow = 7
  c SA, SB, BC, BF = 7

2 a Max flow into B is 11, of this, 4 must go to A and 2 to C, leaving only 5 for D. If flow into D is only 5 (and there are no other flows in) then there cannot be a flow of 6 out of D to A.

b Minimum flow into A is 18, which exceeds the maximum possible out, of 14, on AC.

c $14 + 3 + 10 - 6 = 21$

3 a You should add edges SS_1 SS_2, SS_3 and T_1T, T_2T where S and T represent the super-source and super-sink.

b 40

c many answers

d i many answers must have flow = 30, with AB = 5, BC = 5, AF = 5, CD = 5, SE = 10

4 a 19

b For any vertex, flow in = flow out. $x = 13$, $y = 9$, $z = 4$

c flow can be increased along S A D E T

d Max flow = 74

e changed flows: SA = 34, AD = 23, DE = 13, ET = 24

f cut: SA, BD, BF

5 a $C_1 = 40$ $C_2 = 56$

b 40

c 24 because AF, DF are at maximum capacity (16), so FG = 16. DG is also saturated (at maximum capacity).

d 19 or 20

e For both parts, all edges on cut are at maximum FG = 16, GT = 24 and HT = 16.

f total possibilities are 4: SA = 19 or 20; CE = 11 or 12. These choices are independent of each other.

14 Dynamic Programming

14.1 Technique (p. 233)

1 SADT = 8

2 SBCT = 25

3 SACFT = 30

4 SAEHT = 20

14.2 Technique (p. 237)

1 a SBCT or SBDT; min = 3
  b SADT; max = 4

2 a SACT or SADT; min = 6
  b SACT; max = 11

3 a SBDFT; min = 7
  b SBDFT; max = 9

4 a SADGT; min = 4
  b SADGT; max = 8

Consolidation A (p. 237)

1   SADT = 10

2   **a**   SAECT; min = 3   **b**   SAECT; max = 4

3   **a**

Stage	State	Action	Cost	Total cost
2	0	C	3	3*
	1	A	2	2
		B	3	3
		C	6	6*
	2	A	1	1
		B	2	2*
1	0	B	2	5
		C	3	9*
	1	A	1	4
		B	3	9*
		C	6	8
	2	A	5	11*
		B	5	7
0	0	A	4	13
		B	3	12
		C	5	16*

CAC; max profit = £16,000

4   CAB; cost = £32,000

5   AEI; profit = £140,000

Consolidation B (p. 240)

1   SBFHT = 25

2   **a**   SBEHT; min = 9   **b**   SADIT; max = 13

3

Stage	State	Action	Route minimum	Current maximum
	0	0	3	3
2	1	0	4	4
	2	0	6*	6*
	0	0	3	4
		1	4*	
		0	3	
1	1	1	2	4
		2	4*	
	2	1	3	5*
		2	5*	
	0	0	4	4
0	1	1	3	3
	2	2	5*	5*

b   Maximum route: (0;0), (1;2), (2;2), (3;0)
maximum = 5

4   **a**

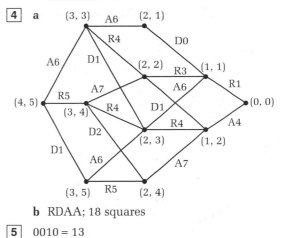

b   RDAA; 18 squares

5   0010 = 13

15 Game Theory

Review (p. 244)

1

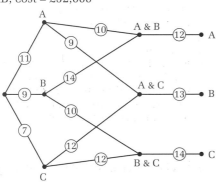

2   **a**

	A	B	C
Andy	12	21	9
Charlie	9	16	4
Seren	7	15	6

b   Maximise $12p_1 + 21p_2 + 9(1 - p_1 - p_2)$
subject to
$9p_1 + 16p_2 + 14(1 - p_1 - p_2) \leqslant 12$
$7p_1 + 15p_2 + 6(1 - p_1 - p_2) \geqslant 8$

15.1 Technique (p. 247)

1   1 saddle; value = −2

2   2 saddles; value = −2

3   none

4   none

5   none

6   1 saddle; value = 2

7   none

8   1 saddle; value = −1

15.2 Technique (p. 248)

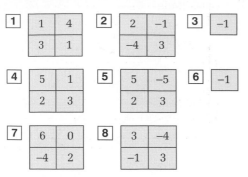

1
1	4
3	1

2
2	−1
−4	3

3
−1

4
5	1
2	3

5
5	−5
2	3

6
−1

7
6	0
−4	2

8
3	−4
−1	3

15.3 Technique (p. 252)

All answers give the probability with which player A should choose row 1, unless otherwise stated.

1 $p = \frac{3}{4}$; value = 2.5

2 $p = \frac{2}{3}$; value = $3\frac{2}{3}$

3 $p = \frac{1}{2}$; value = −1.5

4 $p = \frac{1}{3}$; value = 1

5 row 1 with $p = \frac{1}{2}$; row 2 with $p = \frac{1}{2}$ value = 0.5

6 $p = \frac{1}{2}$; value = 2.5

15.4 Technique (p. 254)

1 max v
st $v \leqslant 3p_1 + 5p_2 + 7p_3$ $p_2 = \frac{2}{5}$
    $v \leqslant 5p_1 + 4p_2 + 6p_3$ $p_3 = \frac{3}{5}$
    $v \leqslant 7p_2 + 4p_3$ value = $2\frac{1}{5}$
  $p_1 + p_2 + p_3 = 1$

2 max v
st $v \leqslant 6p_1$ $p_1 = 0.7$
    $v \leqslant 3p_1 + 2p_2 + 7p_3$ $p_3 = 0.3$
    $v \leqslant 8p_1 + 4p_2 + 5p_3$ value = $\frac{1}{5}$
  $p_1 + p_2 + p_3 = 1$

3 max v
st $v \leqslant 10p_1 + 6p_2 + 7p_3$ $p_2 = 1$
    $v \leqslant p_1 + 4p_2 + 3p_3$ value = −1
    $v \leqslant 8p_2 + 3p_3$
  $p_1 + p_2 + p_3 = 1$

4 max v
st $v \leqslant 5p_1 + 2p_2 + p_3$ $p_1 = 0.2$
    $v \leqslant p_1 + 3p_2$ $p_2 = 0.8$
    $v \leqslant 4p_1 + 6p_2$ value = 2.6
  $p_1 + p_2 + p_3 = 1$

5 max v
st $v \leqslant 10p_1 + p_2 + 7p_3$ $p_1 = \frac{1}{11}$
    $v \leqslant 8p_3$ $p_3 = \frac{10}{11}$
    $v \leqslant 7p_1 + 7p_2 + 9p_3$ value = $7\frac{3}{11}$
  $p_1 + p_2 + p_3 = 1$

6 max v
st $v \leqslant p_1$ $p_1 = 1$
    $v \leqslant 2p_1 + 3p_2 + p_3$ value = −1
    $v \leqslant 4p_1 + 5p_3$
  $p_1 + p_2 + p_3 = 1$

7 max v
st $v \leqslant 10p_1 + 6p_3$ $p_1 = \frac{1}{2}$
    $v \leqslant 5p_1 + 7p_2 + p_3$ $p_2 = \frac{1}{2}$
    $v \leqslant 4p_1 + 6p_2 + 3p_3$ value = 1
  $p_1 + p_2 + p_3 = 1$

8 max v
st $v \leqslant 7p_1 + 3p_2 + p_3$ $p_1 = \frac{4}{11}$
    $v \leqslant 8p_1 + 6p_2 + 5p_3$ $p_2 = \frac{7}{11}$
    $v \leqslant 7p_3$ value = $4\frac{5}{11}$
  $p_1 + p_2 + p_3 = 1$

Consolidation A (p. 254)

1   **a** No column maximum = row minimum
   b Z dominates X.
   c Y with prob $\frac{6}{7}$, Z with prob $\frac{1}{7}$.

2   A choose 1 with $p = \frac{11}{17}$, 2 with $p = \frac{6}{17}$.
   B choose 1 with $q = \frac{8}{17}$, 2 with $q = \frac{9}{17}$ value $\frac{14}{17}$ to A.

3   **a** Both stick on play-safe, but not same value.
   b   **i** Twist
      ii Stick
   c $-2 + 5p$
   d $\frac{2}{3}$

4   **a** Rose = Hide, Computer = Shoot. Not same value.
   b each delay value < corresponding hide value.
   c Track
   d Fight: $5 - 2p$, Shoot: $-1 + 5p$, Track: $2 + 4p$
   e $\frac{6}{7}$

5   **a** max v
    st $v \leqslant 3p_1 + 8p_3 + 10p_3$
       $v \leqslant 9p_2 + 4p_3$
       $v \leqslant 6p_1 + 11p_2 + 7p_3$
      $p_1 + p_2 + p_3 = 1$

   b max v
    st $v \leqslant 4p_1 + 6p_2$
       $v \leqslant 5p_1$
      $p_1 + p_2 = 1$

   $p_1 = \frac{6}{7}$, $p_2 = \frac{1}{7}$, value = $\frac{23}{7}$; Hide = $\frac{6}{7}$,
   Negotiate = $\frac{1}{7}$

Consolidation B (p. 256)

1   **a** Richard–strategy A, value −2.
    Carol–strategy 2, value 1.
    Values not equal, so not stable.
   b Let Richard play A with probability p_1, B with probility p_2 and C with probability p_3.
    Let v = value of the game.
    max v
    st $v \leqslant 7p_1 + p_2$
       $v \leqslant 8p_1 - 4p_2 + 5p_3$
       $v \leqslant 3p_1 + 4p_2 + 6p_3$
      $p_1 + p_2 + p_3 = 1$

2 Whatever the audience, which one of old or new songs scores higher.

a Young = $p + 8(1 - p) = 8 - 7p$
Mixed = $3p + 5(1 - p) = 5 - 2p$
Older = $8p + 3(1 - p) = 3 + 5p$

b $p = \frac{2}{7}$

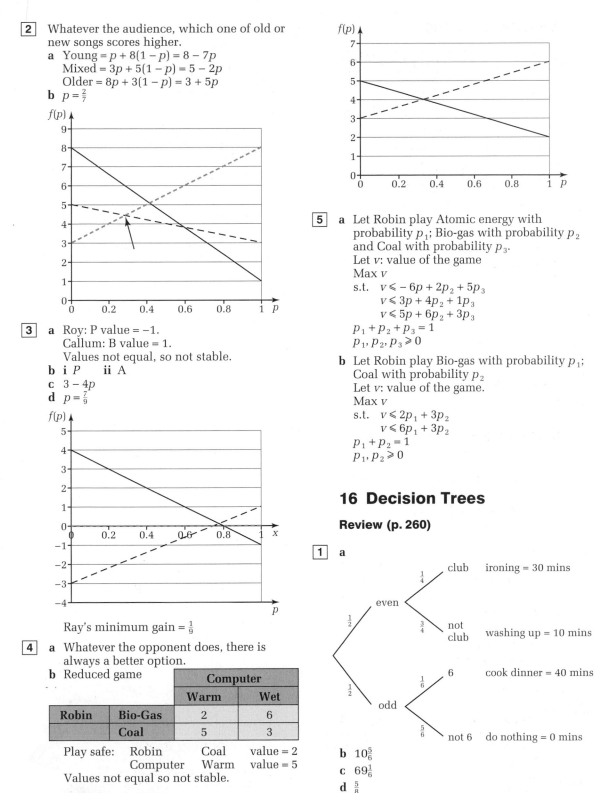

3 a Roy: P value = -1.
Callum: B value = 1.
Values not equal, so not stable.

b i P ii A

c $3 - 4p$

d $p = \frac{7}{9}$

Ray's minimum gain = $\frac{1}{9}$

4 a Whatever the opponent does, there is always a better option.

b Reduced game

Robin		Computer	
		Warm	Wet
Robin	Bio-Gas	2	6
	Coal	5	3

Play safe: Robin   Coal   value = 2
          Computer   Warm   value = 5
Values not equal so not stable.

c $6p + 3(1 - p) = 3 + 3p$

d $p = \frac{1}{3}$; expected game = 3

5 a Let Robin play Atomic energy with probability p_1; Bio-gas with probability p_2 and Coal with probability p_3.
Let v: value of the game
Max v
s.t. $v \leqslant -6p + 2p_2 + 5p_3$
      $v \leqslant 3p + 4p_2 + 1p_3$
      $v \leqslant 5p + 6p_2 + 3p_3$
$p_1 + p_2 + p_3 = 1$
$p_1, p_2, p_3 \geqslant 0$

b Let Robin play Bio-gas with probability p_1; Coal with probability p_2
Let v: value of the game.
Max v
s.t. $v \leqslant 2p_1 + 3p_2$
      $v \leqslant 6p_1 + 3p_2$
$p_1 + p_2 = 1$
$p_1, p_2 \geqslant 0$

16 Decision Trees

Review (p. 260)

1 a

b $10\frac{5}{6}$

c $69\frac{1}{6}$

d $\frac{5}{8}$

16.1 Contextual (p. 261)

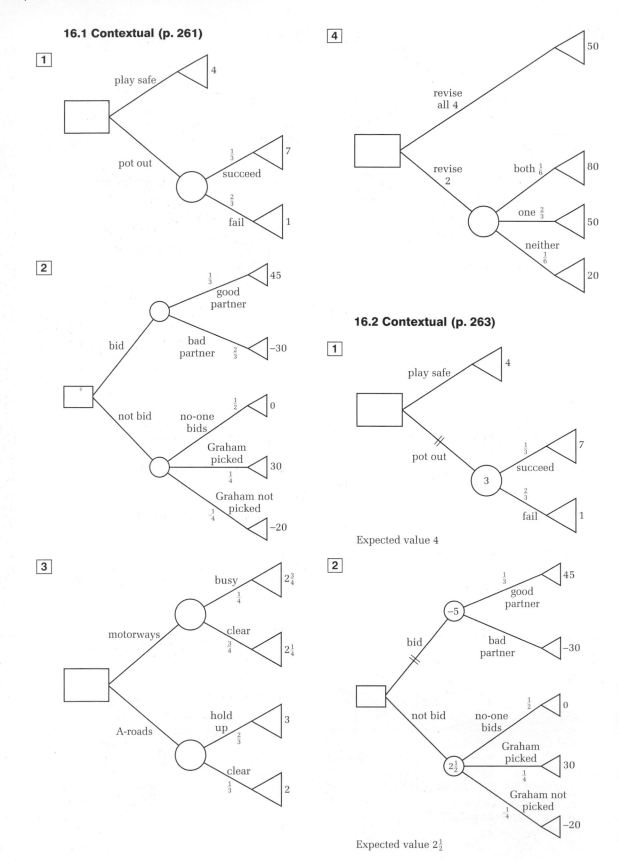

1

play safe — 4

pot out
succeed $\frac{1}{3}$ — 7
fail $\frac{2}{3}$ — 1

2

bid
good partner $\frac{1}{3}$ — 45
bad partner $\frac{2}{3}$ — −30

not bid
no-one bids $\frac{1}{2}$ — 0
Graham picked $\frac{1}{4}$ — 30
Graham not picked $\frac{1}{4}$ — −20

3

motorways
busy $\frac{1}{4}$ — $2\frac{3}{4}$
clear $\frac{3}{4}$ — $2\frac{1}{4}$

A-roads
hold up $\frac{2}{3}$ — 3
clear $\frac{1}{3}$ — 2

4

revise all 4 — 50

revise 2
both $\frac{1}{6}$ — 80
one $\frac{2}{3}$ — 50
neither $\frac{1}{6}$ — 20

16.2 Contextual (p. 263)

1

play safe — 4

pot out
3
succeed $\frac{1}{3}$ — 7
fail $\frac{2}{3}$ — 1

Expected value 4

2

bid
−5
good partner $\frac{1}{3}$ — 45
bad partner — −30

not bid
$2\frac{1}{2}$
no-one bids $\frac{1}{2}$ — 0
Graham picked $\frac{1}{4}$ — 30
Graham not picked $\frac{1}{4}$ — −20

Expected value $2\frac{1}{2}$

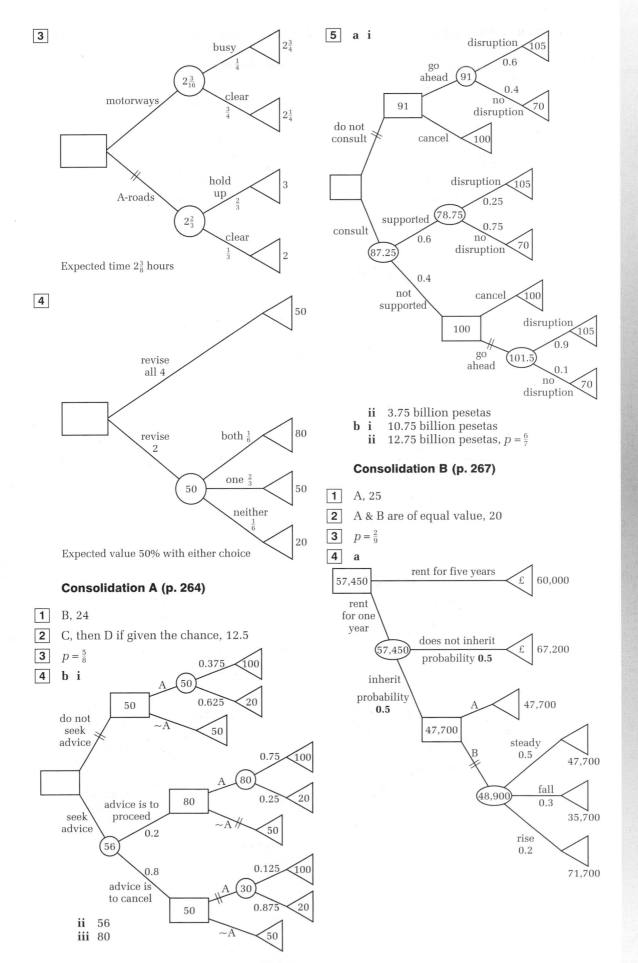

3

motorways

busy $\frac{1}{4}$ → $2\frac{3}{4}$

clear $\frac{3}{4}$ → $2\frac{1}{4}$

$2\frac{3}{16}$

A-roads

hold up $\frac{2}{3}$ → 3

clear $\frac{1}{3}$ → 2

$2\frac{2}{3}$

Expected time $2\frac{3}{8}$ hours

4

revise all 4 → 50

revise 2

both $\frac{1}{6}$ → 80

one $\frac{2}{3}$ → 50

neither $\frac{1}{6}$ → 20

50

Expected value 50% with either choice

Consolidation A (p. 264)

1 B, 24

2 C, then D if given the chance, 12.5

3 $p = \frac{5}{8}$

4 **b i**

do not seek advice

50

A 50

0.375 → 100

0.625 → 20

~A → 50

seek advice

56

advice is to proceed 0.2

80

A 80

0.75 → 100

0.25 → 20

~A → 50

advice is to cancel 0.8

50

A 30

0.125 → 100

0.875 → 20

~A → 50

ii 56
iii 80

5 **a i**

go ahead

91

disruption 0.6 → 105

no disruption 0.4 → 70

91

do not consult

cancel → 100

consult

87.25

supported 0.6

78.75

disruption 0.25 → 105

no disruption 0.75 → 70

not supported 0.4

100

cancel → 100

go ahead

101.5

disruption 0.9 → 105

no disruption 0.1 → 70

ii 3.75 billion pesetas
b i 10.75 billion pesetas
ii 12.75 billion pesetas, $p = \frac{6}{7}$

Consolidation B (p. 267)

1 A, 25

2 A & B are of equal value, 20

3 $p = \frac{2}{9}$

4 **a**

57,450

rent for five years → £ 60,000

rent for one year

57,450

does not inherit probability **0.5** → £ 67,200

inherit probability **0.5**

47,700

A → 47,700

B

48,900

steady 0.5 → 47,700

fall 0.3 → 35,700

rise 0.2 → 71,700

363

b rent for one year then option A (if she inherits)
Expected cost = £57,450
c as above, cost now £59,400
d 36.9% (3 s.f.)

5 **a**

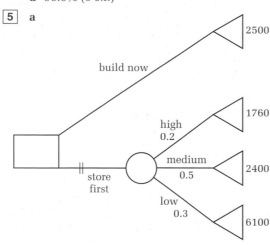

build now, cost advantage £882 million
b store first, cost advantage £420 million
c

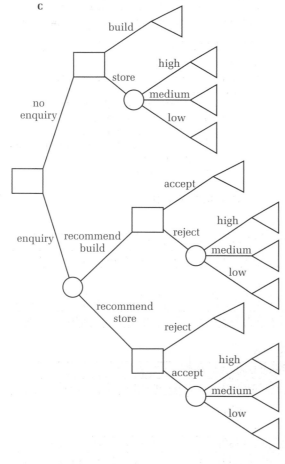

17 Simulation

Review (p. 272)

1 33125

17.1 Contextual (p. 275)

1 **a**

Mins	0	3	8	13	23
Random Nos	00–19	20–59	60–79	80–89	90–99

c Likely to be approx. 128 minutes

2 **a**

Weather	Sunny	Raining	Snowing	Foggy
Random Nos	00–26	27–74	75–83	84–92

reject 93–99

4

No of Drinks	0	1	2	3	4
Random Nos	00–22	23–57	58–79	80–92	93–99

17.2 Contextual (p. 277)

1 **a**

Inter-arrival time	1 min	2 min	3 min	4 min
Random Nos	00–29	30–49	50–79	80–99

Service time	30 sec	1 min	90 sec	2 min
Random Nos	00–49	50–79	80–89	90–99

2 **a**

Service time	1 min	2 min	3 min	4 min
Random Nos	00–23	24–59	60–77	78–89

reject 90–99

Service time	30 sec	1 min	90 sec	2 min
Random Nos	00–17	18–53	54–80	81–98

reject 99

3 **a**

Inter-arrival time	0	1	2	3
Random Nos	00–15	16–55	56–79	80–95

reject 96–99

Service time	30 sec	1 min	90 sec	2 min
Random Nos	00–29	30–64	65–79	80–89

reject 90–99

17.3 Contextual (p. 279)

1 19

2 **a** 4   **b** 31

Consolidation A (p. 280)

1 **a**

Inter-arrival time	1	2	3	4
Random Nos	00–39	40–59	60–89	90–99

b

Service time	30 sec	1 min	90 sec	2 min
Random Nos	00–49	50–79	80–89	90–99

2 **a**

Inter-arrival time	1	2	3	4
Random Nos	00–20	21–55	56–76	77–90

reject 92–99

b

Service time	30 sec	1 min	90 sec	2 min
Random Nos	00–17	18–53	54–80	81–90

reject 99

3 **a i**

Random numbers	00–09	10–49	50–69	70–89	90–99
Time (minutes)	$\frac{1}{2}$	1	$1\frac{1}{2}$	2	$2\frac{1}{2}$

ii

Car number	1	2	3
Time (minutes)	2	$2\frac{1}{2}$	1

b i

Random numbers	00–31	32–79	80–95
Time (minutes)	$\frac{1}{2}$	1	$1\frac{1}{2}$

ii

Order number	1	2	3
Time	$\frac{1}{2}$	$\frac{1}{2}$	1

c Rule 1

Car	a-t	window 1 or 2	To a 1 or 2	To b c p	To L 1 or 2	To L system
1	12:00	2	12:00	12:02	12:02	$12:02\frac{1}{2}$
2	$12:01\frac{1}{2}$	1	$12:01\frac{1}{2}$	12:04	12:04	$12:04\frac{1}{2}$
3	12:02	2	12:04 (A)	12:05	12:05	12:06

Rule 2

1	12:00	2	12:00	12:02	12:02	$12:02\frac{1}{2}$
2	$12:01\frac{1}{2}$	2	12:02 (B)	$12:04\frac{1}{2}$	$12:04\frac{1}{2}$	12:05
3	12:02	1	12:02	12:03	$12:04\frac{1}{2}$ (C)	12:05 (D)

d Rule 2 is quicker overall but slower for car 2

4 **i** 16

ii 00–47   2 seconds
48–63   7 seconds
64–95   35 seconds
reject 96–99

iii

i	1	2	3	4	5	6	7	8	9	10	11	12	13	14	15
l	2	2	7	7	7	35	2	2	35	35	2	2	35	2	35
ct	2	4	11	18	25	60	62	64	99	134	136	138	173	175	210

iv 25–60 seconds

car	1	2	3	4	5	6
time of arrival	0	10	20	30	40	50
time of dep	25	29	33	37	40	50

v 3
vi Run the simulation for a longer period than 1 minute
Include realistic variation in the arrival times from the side road
Use a finer (more smaller groups) probability distribution for the interval time on the main road.
[any two of these].

Consolidation B (p. 285)

1 **a**

Inter-arrival time	1	2	3	4
Random Nos	00–19	20–49	50–69	70–99

b

Service time	30 sec	1 min	90 sec	2 min
Random Nos	00–49	50–79	80–89	90–99

2 **a**

Inter-arrival time	1	2	3	4
Random Nos	00–06	07–55	56–90	91–97

reject 98, 99

b

Service time	30 sec	1 min	90 sec	2 min
Random Nos	00–17	18–53	54–80	81–98

reject 99

3 **i** Wet 00–27; Dry 28–97; reject 98, 99.
ii DDDWWDWWDDWDDD
iii $\frac{5}{14}$
iv $\frac{8}{14}$
v Run for more days, include seasons.

4 **a**

Inter-arrival time	2	3	4
Random Nos	00–24	25–74	75–99

3, 2, 2, 4, 2

b

Length of service	1	2	4
Random Numbers	00–31	32–79	80–95

2, 5, 2, 1, 1, 1

c

Customer no.	Arrival time	Start of service	End of service
1	0	0	2
2	3	3	8
3	5	8	10
4	7	10	11
5	11	11	12
6	13	13	14

d mean queuing time 1 min, mean queue length $\frac{6}{14}$ people, server utilisation 86%
e run for longer (more customers)

18 Recurrence Relations

18.1 Contextual (p. 290)

1 3, 9, 21, 45, 93 **4** 2, 14, 98, 686, 4802

2 3, 11, 35, 107, 323 **5** 3, −1, 3, −1, 3

3 2, 11, 56, 281, 1406 **6** 3, 5, 7, 9, 11

18.2 Technique (p. 291)

1 $u_n = 6 \times 2^n - 3$ **4** $u_n = 2 \times 7^n$

2 $u_n = 4 \times 3^n - 1$ **5** $u_n = 2 \times (-1)^n + 1$

3 $u_n = 2.25 \times 5^n - 0.25$ **6** $u_n = 3 + 2n$

18.3 Technique (p. 293)

1 **a** $u_n = A \times 3^n + B(-1)^2$
  b $A = \frac{3}{4}\ B = \frac{1}{4}$

2 **a** $u_n = = A \times 2^n + B$
  b $A = -2\ B = 5$

3 **a** $u_n = A + B(-2)^n$
  b $A = 4\ B = 0$

4 **a** $u_n = (A + B_n) \times 3^n$
  b $A = 2\ B = -1$

5 **a** $u_n = A \times 1.5^n + B \times 0.5^n$
  b $A = 0\ B = 2$

18.4 Technique (p. 295)

1 $u_n = \frac{11}{8} \times 3^n + \frac{5}{8}(-1)^n - \frac{1}{2}n - 1$

2 $u_n = \frac{1}{24}(39 - 13n)3^n + \frac{n}{8} + \frac{3}{8}$

3 $u_n = -82(1.5)^n + 8n^2 + 32n + 84$

Consolidation A (p. 295)

1 **a** $u_3 = 18$
  b $u_{n+1} = u_n$ (previous year) $+ u_{n-1}$ (new twigs = number at least 2 years old)
  c **i**
  $u_n = (3 + \frac{3}{\sqrt{5}})((1 + \sqrt{5})/2)^n + (3 - \frac{3}{\sqrt{5}})((1 - \sqrt{5})/2)^n$
  ii $u_2 = 12$
  d $u_4 = 30,\ u_5 = 48,\ a$
  e would require $19\frac{1}{2}$ to be pruned.

2 **a** $wx;\ x + x^2$
  b No. of new letters $= x/w$ times u_n, each sending w letters $= xu_n$ $u_n = x^{n-1}w$
  c Amount of new money at level $n = x/w$ times $u_{n+1} = x^{n+1}$ $v_n = x(x^n - 1)/(x - 1)$
  d $u_{10} = 118098,\ v_{10} = 88572$. No – not all unique people.

3 **a** $u_n = a^n(c + b/(a - 1)) - b/(a - 1)$
  b $u_n = 20(1 - 0.5^n)$

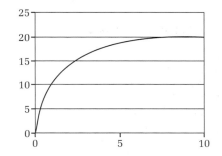

4 **a** 1220
  b $p_{n+1} = 1.2p_n - 100;\ p_n = 500(1.2^n + 1)$
  c 17

5 **a** $c_1 = 9;\ c_2 = 8.1$
  b $c_{n+1} = 0.9c_n;\ 22$

Consolidation B (p. 297)

1 **a** length at end of today = length at end of yesterday + growth today
  b $L_{n+1} = 1.8L_n - 0.8L_{n-1}$
  c $L_n = 6 - 5(0.8^n)$
  d 4
  e 148 cm (3 s.f.)
  f 122 cm (3 s.f.)

2 **a** 2.5%
  b 25 ml
  c 475 ml (4.75%)
  d $u_{n+1} = 0.9u_n + 250$
  e $C_{n+1} = \dfrac{9000C_n + 250}{10\,000} = \dfrac{36C_n + 1}{40} = 0.9C_n + 2.5$
  f 25%

3 **a** $u_2 = 700,\ u_3 = 850$
  b $u_{n+1} = 1.5u_n - 200$
  c $u_n = 133\frac{1}{3} \times 1.5^n + 400$

4 **a** $u_{n+1} = 1.02u_n - X$
  b $u_n = (1000 - 50X)(1.02)^n + 50X$
  c £66.70

5 **a** $u_2 = 7\ u_3 = 20$
  b $u_n = \frac{3}{4}(3^n) + \frac{1}{4}(-1)^n$

19 Propositional Logic

19.1 Technique (p. 301)

1
  a If I am carrying an umbrella then it is raining.
  b It is raining and I am on holiday.
  c I am not carrying an umbrella.
  d It is raining and I am not on holiday.
  e If it is raining and I am not carrying an umbrella then I am on holiday.
  f If it is not raining then I am not on holiday.
  g If I am on holiday then it is raining.

2
  a $p \Rightarrow \sim q$
  b $p \vee r$
  c $q \vee r$
  d $p \Rightarrow (r \wedge \sim q)$
  e $\sim q \Rightarrow p$
  f $r \Rightarrow p$

19.2 Technique (p. 303)

1
  a $a \vee b$
  b $(a \wedge b) \vee (a \wedge c)$
  c $(a \wedge b) \vee (\sim a \wedge c) \vee (b \wedge c)$
  d $(a \vee b) \vee c$
  e $((a \wedge b) \vee \sim a) \vee \sim b$

2
  a
  b

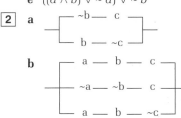

19.3 Technique (p. 308)

1 **b** and **c**   **d** and **f**

2 **a**

b	c	~b ∧ c	∨	b ∧ ~c
0	0	0	0	0
0	1	1	1	0
1	0	0	1	1
1	1	0	0	0

b

a	b	c	(a ∧ b ∧ c)	∨	~a ∧ ~ b ∧ c)	∨	a ∧ b ∧ ~c
0	0	0	0	0	0	0	0
0	0	1	0	1	1	1	0
0	1	0	0	0	0	0	0
0	1	1	0	0	0	0	0
1	0	0	0	0	0	0	0
1	0	1	0	0	0	0	0
1	1	0	0	0	0	1	1
1	1	1	1	1	0	1	0

3
  a tautology   **b** tautology
  c neither   **d** tautology
  e tautology   **f** tautology
  g tautology

19.4 Technique (p. 310)

1
  a $(a \wedge b) \vee (b \vee c)$ **b** $(a \vee b) \vee (c \vee d)$
  e $\sim(a \wedge b) \wedge c$ **d** $(\sim a \wedge b) \vee \sim c$

2
  a
  b

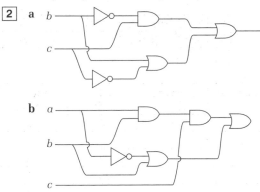

19.5 Technique (p. 313)

1 $(a \wedge b) \wedge (a \wedge c)$
  $= a \wedge (b \vee c)$ distributive

2 $(a \vee b) \wedge (a \wedge b)$
  $= [(a \vee b) \wedge a] \wedge [(a \vee b) \wedge b]$ distributive
  $= a \vee b$ adsorption

3 $(a \wedge b) \vee (a \wedge \sim b) = a \wedge (b \vee \sim b)$ distributive
  $= a \wedge 1$ identity
  $= a$ identity

4 $a \wedge [(b \wedge c) \vee (b \wedge \sim c)] = a \wedge b$ using method for Q3

5 $\sim a \wedge (\sim b \vee a)$
  $= (\sim a \wedge \sim b) \vee (\sim a \wedge a)$ distributive
  $= (\sim a \wedge \sim b) \vee 0$ identity
  $= (\sim a \wedge \sim b)$ identity
  $= \sim(a \vee b)$ de Morgan

Consolidation A (p. 313)

1 let n = 'the north wind blows'
  let p = 'we have snow'

n	p	~n	~n	n ⇒ p	~p ⇒ n
0	0	1	1	1	1
0	1	1	0	1	1
1	0	0	1	0	0
1	1	0	0	1	1

2 **a** $a \vee (\sim a \wedge b)$

3 **a** The light changes state i.e.: if it was on, it goes off, and vice versa).

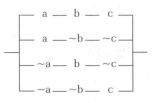

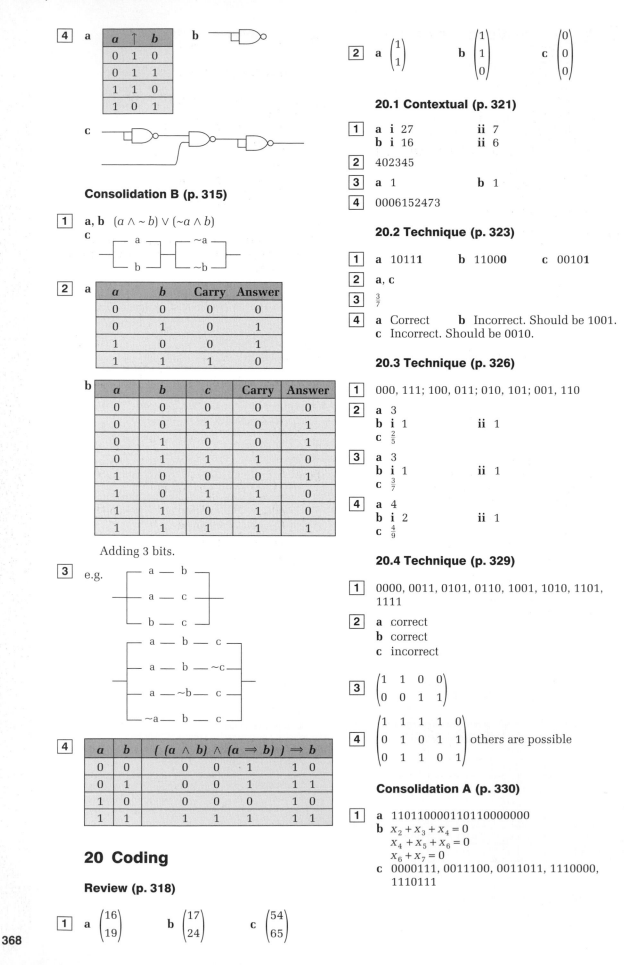

4 a

a	$\uparrow$	b
0	1	0
0	1	1
1	1	0
1	0	1

b

c

Consolidation B (p. 315)

1 **a, b** $(a \wedge \sim b) \vee (\sim a \wedge b)$

c

2 a

a	b	Carry	Answer
0	0	0	0
0	1	0	1
1	0	0	1
1	1	1	0

b

a	b	c	Carry	Answer
0	0	0	0	0
0	0	1	0	1
0	1	0	0	1
0	1	1	1	0
1	0	0	0	1
1	0	1	1	0
1	1	0	1	0
1	1	1	1	1

Adding 3 bits.

3 e.g.

4

a	b	$((a \wedge b) \wedge (a \Rightarrow b)) \Rightarrow b$			
0	0	0	0	1	1 0
0	1	0	0	1	1 1
1	0	0	0	0	1 0
1	1	1	1	1	1 1

20 Coding

Review (p. 318)

1 a $\begin{pmatrix} 16 \\ 19 \end{pmatrix}$ b $\begin{pmatrix} 17 \\ 24 \end{pmatrix}$ c $\begin{pmatrix} 54 \\ 65 \end{pmatrix}$

2 a $\begin{pmatrix} 1 \\ 1 \\ 1 \end{pmatrix}$ b $\begin{pmatrix} 1 \\ 1 \\ 0 \end{pmatrix}$ c $\begin{pmatrix} 0 \\ 0 \\ 0 \end{pmatrix}$

20.1 Contextual (p. 321)

1 **a i** 27   **ii** 7
  b i 16   **ii** 6

2 402345

3 **a** 1   **b** 1

4 0006152473

20.2 Technique (p. 323)

1 **a** 10111   **b** 11000   **c** 00101

2 **a, c**

3 $\frac{3}{7}$

4 **a** Correct   **b** Incorrect. Should be 1001.
  c Incorrect. Should be 0010.

20.3 Technique (p. 326)

1 000, 111; 100, 011; 010, 101; 001, 110

2 **a** 3
  b i 1   **ii** 1
  c $\frac{2}{5}$

3 **a** 3
  b i 1   **ii** 1
  c $\frac{3}{7}$

4 **a** 4
  b i 2   **ii** 1
  c $\frac{4}{9}$

20.4 Technique (p. 329)

1 0000, 0011, 0101, 0110, 1001, 1010, 1101, 1111

2 **a** correct
  b correct
  c incorrect

3 $\begin{pmatrix} 1 & 1 & 0 & 0 \\ 0 & 0 & 1 & 1 \end{pmatrix}$

4 $\begin{pmatrix} 1 & 1 & 1 & 1 & 0 \\ 0 & 1 & 0 & 1 & 1 \\ 0 & 1 & 1 & 0 & 1 \end{pmatrix}$ others are possible

Consolidation A (p. 330)

1 **a** 110110000110110000000
  b $x_2 + x_3 + x_4 = 0$
    $x_4 + x_5 + x_6 = 0$
    $x_6 + x_7 = 0$
  c 0000111, 0011100, 0011011, 1110000, 1110111

2   **b**   1   **c**   2 from answers to d

     d   80268024
        59268024
        50568024
        50258024
        50261024
        50268924
        50268954
        50268923

     e $\frac{1}{10}$ of $10^8 = 10^7$ are valid, 9×10^7 invalid

3   **b**   E.g. test 00001

     c   E.g.: test 01000

     d   E.g.: 01001

     e   Detect but not correct.

4   **a**   **i**   3 bits gives $2^3 = 8$ words

          ii   000
              001
              010
              011
              100
              101
              110
              111

     b   **i**   4th column   0
                          1
                          1
                          0
                          1
                          0
                          0
                          1

          ii d = detect 1, correct 0

     c d = 2: detect 1, correct 0

     d   Any pair of codewords added together should give a codeword.

     e d = 3; detect 1, correct 1

     f   E.g.:

$$\begin{pmatrix} 1 & 0 & 0 & 0 & 1 & 0 & 0 \\ 0 & 1 & 0 & 0 & 0 & 1 & 0 \\ 0 & 0 & 1 & 0 & 0 & 0 & 1 \\ 1 & 1 & 1 & 1 & 0 & 0 & 0 \end{pmatrix}$$

     g   E, SW, W

5   **a** 2^6 **b**   8

Consolidation B (p. 332)

1   **a** $\frac{3}{7}$ **b**   3   **c**   1   **d**   1

     e   E.g.:

$$\begin{pmatrix} 1 & 1 & 0 & 0 & 0 & 0 & 0 \\ 0 & 0 & 1 & 1 & 0 & 0 & 0 \\ 0 & 0 & 0 & 0 & 1 & 1 & 0 \\ 1 & 0 & 1 & 0 & 1 & 0 & 1 \end{pmatrix}$$

     f   correct word: 1100110

2   30

3   **a**   111001 is correct; 2nd word 001011

     b   000000, 001011, 110010, 111001, 001111, 000100.

4   **a**

        A   B   C   D

     b   B

     c   01011011

5   **a**   E.g.:

$$\begin{pmatrix} 1 & 0 & 0 & 0 & 1 & 0 & 0 \\ 0 & 1 & 0 & 0 & 0 & 1 & 0 \\ 0 & 0 & 1 & 0 & 0 & 0 & 1 \\ 1 & 1 & 1 & 1 & 0 & 0 & 0 \end{pmatrix}$$

     b   S T A T E

Index

absorption rules   311
accuracy required   278, 288
adjacency matrix   27, 28, 44
Algebra, Boolean   307, 311–13
algorithms   1–6, 71
   alternating path   178–9, 187
   complexity (order)   4–5, 69
   "divide and conquer"   18–19, 25
   exchange sort   16
   factorial   2, 4–5
   flow augmenting   219–20, 229
   Floyd's   71–3, 79, 91
   greedy   47, 63, 198–9, 233
   heuristic   21, 93, 110, 188, 196
   Hungarian   191–5, 211
   "improvement"   177–9
   insertion sort   14
   Kruskal's   47–50, 62, 63
   labelling   219–22
   linear   4, 11–22
   lowest cost   198–9
   maximum matching   177–9
   nearest neighbour   93–5, 97–9, 102, 110
      improvements   97–8
      lower bounds   99–101, 102, 110
      upper bounds   97–8, 102, 110
   north west corner   196–8, 201, 211
   order (complexity) of   4–5, 69
   planarity   37–8
   Prim's   51–3, 54–5, 63, 102
      with a matrix   54–7
   properties of   4–5
   recursive   6
   selection with interchange   15–16
   simplex   157–62, 165, 172, 173, 253
      for sorting numbers   5
   stopping conditions   4
   two-stage   163–6, 173
allocation matrix   188–90, 192–3, 211
allocations
   Hungarian   algorithm   191–5, 211
   minimum cost   188–90, 192–3
alternating path algorithm   178–9, 187
and (∧)   300, 302
AND gates   308, 309, 310
answers   335–69
arcs (edges, lines)   26, 44, 62, 88
activity on   112–14, 117–19, 122, 129, 137
arguments   316
associative rules   311

back flow   219, 220, 221, 229
barcodes   319, 330, 334
battleships game   24
Bellman, Richard   230
Bellman's principle   230
Big-M method   167–8, 173
binary   318
   codes   322–3, 324, 325, 334
   counting in   327

   input   308–10
   search   25
bin-packing   20–2, 25
bipartite graphs   32–3, 45
   modelling with   174–5, 187
bits   322, 323, 328
Boole, George   311
Boolean Algebra   311–13
   rules   307, 311
Boolean expressions   300, 302, 309–10, 311, 317
bottleneck (minimum cut)   217, 229
brackets, use of   306
Braille   332
breakthrough   178
bubble sort   12–13, 17, 18
bus times problem   272–3

calculators, scientific   275
capacity   217–19, 229
car wash   276–7
card games   245–6, 247–8, 249–51
Cascade (Gantt) Charts   124, 125, 126, 138
   to produce a schedule   125–7
check digits   319–21, 323, 327, 334
Chinese post person problem (route inspection)   80–2, 87–8
circuits
   combinatorial   308–10, 317
   equivalent   303
   lighting   316
   switching   302–3, 317
Classical Problem   89–92, 93, 110
clock (modulus) arithmetic   318
coach problem   232–3
codes   319, 334
   binary   322–3, 324, 325, 334
   correction capability   334
   errors in   324–5, 328, 334
   Huffman   333, 334
   linear   326–7, 334
   Morse   333
   structured   2
codewords (words)   322, 324, 326–9, 334
coding   318–34
   check digits   319–21, 323, 327, 334
   hamming distance   324–5, 334
   parity check matrices (H)   326, 327–8, 334
colouring problem   43
column vectors   318, 328, 334
combinatorial circuits   308–10, 317
commutative rules   311, 312
complement rules   312
complete graphs   33, 45
complexity (order) of algorithms   4–5, 69
computer packages   173, 186
computers   308, 322
computing principles   304–5
connected graphs   33, 44
connectivity   27

constraints (limitations, restrictions)   139–41,
    143, 144, 148, 149, 156, 158
contradiction   304, 306, 312
correcting mistakes   319–20
correction capability of a code   334
cost, demand   201–2, 203
cost, supply   201–2, 203
crashing a network   128–9, 138
critical activities   117, 119, 121, 124
critical path   121, 137
Critical Path Analysis   111–38
    activity on arc (edge)   112–14, 117–19, 122,
        129, 137
    activity on node (vertex)   114–15, 119–21, 122,
        129, 137
    algorithm to draw network   112
    Cascade (Gantt) Charts   124, 125, 126, 138
    float   121–3, 124, 137
    formulation   111–15
    notation   111
crop problem   194–5
cuts (into networks)   217–19, 229
cycles   26, 44
    Hamiltonian   36–8, 44, 89, 90, 101–2, 107, 110

data, normally distributed   278
de Morgan, Augustus   311
de Morgan's rules   307, 311
decision trees   260–71
degenerate solutions   201, 203, 205
demand cost   201–2, 203
deterministic problems   230
deviation, standard   278, 279
Dijkstra, Edsger Wybe   64
Dijkstra's algorithm   64–8, 69–70, 78, 79
    for all paths   69–70
directed edges   88
distance matrix   30, 44
distributed data   278
distribution, probability   281
distributive rules   311, 312
"divide and conquer" algorithm   18–19, 25
double negation   311
dummy activity   113–14, 137
dummy column in a matrix   189–90
duplicate values   14–15
dynamic programming   230–43
    common applications   234–7
    recursive definition   230
    sub-optimal strategy   230, 232, 235, 243

EDEXCEL   209
edges (arcs, lines)   26, 44, 62, 88
    activity on   112–14, 117–19, 122, 129, 137
electrical circuits   302–3
equations   250, 292, 294, 299
equivalent circuits   303
equivalent statements   304, 306–7, 309, 311,
    312–13
errors in a code   324–5, 328, 334
errors, standard   278, 279, 288
Euler, Leonhard   32
Eulerian graphs   32, 45, 88
evaluating arguments   316
event times   117–21, 137
exam boards   182

exchange sort algorithm   16
expected monetary values (EMVs)   261, 263, 271
exponential functions   18

factorial algorithms   2, 4–5
factorials, calculating   1, 2–3
false   304
family tree   11
fantasy football   155
fast food restaurant   281–2
feasible regions   140, 141, 144, 146, 150, 156
first fit   20, 21–2, 25
float   121–3, 124, 137
    independent   122, 123, 137
    interfering   122, 123, 137
    shared   122, 123
    total   122, 123, 137
flow   217–19, 220–2, 228, 229
    back   219, 220, 221, 229
    maximum   228
    optimal   219
    potential   219, 221, 229
flow augmenting algorithm   219–20, 229
flow augmenting paths   216, 220–2, 229
flow charts   1–2
Floyd's Algorithm   71–3, 79, 91
formal (propositional) logic   300–10
Fossil fuel problem   212–13, 215–16, 217–19,
    228
fractions, improper   162
functions, exponential   18
functions, objective   143–4, 156

game of life   287
game theory   244–59
    mixed strategies   249–51
    strategy dominance   247–8
    zero–sum   244–7, 259
games
    battleships   24
    card   245–6, 247–8, 249–51
Gantt, Henry   124
Gantt (cascade) charts   124, 125, 126, 138
    to produce a schedule   125–7
gas plant problem   213–14
graph theory   26–45
graphs   44, 140
    bipartite   32–3, 45
        modelling with   174–5, 187
    complete (K)   33, 45
    connected   33, 44
    modelling networks with   30–3
    notation   26–8
    planar   35–8, 45
    semi–Eulerian   32
    simple   44
    sparse   88
greedy algorithm   47, 63, 198–9, 233

half adder   315
Hamilton, Sir William Rowan   89
Hamiltonian Cycle   36–8, 44, 89, 90, 101–2, 107,
    110
Hamming, RW   324
hamming distance   324–5, 334
handshaking   31

heuristic algorithms   21, 93, 110, 188, 196
histogram, resource   126–7, 138
Hong Kong   26–7
Horsey Weavers problem   140–1, 143–4
Huffman code   333, 334
Hungarian Algorithm   191–5, 211

identity rules   312
if and only if   300, 301, 307
if...then   300, 301, 305
implication   301, 307
improper fractions   162
"improvement" algorithms   177–9
improving a solution   202, 203, 204–6, 211
indexed search   25
indicator variables   79, 88, 186
inequalities   139–41, 158
infinity sign   72
innocent until proven guilty   305
in–order search   9, 10, 25
input   309, 310, 317
    binary   308–10
insertion sort   13–15
    algorithm   14
integer solutions   145–6
ISBN numbers   320, 321
isomorphism   27, 45

junctions (nodes)   9, 25, 261

k (integer counter)   18
K (complete) graphs   33, 35
knapsack problem   211, 235–7
Konig   191
Kruskal, JB   47
Kruskal's algorithm   47–50, 62, 63
Kuratowski's theorem   35

labelling algorithm   219–22
law, assumption in   305
lighting circuits   316
limitations, (constraints, restrictions)   139–41,
    143, 144, 148, 149, 156, 158
linear algorithms   4, 11–22
linear codes   326–7, 334
linear programming   139–156
    integer solutions   145–6
    minimisation   150
    multiple solutions   147–8
    optimisation   143–4, 156
    slack variables   148–9
    solutions   252–3
    three dimensions   156
linear search   7–8, 25
logarithms   4, 18, 299
logic, propositional (formal)   300–10
    circuits   302–3, 308–10, 316, 317
    truth tables   304–7, 309, 316, 317
logic gates   308–10
lowest cost algorithm   198–9

maps   26, 28, 43
matchings   174–87
    complete   187
    maximum   187
    modelling with bipartite graphs   174–5, 187

multi–task   186
mathematicians   32, 47, 80, 89, 191, 311
matrices
    adjacency   27, 28, 44
    allocation   188–90, 192–3, 211
    distance   30, 44
    dummy column in   189–90
    multiplying   318
    parity check (H)   326, 327–8, 334
    pay-off   245–6, 250, 251
Max flow/Min cut theorem   217, 221, 229
maximin problem   234–5, 252–3
maximisation   156, 161, 194–5
maximum matching algorithms   177–9
measuring jug problem   43–4
mileage charts   54
minimax problems   234
minimisation problems   150, 156, 161
minimising risk   245
minimum cut (bottleneck)   217, 229
minimum spanning tree (MST)   53, 56, 62, 97–8,
    100, 102, 110
mistakes, correcting   319–20
modelling with graphs   30–3, 174–5, 187
models, single event   272–4
modulus (clock) arithmetic   318
Morse code   333
MS Excel   3, 287
MS Project   124
multiple solutions to linear programming   147–8
multistage problems   230
multi–task matching   186

NAND gates   308–9
nearest neighbour algorithm   93–5, 97–9, 102,
    110
    improvements   97–8
    lower bounds   99–101, 102, 110
    upper bounds   97–8, 102, 110
network flow   212–29
    cuts   217–19, 229
    labelling algorithm   219–22
    optimality   217–18
networks   30, 44
    crashing   128–9, 138
    cuts into   217–19, 229
    modelling with graphs   30–3
nodes (junctions)   9, 25, 261
    activity on   114–15, 119–21, 122, 129, 137
normally distributed data   278
North West Corner algorithm   196–8, 201, 211
not (~)   300, 301
NOT gates   308, 309, 310

objective function   143–4, 156
optimality, testing for   201–3, 204, 205–6
optimisation
    of linear programmes   143–4, 156, 186
    of network flow   215–16, 217–18, 221
optimum probability   250
or (∨)   300, 301, 302, 305
OR gates   308, 309, 310
orchard problem   196–9, 202–3
order (complexity) of algorithms   4–5, 69
order (valency) of vertices   32, 33, 44
outcome   287–8

output   309

parity check matrices (H)   326, 327–8, 334
pay-off matrices   245–6, 250, 251
pension funds   155–6
phone numbers, checking   319–21
pivot column   159
pivot value   18
planar graphs   35–8, 45
planarity   35–8
   algorithm   37–8
playing cards   245–6, 247–8, 249–51
play-safe strategy   245–6, 248, 259
post-optimal analysis   173
pre- and post-order search   25
Prim, R C   51
Prim's algorithm   51–3, 54–5, 63, 102
   with a matrix   54–7
principles
   Bellman's   230
   of computing   304–5
prisoner's dilemma   258
probability   244, 252–3, 272
   distribution   281
profit function   143–4, 145
profit line   144
project management   124
propositional (formal) logic   300–10
   circuits   302–3, 308–10, 316, 317
   truth tables   304–7, 309, 316, 317

quadratic equations   292
queuing   276–7, 287, 288
Quicksort   15, 18–19, 25

random events   287
random numbers   275
random walk   273–4
ratio test   159
recurrence relations   289–99
   first order   290–1, 299
   second order   292–3, 294–5, 299
   sequences   289
redundancy   62
reliability of simulations   278–9, 288
required accuracy   278, 288
resource histogram   126–7, 138
resource levelling   125–7, 138
resource schedule   125–7, 138
risk, minimising   245
restrictions (constraints, limitations)   139–41,
      143, 144, 148, 149, 156, 158
rounding up   21
route inspection   (Chinese post person problem)
      80–2, 87–8
rug problem   140–1, 143–4
rules   307, 311, 312

saddle point   246, 259
sailing regatta   260–1, 262–3
satellite transmissions   322–3
scheduling   101–2, 110, 125–7
searching   7–11, 24–5
   binary   8–9
   indexed   7–8
   in-order   9, 10, 25

linear   7–8, 25
   pre- and post-order   25
   tree   8–10
selection with interchange algorithm   15–16
semi-Eulerian graphs   32
sequences   289–95   see also recurrence relations
shaker sort   13
shell sort   17–18, 24, 25
   algorithm   17
shortest paths   64–79
   Dijkstra's algorithm   64–8, 69–70, 78, 79
      for all paths   69–70
   Floyd's algorithm   71–3, 79, 91
   problems   230–1, 232
   refinements   78, 79
shuttle sort   13–14
silicon chips   308
simple graphs   44
simplex algorithm   157–62, 165, 172, 173, 253
   big-M method   167–8, 173
   two-stage   163–6, 173
simplex tableau   158–62, 164–6, 167–8, 173, 253
simulation   272–88
   multi-stage   276–7, 287, 288
   queuing   276–7, 287, 288
   reliability   278–9
   single event models   272–4
simultaneous equations   250
sink (T)   213, 217, 229
slack (surplus) variables   148–9, 156, 158, 159,
      173
software   173, 186
solutions
   degenerate   201, 203, 205
   improving   202, 203, 204–6, 211
   by inspection   215–16
   integer   145–6
   multiple, to linear programming   147–8
   stable   246, 249, 259
   uniqueness of   50
sorting   11–25
   algorithms   17, 25
   bubble   12–13, 17, 18
   insertion   13–15
   shaker   13
   shell   17–18, 24, 25
      algorithm   17
   shuttle   13–14
source (S)   213, 217, 229
spanning trees   46–63
   Kruskal's algorithm   47–50, 62, 63
   minimum spanning (MST)   53, 56, 62, 97–8,
      100, 102, 110
   Prim's algorithm   51–3, 54–5, 63, 102
      with a matrix   54–7
sparse graphs   88
spreadsheets   3, 275, 287, 299
stable solution   246, 249, 259
standard deviation   278, 279
standard error   278, 279, 288
statisticians   278
stopping conditions (in algorithms)   4
strategy dominance   247–8, 259
strategy, mixed   249–51, 259
strategy, play safe   245–6, 248, 259
strawberry plants   292–3

structured code   2
sub-graphs   35, 36, 229
supersink   214, 229
supersource   214, 229
supply cost   201–2, 203
switching circuits   302–3, 317
symbols   72, 300–1, 302, 305, 307, 317

tableau, Simplex   158–62, 164–6, 167–8, 173, 253
tautology   304, 306, 307, 312
taxi service problem   188–90, 192–3
testing for optimality   201–3, 204, 205–6
theatre act problem   101–2
theorem, Kuratowski's   35
theorem, Max flow/Min cut   217, 221, 229
tour of vertices   143, 146
traffic flow   283–4
train problem   234–5
transportation problems   196–9, 211
   coaches   232–3
   improving a solution   202, 203, 204–6, 211
   taxi service   188–90, 192–3
   testing for optimality   201–3, 204, 205–6
   trains   234–5
Travelling Salesperson Problem (TSP)   89–110
   Classical problem   89–92, 93, 110
   constraints   109
   Hamiltonian Cycle   36–8, 44, 89, 90, 101–2, 107, 110
   nearest neighbour algorithm   93–5, 97–9, 102, 110
      improvements   97–8
      lower bounds   99–101, 102, 110
      upper bounds   97–8, 102, 110

scheduling   101–2, 110
tree diagrams   9, 260, 261, 263
tree search   25
trees, decision   260–71
trees, spanning   46–63
   minimum (MST)   53, 56, 62, 97–8, 100, 102, 110
true   304
truth tables   304–7, 309, 316, 317

uniqueness of solutions   50

valency (order) of vertices   32, 33, 44
valid arguments   316
variables   139–40, 156, 158
   artificial   163, 164, 165, 167
   decision   231
   indicator   79, 88, 186
   probability   249
   slack (surplus)   148–9, 156, 158, 159, 173
   stage   230, 235, 243
   state   230, 235, 243
vectors, column   318, 328, 334
Venn diagrams   312–13, 317
vertices (nodes, points)   26, 44
   activity on   114–15, 119–21, 122, 129, 137
   order (valency) of   32, 33, 44
   tour of   143, 146

weaver problem   140–1, 143–4
weight of a word   322
worst case scenario   325

zero–sum games   244–7, 259